THEORIES OF LITERATURE IN THE
TWENTIETH CENTURY

D. W. FOKKEMA
ELRUD KUNNE-IBSCH

Theories of Literature in the Twentieth Century

Structuralism
Marxism
Aesthetics of Reception
Semiotics

C. HURST & COMPANY · LONDON

First published in the United Kingdom in 1978
by C. Hurst & Co. (Publishers) Ltd.,
1-2 Henrietta Street, London WC2E 8PS.
© 1977, by D. W. Fokkema and E. Kunne-Ibsch
Second impression, corrected, March 1979

ISBN 0-903983-83-4 *(cased)*

ISBN 0-905838-09-2 *(paper)*

Typeset by A. Brown & Sons Ltd., Hull, and
Printed in Great Britain by offset lithography by
Billing & Sons Ltd., Guildford, London and Worcester

To Jan Brandt Corstius

ACKNOWLEDGEMENTS

Chapter 2 originally appeared under the title "Continuity and Change in Russian Formalism, Czech Structuralism, and Soviet Semiotics" in *PTL 1* (1976), pp. 153–96 (North-Holland Publishing Company, Amsterdam). Chapter 5 appeared in a German version under the title: "Rezeptionsforschung: Konstanten und Varianten eines literaturwissenschaftlichen Konzepts in Theorie und Praxis" in *Amsterdamer Beiträge zur neueren Germanistik* 3 (1974), pp. 1–37 (Rodopi N.V., Amsterdam). We wish to express our thanks to Mr J. K. W. van Leeuwen, of North-Holland Publishing Company, and to Dr G. Labroisse, editor of *Amsterdamer Beiträge,* for their kind permission to republish these articles.

We also thank Professor Ralph Cohen for permission to reprint several paragraphs from "The Forms and Values of Contemporary Chinese Literature", originally published in *New Literary History* 4 (1972–3), pp. 591–603 (University of Virginia, Charlottesville, Virginia).

CONTENTS

Acknowledgements   *page* vii

Foreword   xi

1. Introduction   1

2. Russian Formalism, Czech Structuralism and Soviet
   Semiotics   10
   *The Claim of Scientific Reliability—The Devices of
   Literature—The System of Literature—Motif Analysis—
   Czech Structuralism—Soviet Semiotics—Concluding
   Remarks*

3. Structuralism in France: Criticism, Narratology and
   Text Analysis   50
   *Structuralist Criticism—Structuralist Narratology—
   Linguistic-Structuralist Text Description*

4. Marxist Theories of Literature   81
   *Marx, Engels, and Lenin—Theory and Practice after the
   October Revolution—The Chinese Reception of Marxist
   Literary Theories—Lukács and Neo-Marxist Criticism*

5. The Reception of Literature: Theory and Practice of
   "Rezeptionsästhetik"   136
   *Theoretical Discussion—Historical Study of Reception—
   Empirical Study of Reception—The Implicit Reader—The
   Social-Political Approach—Concluding Observations*

6. Prospects for Further Research   165
   *The Challenge of Semiotics—Epistemological Assumptions
   of the Historical Sciences—Jauss and the Sociology of
   Knowledge—A Semiotic Analysis of Structures of
   Communication—Conclusion*

Notes   184

Bibliography   195

Index   215

FOREWORD

Publications in the field of literary theory have grown in number over the past ten years and the time now seems ripe for stock-taking. One may wonder whether the recent proliferation of concepts, models and theories has been of any avail to the study of literature. However, the authors of this book consider the search for a theory of literature a condition of the scientific study of literary texts.

We assume that students of literature—whether under-graduates, postgraduates or teachers—would like to judge the foundations of their discipline for themselves. In the present book we have tried to present the most relevant materials for such a judgement. Of course we know that our selection of theories and their presentation is shaped by certain assumptions that will not be shared by every reader. One of these assumptions is that there are various ways towards knowledge, whereas we may never reach the certainty of perfect knowledge. Another assumption is that it is worthwhile to aim at the highest possible level of knowledge, since not to do so would throw the door open to subjectivism and irrationalism. In our view, the attempt to establish a system of falsifiable hypotheses or statements about literature implies an attempt to distinguish between the facts and values of literature. The respective functions of literary theorist and literary critic should be distinguished as clearly as possible. We shall elaborate on this position in our introductory chapter.

Our intention has been to present the outlines of current theories of literature, and to arrange them in such a way that their underlying assumptions and implied value judgements become explicit. This will enable the reader to select a theory, the assumptions and criteria of which he finds agreeable; but we do not intend to promote this kind of self-affirmation. We do hope that the reader will detect the sometimes arbitrary and always hypothetical nature of the foundations of the very theory he wishes to work with. The question whether there is one ultimate truth remains outside the scope of this book. We have preferred, in the words of Proust, to provide "méticuleusement des renseignements précis".

It is only in the concluding chapter that we seem to abandon this point of view. We have indicated which theories appear to contain fertile insights that can be developed further, and in what directions research may be undertaken with some promise of satisfactory results.

A final word on our division of labour. Although we wish to share the responsibility for the whole book equally, the reader may want to know that the first draft of chapters 3, 5 and 6 was written by the first of the undersigned, and the first draft of chapters 1, 2 and 4 by the second.

ELRUD KUNNE-IBSCH
(Free University, Amsterdam)

D. W. FOKKEMA
(University of Utrecht)

1

INTRODUCTION

"In order to become, finally a science, literary history must lay claim to reliability."

—Ju. Tynjanov (1927)

"In fact, to concede that a result of inquiry may be only an uncertain approximation is, in itself, a way of achieving exactitude in results, a way of making knowledge exact."

—E. D. Hirsch, Jr. (1972)

This book is based on the assumption that we need theories of literature in our attempts to interpret literary texts and to explain literature as a specific mode of communication. The scientific study of literature is inconceivable without relying on a particular theory of literature. Before we review the main contemporary theories of literature, it is necessary to identify and refute certain trends which are incompatible with a systematic study of literary theory. Therefore, this introductory chapter will have a somewhat negative character. However, the criticism of a number of views which in our opinion are mistaken provides us at the same time with an opportunity to emphasize the historical perspective. Recent developments in literary theory are the outcome of research by several generations of scholars. Present reactions to past ideas can be clarified by a study of the latter.

First, the suggestion that literary scholarship is heavily dependent on the prevailing trends in creative literature should be discussed. The theory of Classicism, it has been argued, should be understood as a generalization of the drama and epic of the time. The biographical method in criticism is viewed as one of the effects of Romanticism, which drew largely on autobiographical material. The psychological novel is considered to be responsible for the psychological approach in literary criticism. Similarly, the view has been defended that Russian Formalism is indebted to the ideals and slogans of Futurism (Pomorska, 1968).

But one may very well argue differently. New trends in literary theory can also be related to new developments in science and society. There is an unmistakable influence of Freudian psychology in psychologically-oriented literary criticism. Marxist literary

1

criticism has been intertwined with particular political and sociological views. The search for a literary system or structure has certainly been inspired by *Gestalt* psychology. Russian Formalism is not only indebted to Futurism, but also to new developments in linguistics. Some schools of literary theory are closer to new trends in creative literature, others are directly related to current developments in scholarship and society. Still others are somewhere in between. It would seem rather unprofitable to generalize on the genetic explanation of the existing differences between the various schools of literary theory. Although a genetic explanation in each particular case may clarify some aspects of the schools under review, it does not release us from the obligation to study the various literary theories on their own merits and to establish their more or less restricted validity.

Another trend that should be signalled is the Wittgensteinian idea that art defies definition (Weitz, 1956; 1972). In its application to literature, this position has been eloquently defended by George Watson in his book *The Study of Literature* (1969). Watson not only refuses to define his own concepts, but also challenges the usefulness of the definition of period concepts such as have been developed by René Wellek. The reason why Watson and Wellek differ on this basic question seems to be that they each adhere to different conceptions of what a definition should be. Watson confusingly refers to the *real* definition, when he defines the term "definition" as "a verbal formula which includes all the cases and excludes all the non-cases", and further holds that "the realities of literature" are not "amenable to definition" (Watson, 1969: 36–7). Wellek, on the other hand uses *descriptive* definitions in order to explain the meaning of such words as Classicism, Romanticism, Realism, Symbolism and other period concepts.[1] His period terms are "names for systems of norms which dominate literature at a specific time of the historical process". The period term is "a regulative idea, an ideal type which may not be completely fulfilled by any single work and will certainly in every individual work be combined with different traits, survivals from the past, anticipations of the future and quite individual peculiarities" (Wellek, 1963: 129, 252). The period concept, though correlated with certain observable facts, is a construction, indispensable to any discussion of literary history that attempts to transcend the stage of loose conversation about individual texts. Watson's belief that "it is in no way necessary for knowing what romanticism is to be able to say what it is" and that "pointing" to supposedly romantic authors will be enough (Watson, 1969: 39), would make us speechless and the results of our investigations impervious to criticism. Shirking the definition of literary concepts means the end of a systematic approach to the study of literature.

Similar criticism of Morris Weitz's publications has been published by Joseph Margolis (1965), Lee B. Brown (1968), M. H. Abrams (1972) and others. Margolis sees a contradiction in Weitz's argument. On the one hand, art is held to be logically impossible to define, and, on the other, it is held to be an empirical matter. Lee B. Brown detects essentialist strains in Weitz's theorizing and convincingly defends the "descriptive generalization" as "a perfectly respectable kind of definition" (Brown, 1968: 412). Abrams quite convincingly argues that Weitz claims not to be in need of a theory but is in fact using one.

So far Wittgenstein's theory of the "family resemblance" of related phenomena which seemingly cannot be covered by one definition has been of no avail to the study of literature. Abrams rightly emphasizes that the more diverse the family of objects, "the more important it becomes, if we are to talk to some effect, that we specify and limit our use of the term" (Abrams, 1972: 17). Without further clarification it is not at all clear how the family of literary texts can be recognized. Should one decide that a text belongs to that family as soon as the term "literature" is applied? This cannot be the case, as the word is of recent coinage and in many languages has no equivalent. The concept of family resemblance can hardly help us to distinguish between different kinds of objects, and has not led to new findings or insights. The ideal of the "true and real definition of the necessary and sufficient properties of art", which Morris Weitz looked for and could not find (Weitz, 1956), must be replaced by the modest attempt to delimit the boundaries of the corpus of materials one is talking about. That modest ideal and the habit of being explicit about the meaning of the concepts one uses have much more chance of furthering the study of literature than the regression to unexplained "pointing", "looking and seeing".

The success of the family resemblance theory is, of course, due to the fact that the concept of literature has different meanings in different periods and cultures. However, the difference between these meanings can largely be explained by reference to the various historical conditions and the corresponding cultural and literary conventions. Literature is certainly not a static concept, but should be determined in both synchronic and diachronic terms. That is what made Ju. Tynjanov (1924a) describe literature as a dynamic linguistic construction. Instead of abandoning all attempts to define literature, any definition of literature should take account of the fact that certain texts at a certain time and place have been *accepted* as literary, whereas in other times and places they have not.[2] Literary devices wear out. Horace had already observed that "words die out with old age" (Dorsch, 1970: 81). Like Horace, a third-century Chinese treatise on poetry argues that the poet recurs to newly coined or long forgotten terms.[3] Although at different times and places literary devices and conventions may differ, it seems an adequate generalization to say that they all aim at intensified perception. In different situations different elements have been used to achieve that aim; different factors have constituted one and the same literary function. The literary theories we shall review consider the constituents of the aesthetic function of literature as the pivotal problem and, in varying degrees, focus on the variability of these constituents and the invariability of the aesthetic effect.

A third trend which has impeded the development of literary theories derives from a—quite understandable—reaction to German historicism. Various scholars have stressed the impossibility or, at least, the impracticableness of separating the exegesis of meaning (interpretation) from the judgement of value (evaluation). Here, historicism or historical relativism is understood as an individualizing view, which interprets and evaluates the historical phenomena of a certain period on the basis of the norms and in relation to the other historical phenomena of that period.[4] One of the main arguments against the historicist method was the belief that one would never be able to reconstruct the historical norms with certainty; and that, if such a reconstruction were possible at all, a value judgement based on these historical norms would be meaningless to the modern reader. Historicism determined the value of a work of art with reference to the historical context and tended to reduce its significance to its time of origin.

The criticism by Wolfgang Kayser of that attitude has often been mentioned. Quoting an article by Karl Viëtor of 1945, Kayser resented the extreme historicizing of the *geistesgeschichtliche Schule,* as it entailed a decreasing attention to artistic quality and critical judgement (Kayser, 1958: 40). Kayser advocated a separation between literature and history instead. The interpretation of a literary work, he argued, focusses on the work as art and needs a particular orientation towards the poetic aspect, which is essentially different from the historical orientation.[5] The critical judgement, according to Kayser, should be provided in and through the interpretation. His correct belief that each system of evaluation is explicitly or implicitly based on a theory of literature, and that each interpreter is a product of his own time did not, however, result in relativism.[6] Rather inconsequently, Kayser advocates a method of interpretation that ostensibly does not aim at any evaluation at all but attempts to detect a unity of tensions *(Einstimmigkeit)* in the literary work. The assumption, of course, is that unity is a distinctive feature of art and hence a primary criterion in an adequate evaluative system. Although Kayser, on at least one occasion,[7] is explicit on this, his repeatedly expressed view that interpretation provides enough evaluation and that the literary work must reveal the criteria with which it should be evaluated, has rather tended to cloud the distinction between interpretation and evaluation. For, as Kayser said: "Evaluation is inherent in the interpretation."[8] In Europe similar views were held by Emil Staiger (1971: 9–12), H. P. H. Teesing (1964) and others.

In American criticism a similar trend to identify interpretation and evaluation can be detected, although historical relativism never gained a strong foothold in the New World and, therefore, did not call either for a strong reaction. In fact, this may be the reason why the debate on historicism has been a protracted affair in the United States (cf. Roy Harvey Pearce, 1969; Wesley Morris, 1972). It also explains why in this respect Austin Warren expresses himself in a rather moderate way, acknowledging that a separation between interpretation and evaluation "can certainly be made", although it is rarely practised or practicable (Wellek and Warren, 1956: 240). Warren adds that understanding poetry passes readily into judging poetry, judging while analysing. He mentions Eliot's essays as an example, whereas the words "understanding poetry" evidently refer to the well-known book by Cleanth Brooks and Robert Penn Warren (1938). Much more aware of the negative effects that a separation of analysis and evaluation, as in German historicism, can have, René Wellek held somewhat stronger views. Analysis can never stand alone: "There is simply no way of avoiding judgment by us, by myself." "Evaluation grows out of understanding; correct evaluation out of correct understanding" (Wellek, 1963: 17–18).

The doctrine of the inseparability of interpretation and evaluation loses much of its strength as soon as literary works of past ages or of various civilizations are involved. Whereas Kayser rightly still considered the examination of historical conditions to be a necessary preparation for literary interpretation, Wellek seems to underestimate the problems which an older text may hold for the reader when he says that with literary texts "we can experience quite directly how things are" (Wellek and Warren, 1956: 244). Too readily he has supported Eliot's misleading thesis "that the whole of the literature of Europe from Homer [. . .] has a simultaneous existence and composes a simultaneous order" (ibid.: 244). It means "that one recognizes that there is one poetry, one literature, comparable in all ages" (ibid.: 32). This is a position with which one could agree; in fact, it is the inevitable hypothesis of any student of comparative literature. However, it is a hypothesis which, without further elaboration, does not solve anything, but poses the problem of how this concept of one united literature should be constructed. And accepting this position, as we do, does not mean that one should accept its paraphernalia: the derogatory view of literary reconstruction as an attempt to enter into the mind and attitude of past periods, the defeatist rejection of methods which do not guarantee fixed results, the absolutist clinging to aesthetic imperatives for fear of an anarchy of values (cf. Wellek, 1963: 1–21). Wellek's repeated warning that historical relativism will lead to an anarchy of values ignores the fact that relativism as such represents a principal value. His assumption that well-established ethical and aesthetic norms should be and are at the basis of our method can certainly be questioned.

This is not in defence of a restoration of historicism. For historicism deprives the student of literature of the possibility to pronounce a judgement of his own, whereas he, more than the common reader, seems qualified to do so. A purely historicist approach prevents the literary scholar from actively participating in contemporary society. A negative effect of historical relativism is also that literary history may be conceived as a series of isolated periods, which have no relation and often no meaning for the present.

On the other hand, we cannot see how a normative view of literature can do justice to contemporary and ancient literary texts in foreign cultures, where different traditions and ideologies reign. Our discipline demands from us that we investigate the literature of ancient Greece and Rome, of Mesopotamia, Africa, India, China and Japan, if we wish to avoid the accusation of modernist or eurocentric prepossession and to uphold a pretension to universality. That means that we will have to study what texts were acceptable as literature to readers in completely alien cultures.

We will have to study their ways of evaluating texts and to reconstruct their value systems, while preventing for the time being our own value system from interfering. When the structures of these alien value systems have been ascertained, they may be compared with other value systems, including our own. The mutual confrontation of these value systems will yield both differences and similarities. Such a confrontation may reveal the relativity of our own value system, provide us with alternative solutions to familiar problems and unsettle the habit of ethnocentrism. This method can be called cultural relativism (cf. Fokkema, 1972: 59–72). It may also be practicable to analyse the coexisting or successive value systems of one and the same culture. In the Soviet Union, for instance, for some time the assumptions and values of Russian Formalism coexisted with those of Marxist criticism, whereas in a later stage Marxist criticism almost exclusively dominated the scene.

Recently the doctrine of the inseparability of evaluation and interpretation has been questioned by Monroe C. Beardsley (1970), E. D. Hirsch (1972; 1976) and others. But there was a good reason for the long-lasting success of the doctrine of the inseparability of interpretation and evaluation, which normative critics, including the Marxists, have defended. They have been acting in reaction to the inadequacy of the historicist creed. Unfortunately, however, they have been unwilling to scrutinize and discuss the status of their own values. Indeed, they have acted on the basis of ethical and aesthetic imperatives. We reject this dogmatic attitude. Our concept of the scientific study of literature implies the necessity to distinguish between evaluation and interpretation. Any theory of literature should develop methods to guarantee that the observations and conclusions of the scholar are not obstructed by his personal preferences and values. The very first step into that direction depends on the will to avoid such interference by subjective conditions.

Having signalled the dangers of merely genetic explanations, of renouncing the definition of concepts, and of blending evaluation and interpretation, one may wonder what positive criteria can be formulated that theories of literature have to satisfy. What should one expect from a literary theory? One may, of course, subscribe to René Wellek's view that literary theory is "the study of the principles of literature, its categories, criteria, and the like", in contradistinction to literary criticism, which deals with concrete works of art (Wellek, 1963: 1). But if one adheres to a stricter concept of theory and assumes, with C. G. Hempel, that "theories are usually introduced when previous study of a class of phenomena has revealed a system of uniformities that can be expressed in the form of empirical laws" (Hempel, 1966: 70), one wonders whether any literary theory exists at all, except in extremely trivial or merely programmatic statements.

The crucial question is to what extent hypotheses pertaining to literature have been formulated with a claim to universal, or at least general validity. A quick review of the results in this respect is so disappointing that one wonders whether they will ever lead to a decent theory.[9] The literary theorist can boast only of having assigned names to certain phenomena and groups of phenomena (metres, rhymes, figures, narrative structures, genres, period concepts, conventions, codes), but the interrelationship of these phenomena too often reveals arbitrariness and chance. Conventions do play a foremost role in literature, and they do not obey a simple logic. If Max Rieser is correct in saying that "the law of form or of order or of structure which produces the work of art is not logical in character; it is more akin to the laws of natural processes, life processes" (Rieser, 1968: 262),—then we should not exclusively rely on developing general hypotheses and the logical inferences based upon them.

On the other hand, the aim to phrase universally valid hypotheses should not be dismissed too easily. Musing on the theme that "yesterday's daring metaphors are todays clichés", Arthur Koestler recently pleaded that the law of diminishing returns also applies to literature. He argues that the "wearing out" of words is an inevitable consequence of a property of our nervous system. The phenomenon psychologists have called "habituation" has the same neurological basis (Koestler, 1970). Convincing though the argument may seem, Koestler's law does not specify *when* precisely the returns will diminish and therefore has no predictive value. His law is unfalsifiable. One could as well argue that every phase of diminishing returns is preceded by a phase of *increasing* returns. A new metaphor must first be accepted by a growing public before its returns will diminish. One might invent the law of increasing returns and try to apply it to literature. Again, it would be unclear *when* this law should be applied. However, if we cannot refer yet to universal empirical laws in literature,[10] there is still no reason to renounce the attempt to find them.

Like Hempel's concept of a theory, the claim of universal validity is very much a product of natural science. Even if one decidedly subscribes to Popper's defence of a "unity of method" (Popper 1969a: 130–43), as we do, that does not imply that this one method will lead us equally far in all disciplines. The "unity of method" does not deny, of course, the existence of different methods of investigation in the various disciplines, but refers to the application of one method of falsification and provisional confirmation of hypotheses in all disciplines. In literary studies these hypotheses will often have a modest character and restrict themselves to establishing singular facts of authorship, chronology, influence, reception, literary devices and interpretation. Although these hypotheses deal with individual facts, they have to resort to general principles belonging to a literary theory if they wish to explain anything at all.

To begin with, literary theory must create a reservoir of universal or, at least, general concepts by means of which individual facts can be described and explained.[11] If we cannot detect general laws of any relevance, we certainly will be able to see that literature is determined by *relations* that are universal in character. There is the relation between originality and tradition, form and meaning, fictionality and reality, addresser and addressee, combination and selection of the material. Of these pairs, the number of which can be increased, at least one element is historically conditioned. Every literary theory must take this into consideration. Theorizing which reduces literature to abstract, a-historical form and on that basis attempts to phrase universal laws, has so far remained in the programmatic stage. On the other hand, the hermeneutic position that deals only with the interpretation of individual works and shirks all generalization cannot further our understanding of the literary process either. The only way open for future development of our discipline is the construction of general concepts and models, which allow for individual deviations and take account of the historical basis of all literature. Most of the theories that will be reviewed in the next four chapters have contributed to the construction of a *metalanguage*, in terms of which literature can be systematically discussed. Without conceptualization and generalization, and without the terminology of a metalanguage, no scientific discussion of the components of literature and literary history seems possible.

2

RUSSIAN FORMALISM, CZECH STRUCTURALISM AND SOVIET SEMIOTICS

In an essay published in St. Petersburg in 1914 Šklovskij wrote: "At present the old art is dead already, whereas the new art is not yet born. Things are dead as well—we have lost a feeling for the world. [...] Only the creation of new artistic forms may restore to man awareness of the world, resurrect things and kill pessimism" (Šklovskij, 1914: 13). This essay has been considered the first introduction to Formalism, and it certainly may be regarded as a link between the Futurist theorizing of Aleksej Kručěnych and Viktor Chlebnikov on the one hand (Markov, 1968) and the rich tradition of more mature studies which are commonly grouped together as Russian Formalism on the other. Around 1930 the history of Formalism—or, as the protagonists themselves termed it, the "formal method" (formal'nyj metod)—ended abruptly and prematurely due to political circumstances. The nine theses on "Problems of the Study of Literature and Language" formulated by Jurij Tynjanov and Roman Jakobson (1928) summarize the main positions of the later phase of Formalism and contain at the same time some of the incipient views of Czech structuralism.

In the late 1920s Prague had become an important centre for the study of both literature and language, partly because certain members of the Formalist school, or those closely associated with it had settled down there. Again politics intervened: the rise of Nazism forced various scholars to leave Czechoslovakia and silenced others.

Yet the tradition of structuralism was kept alive in some way or another both in the Soviet Union and in other East European countries, notably after the death of Stalin in 1953. After twenty-five or thirty years the threads that were dropped in the late 1920s were taken up again. The earlier Formalist positions were reinvestigated, criticized, expanded and rephrased, often in terms of information theory and semiotics.

In spite of the fact that a new generation came to the fore and in spite of all political interference, the three stages of Russian

Formalism, Czech structuralism and Soviet semiotics show a clear continuity. Today many of the hypotheses and values of Russian Formalism seem more alive than ever before, and they have never had so wide a currency outside the Soviet Union as they do today. There are, of course, marked differences among the various theories expounded by the Russian Formalists, notably between the Moscow and the Leningrad (Petrograd) branch. In 1915 the Moscow Linguistic Circle was established with Roman Jakobson, Pëtr Bogatyrëv and G. O. Vinokur as its principal members. In his Moscow period, Roman Jakobson already regarded literary theory or poetics as an integral part of linguistics. His view that "poetry is language in its aesthetic function" was published in 1921. Forty years later, this position was repeated in an only slightly altered form in his essay on "Linguistics and Poetics" (1960). The group in Leningrad which from 1916 became known as the Society for the Study of Poetic Language or *Opojaz*[1] took a less strictly linguistic point of view. The active participants were Lev Jakubinskij, Viktor Šklovskij, Boris Ejchenbaum and Sergej Bernštejn. Šklovskij and Ejchenbaum were later patronized by Viktor Žirmunskij, who in 1920 became head of the Department for Literary History at the National Institute of Art History in Leningrad, with which Jurij Tynjanov, Boris Tomaševskij and Viktor Vinogradov were also connected. From the very beginning they were more involved with the problems of literary history, including matters of evaluation, than with linguistic questions.[2]

Almost every new school of literary theorists in Europe takes its cue from the "Formalist" tradition, emphasizing different trends in that tradition and trying to establish its own interpretation of Formalism as the only correct one. For that reason alone it would seem timely to investigate once àgain the basic tenets of Formalism. For a more detailed survey of Formalism we must refer to Erlich (1969), Striedter (1969) and Stempel (1972).

The Claim of Scientific Reliability

One of the principal aims of Formalism is the scientific study of literature. This, in fact, is based on the belief that such a study is after all possible and appropriate. Even if this belief was not further discussed, it served as one of the premises of Formalism. But whenever the Formalists questioned the scientific examination of literature, they believed that their studies would enhance the reader's capability to read literary texts in an appropriate way, i.e. with an eye for those properties of the text that were considered "literary" or "artistic". Perception through the artistic form, they reasoned, restores our awareness of the world and brings things to life. Indirectly, the premises of Formalism seem to have a psychological foundation since immediate experience is one of its principal ideals. Only at a later stage, however, was the social function of the immediate experience of art forms emphasized (Jakobson, 1934).

Of course, the belief that a scientific study of literature is possible and appropriate is common to most literary theorists. But few theoreticians have been so emphatic about it as were the Russian Formalists. From his early publications Šklovskij (1916a) was interested in the "laws of poetic language". And Jakobson (1921) emphasized the necessity that the "science of literature" (*nauka o literature*) be a science. Moreover, Tynjanov expressed the view that "in order finally to become a science, the history of literature must lay claim to reliability" (1927: 435).

However, the most elaborate statement on methodological problems can be found in Ejchenbaum (1926). Ejchenbaum presents a modern concept of scientific investigation which resembles the hypothetical deductive method later advocated by Popper. Ejchenbaum writes:

We establish concrete principles and adhere to them to the extent they are proved tenable by the material. If the material requires their further elaboration or alteration, we go ahead and elaborate or alter them. In this sense we are relatively detached from our own theories, as indeed a science ought to be, seeing that there is a difference between theory and convictions. There are no ready-made sciences. The vitality of a science is not measured by its establishing truths but by its overcoming errors (1926: 3–4).

This implies that all scientific assertions about literature are, in principle, revocable. We cannot be certain that there exists a definite and absolute truth. If an assertion proves untenable, it, as well as all other assertions which depend on it, should be eliminated. This shows the interdependence of scientific observations as well as their (in principle) hypothetical status.

The concept of the study of literature as a science forced the Formalists to look for universal or at least general properties of literature. Hence Jakobson (1921) proclaimed "literariness" (*literaturnost'*) to be the object of the science of literature, instead of literature as a whole or individual literary texts. According to Jakobson, the *devices* or constructive principles that make a text into a work of art are the proper objects of the study of literature. Ejchenbaum (1926) and most other Formalists basically agreed with this view, although gradually the study of literature was extended to other aspects as well. In concentrating on the devices of literature Jakobson and Ejchenbaum believed that certain elements or factors should be abstracted from the literary text and studied independently from the text and its context.

On the other hand, the Formalists accepted Kručënych's view that a new form produces a new content, and that content is conditioned by form (Jakobson, 1921). Thus it seems to be the rule that different forms must have different meanings. Synonyms and homonyms are exceptions that allow the poet to draw attention to the sign character of words or, as Jakobson (1921) says, to "emancipate words from meanings". In the case of synonyms the same meaning is distributed over two words, whereas homonyms combine at least two meanings in one word. The poetic play with homonyms and synonyms is possible only against the background of the general rule that new forms must have new meanings, a rule which forbids discussion of content without discussion of form. In effect, there was a tendency to reject any abstracting from the text, which reminds us of the New Critics' rejection of "the heresy of paraphrase".

Šklovskij explicitly disapproved of reducing a literary work to the thought it expressed, and found support for this position from L. N. Tolstoy, who in a letter commenting on *Anna Karenina*, wrote as follows:

If I would want to say in words all that I intended to express in the novel, then I would have to rewrite the very novel which I have written. [...] In all, or almost all that I have written, I was guided by the need to collect thoughts, which were linked to each other in order to express myself. Every thought expressed in words loses its sense and becomes extremely banal, when it is isolated from the concatenation to which it belongs (Sklovskij, 1916b: 109).

In the same vein Tomaševskij warned that "one cannot paraphrase Pushkin"* (Erlich, 1969: 53).

There is a seeming contradiction between Jakobson's view that the devices of literature can be abstracted from the literary texts, and the belief that abstraction from the text is, in fact, unwarranted. This misleading contradiction has created much confusion, with which the contemporary study of literature is still confronted. However, the dilemma between abstraction and the study of the concrete material does not exist only in the study of literature. The natural sciences also deal with individual

*The spelling of familiar names, such as Pushkin, Tolstoy and Chekhov, departs from the internationally accepted system of transliteration of the Russian script which we use elsewhere.

phenomena and yet have discovered general factors at work in or among these individual phenomena. But, in discovering these general factors, the sciences aim at *explanation*, not at the kind of inadequate reproduction which is paraphrase. Explanation calls for a certain degree of generalization. Conceptualization and generalization are justified by our need to discuss things or to explain their meaning in a detached, scientific manner. The recognition of general factors is the very basis of all knowledge. It is also a precondition of the recognition of a literary text as being literary. Therefore, the search for devices that make a text into a literary text, as proposed by Jakobson, is only an explicit operation of the unconscious activity of any reader.

In our opinion, it is not necessary to conclude that the search for the devices or constructive principles of literary texts is incompatible with the rejection of the paraphrase. The Russian Formalists did not wish to "destroy" the literary text or to reproduce it in an inferior form. They only wanted to talk rationally about the principles according to which it had been built. They bridged the gap between abstraction and the individual text by introducing the concept of *function*. They wished to study how certain constructive principles or *devices* are at work in the literary text and how they make the text into an organized whole. This led them first to the concept of the literary *system*, and finally to the concept of *structure*.

The Devices of Literature

Formalist thinking between 1914 and 1930 clearly shows a certain development. The influence of Edmund Husserl (1900), Broder Christiansen (1909) and Ferdinand de Saussure (1915) penetrated gradually into the Formalist writings. But there is also an immanent development. If, however, we deal first with the devices of literature, then with the concept of factor and function, and finally with dominant and system, we seem to invest the findings of the Formalist school with a systematic appearance that is not warranted by its historical development. A strong point of the Formalist school is its close relationship with creative writing. Several Formalist critics were closely associated with Futurist writers. Tynjanov turned to writing fiction when theorizing had become too dangerous politically. But this close relationship with the workshop of literature also had a negative aspect: a denigrating attitude towards definitions and attempts to bring knowledge into a system. The driving force behind Russian Formalism appears to have been the urge to demolish petrified concepts, to discover new forms and to instill into life a quality which should make it worthwhile. A systematic approach is almost incompatible with this attitude. Only if we take into account that our presentation is highly selective, and tends for the sake of clarity to give undue emphasis to conceptualization in Formalist thinking, does it seem warranted to deal with a number of Formalist concepts more or less systematically.

Šklovskij's essay "Art as Device" (1916a) was one of the first to give an outline of several of the main Formalist tenets. He dismisses as incorrect the idea that poetry is mainly characterized by images, and in doing so he rejects the position of the influential nineteenth-century critics Potebnja and Belinskij,[3] as well as the critical tradition of Symbolism. According to Šklovskij, it is not the images that characterize poetry and determine its history, but the introduction of "new devices for the arrangement and processing of verbal material" (1916a: 5). The poetic image is only one of the means of intensifying the impression, and as such its role is similar to that of other devices of poetic language, such as simple and negative parallelism, simile, repetition, symmetry and hyperbole. All serve to enhance the immediate experience *(oščuščenie)* of a thing or of a word, just as words can also become things.

The mistaken view that art is a way of thinking by means of images originated, according to Šklovskij, from the identification of the language of poetry with that of prose. Here Šklovskij's terminology is vague and uncertain, and we know from a reference in the very same essay to Jakubinskij's contributions that he had the opposition between poetic (literary) and practical language in mind, rather than that between poetry and artistic prose. Later, notably in the publications of Roman Jakobson, the opposition between poetic (literary) and practical language gave way to the less rigid distinction between the poetic (literary) and practical *functions* of language. Practical language, writes Šklovskij, tries to be brief. Through habituation, acts (including speech acts) become automatic. This process of automatization may explain why a half-finished sentence or even half a word is often enough in practical language. Under these conditions the image is meant to be a short cut.

Poetic language, on the other hand, defies economy. The poetic image, like other devices of poetic language, aims to destroy the tendency towards habituation and serves to lengthen and intensify the process of perception. Betraying the influence of Bergson (Curtis, 1976), Šklovskij wrote in a famous paragraph,

[. . .] precisely in order to restore the immediate experience of life, to feel things, to make the stone stony, that which is called art exists. The aim of art is to convey the immediate experience of a thing as if it is seen instead of recognized; the device of art is the device of making things strange and the device of the impeded form, which enlarges the difficulty and the length of the perception, as in art the process of perception is self-oriented [*samocelen*] and must be lengthened; art is a means to becoming aware of the making of things, but in art the things made are not important (Sklovskij, 1916a: 15).

Šklovskij explains that, apart from rhetorical figures, there are various other ways of achieving the aim of the impeded form and making things strange. He borrows a number of examples from the works of L. N. Tolstoy. Tolstoy created the experience of estrangement by describing things without mentioning their proper names, as if they were seen for the first time. He depicts a battlefield through the eyes of a civilian (*War and Peace*), and describes the human system of ownership through the eyes of a horse ("Cholstomer"). The effect of these devices is that "an object is transferred from [the sphere of] its usual perception to that of a new perception, which results in a particular semantic shift" (Šklovskij, 1916a: 31).

This is early Formalism in a nutshell, and many attempts have been made to comment on it. First the question has been raised as to what is the relation between the device of making strange and the device of the impeded form (Wolf Schmid, 1973). One does not need to accept the direct influence on Šklovskij of Saussure's or Husserl's semiotics in order to decide that both devices should be located on the level of the *signifiant* (signifier). The difference, however, appears to be that the device of impeded form plays a role mainly in microstructures, and that of making things strange mainly in macrostructures, such as resulting from the point of view. In both cases the writer or poet aims at a new perception of things or a restoration of "the experience of life", and this goal is reached by means of a specific construction of the language. In view of this formal aspect, Šklovskij reaches the conclusion that poetry can be defined as "impeded, curbed language", as "a language construction".

This definition of poetry shows that Šklovskij, as well as other Formalists, focussed his attention on the technical aspects of poetry. His view that art is a means of becoming aware of the making of things, and that "the things made are not important in art", has strengthened the impression of a one-sided interest in technique. Indeed, Šklovskij's comments on Tolstoy rarely, if ever, touch upon the values of his philosophy, and his remarks concerning Turgenev's philosophical essay on Hamlet and Don Quixote are plainly derogatory (Šklovskij, 1925: 101). When, moreover, Roman Jakobson (1921) declares that literariness (*literaturnost'*), or "that which makes a certain work into a literary work", is the only proper object of the science of literature, there seems to be ample ground for criticizing the Formalists, as Erlich did (1969: 90), for being one-sidedly interested in the "sum-total of the stylistic devices"(Šklovskij, 1925: 165).

Yet this criticism is not completely fair. Šklovskij says clearly that "the things made are not important *in art*", which means that they may be important from the non-artistic, i.e. philosophical, religious or social point of view. He further made it abundantly clear that art, including literature, has a psychological function as it restores the immediate experience of life. When Šklovskij posited that "the content (hence, the 'soul') of a literary work is the sum-total of its stylistic devices", he was apparently influenced by Nietzsche, who expressed himself on the problem of form and content as follows: "The price of being an artist is to grasp as *content*, as 'the thing itself', what all non-artists call 'form'" (Kunne-Ibsch, 1974: 1). If not in any other connection, Šklovskij was familiar with Nietzschean thought through Christiansen (1909).

The Formalists did indeed devote most of their attention to the formal aspects of literature. In the field of narratology they investigated the way in which the various episodes of a story are connected; they examined the technique of the frame-story and the relations, often family ones, between characters. Their primary interest was to discover the technique of how a story is made. The conversation between characters is not interpreted in isolation, but seen as a means for advancing the action by introducing new material. And as to the question of why for example, in *Don Quixote* a central place is attributed to the inn, Šklovskij answers by pointing out that it is the epicentre of many episodes, the point where all threads of the novel cross each other. In short, the inn is a *compositional* factor of considerable importance (Šklovskij, 1925).

Various technical terms were introduced and used by Šklovskij, Ejchenbaum, Tynjanov, and others in order to distinguish the main constructive factors in a literary work. The least controversial is the *fabula*, which can be defined as "the description of the events" (Šklovskij, 1921: 297) or, more precisely, as the representation of the action in its chronological order and causal relations. The *fabula* can be distinguished by purely semantic means. The concept of *fabula* is used in opposition to that of *sjužet*, usually translated as "plot" or "narrative structure" (often misleadingly transcribed as "sujet"). According to the Formalists, plot (*sjužet*) is the way in which the semantic material is presented in a given text. Tynjanov came close to this definition when he described plot as the actual composition of semantic elements in a text *(semanatičeskaja gruppirovka)* (1924a: 409). Šklovskij explained that "the *fabula* is merely material for the formation of the plot" (1921: 297). These definitions agree with those proposed by Tomaševskij (1925: 137). In Russian Formalism, plot is a concept which has both a formal and a semantic aspect. Whereas the *fabula* is the product of a rather high level of abstraction, the concept of plot remains closer to the text and requires less abstraction. The *fabula* is abstracted from the semantic material that is a constituent factor of the plot.

Ejchenbaum explains the concept of plot by means of the motif. The plot, then, consists of "the interconnection of the motifs by means of their motivation" (1918a: 123). But among the Formalists there is not much consensus over the meaning of motif. Initially Šklovskij accepted Veselovskij's (1838–1906) not very precise definition of motif as "the most elementary narrative unit" (Šklovskij, 1916a: 39). But gradually the Formalists began to see the motif as a "factor" or "constructive principle", rather than a "unit" or "element" (Bernštejn, 1927: 345). The traditional notion of motif as a thematic concept had changed into a compositional concept (Ejchenbaum, 1926: 15–16). One can describe this shift of emphasis as the development of the notion of motif from "the smallest unit of the *fabula*" to "the smallest constructive principle of the plot".

The Formalists soon discovered that the constituent factors of a story are not limited to motifs and their motivations. Characters, as well as the setting (e.g. the inn in *Don Quixote*), may play that role. The plot is not necessarily the main organizing factor of a story, as is explained by Ejchenbaum in his essay "How Gogol's 'Overcoat' Was Made" (1918a). It appears that in Gogol's story the personal tone of the narrator becomes a constructive factor of primary importance. Ejchenbaum's analysis showed that elements of oral narration and narrative improvisation may enter written literature. The untranslatable name for this device of quasi-oral narration is *skaz* (Ejchenbaum, 1918b).

Vinogradov (1925) regarded *skaz* as an "artistic construction raised to a square", since it consists of an aesthetic superstructure on the basis of language constructions, mainly monologues, which themselves are characterized by stylistic selection and compositional devices. Not all texts dominated by the personal tone of the narrator must resort to *skaz*. In his essay on "Literature Without Plot", Šklovskij discussed the predominance of an intimate tone in the writings of V. V. Rozanov, which he called the "tone of the confession" (1925: 172). Šklovskij emphasized that Rozanov cannot be considered as actually having made a confession in his writings, but he believes that Rozanov used the "tone of the confession" merely as a literary device.

Various constructive factors were distinguished in literary prose. But it took some time before their interrelation was investigated. In the theory of poetry a similar development took place. Whereas in prose the plot as a rule is the "central constructive factor", in poetry that role is fulfilled by rhythm (Tynjanov, 1924a). Plot, characters, setting and thematic elements are reduced to the position of material in poetry and organized by the rhythm.

Initially the Formalists' study of poetry focussed on single devices occurring in verse. Like Šklovskij, Jakobson (1921) emphasized the device of the impeded form. He observed that we perceive contemporary poetry against the background of the prevailing poetic tradition, as well as that of "practical language". In the first instance, literary history shows that the device of the impeded form aims at a disorganization of the established literary form. The result may be a form which appears to be "simple" to us, as in the case of certain verses by Pushkin. Other devices, such as parallellism and the play with synonyms and homonyms, signal the difference from practical language. Jakobson concluded that poetry is "an utterance with a set [*Einstellung*] towards the expression" (*vyskazyvanie s ustanovkoj na vyraženie*), with the result that the "communicative function", which predominates in practical and emotional language, is reduced to a minimum (Jakobson, 1921; 1960).

This view was basically accepted by other Formalists writing on poetry, such as Tynjanov and Brik. The specific focus on the forms of the expression in poetry led Tynjanov and Brik to explore the semantic and syntactical effect of the formal characteristics of poetry, such as rhythm and rhyme. Their findings proved to be of seminal importance, as is apparent from recent studies by Lotman (1964; 1970) and Segal (1968).

Tynjanov (1924b) observed that the word in poetry appears to belong to two series (*rjad*), that of rhythm and that of meaning. Both rhythm and semantics play a role in the selection of words in poetry. In one of his early uses of the word *struktura*, Tynjanov explains that the difference in structure between the respective vocabularies of poetry and prose must be attributed to "the unity and terseness (*tesnota*) of the poetic series, the dynamic role of the word in the poem and the successiveness (*sukcessivnost'*) of poetical speech" (1924b: 133). More than in prose, the position of the word in a line of poetry may have a semantic effect: "Between words a relationship comes into being on the basis of their [successive] position" (1924b: 76). This may result not only in a specific coloration of the word, but even in a shift of meaning.

Like Tynjanov, Brik, in oral reports later incorporated into his study "Rhythm and Syntax" (1927), emphasized the interrelationship between the rhythmic and the semantic factors. In the history of poetry, either the rhythmic or the semantic principle is emphasized at the cost of the other; poetry, however, needs both. Brik (1927) also stressed that in poetry words are organized according to two different laws, viz. the rules of rhythm and those of prose syntax.

Gradually the Russian Formalists came to accept the view that the various factors in verbal art are interrelated. The dominant function of one factor subordinates the importance of other factors and deforms them, but seldom completely annihilates their functions. If the Formalists viewed literature as a system characterized by the interdependence of its elements, this position must be called *structuralist*, although they rarely used that label before 1927.

The structuralist approach to literature ended the one-sidedness of early Formalism. Šklovskij's view that a literary work is nothing else than its construction, or the sum-total of all devices, proved unsatisfactory. A work of literature is not an accumulation of devices but an organized whole, made up of factors of varying importance. The semantic material will nearly always have at least a minor function. This was the firm position of Tynjanov (1924b) and Brik (1927). The idea of "transrational" poetry or poetry without a meaning (*zaum'*), defended by Jakobson (1921), was not taken seriously any more once the conviction had developed that poetry is not the result of rhythm alone, but of the interplay of various factors, dominated by the factor of rhythm. With the subsiding interest in isolated technical matters and with the transition from problems of sound structure and poetry to those of semantics, prose and literary history, the one-sided influence of linguistics apparent in early Formalist writings gradually decreased.

The System of Literature

Bernštejn (1927) concluded that a work of art is characterized by wholeness to such an extent that it cannot be split up into parts. The work of art is not the result of an addition of elements but of factors which, while organizing the material into a whole, are constituents of the structure of the work of art. Although the work of art cannot be split into elements, it is possible to analyse the artistic structure in terms of factors. Bernštejn further posited that the work of art expresses a meaning or, in his own words, can be considered as an "external sign of an emotional–dynamic system of non-perceptible emotions" (1927: 343). The aesthetic object, to which the external sign (the work of art, or the artefact, as Mukařovský was later to call it) refers, is reconstructed by the receiver in the reception of that sign. The work of art, Bernštejn argues, can only function as a sign because of its structure, which can be analysed in recognizable factors.

Bernštejn explains that he has been inspired by Christiansen's *Philosophie der Kunst* (1909), which he quotes from a Russian translation with which Šklovskij (1916b) was also familiar. He likewise acknowledges the influence of the philosopher Gustav Špet (1922), who defined the concept of structure and to whom we will return shortly.[4] Špet appears to be inspired by the phenomenological semiotics of Husserl, who, though avoiding the word "structure" in his *Logische Untersuchungen* (1900–1), in fact describes the simplest form of structure in terminology that comes very close indeed to that of the Russian Formalists. If two elements, says Husserl, are placed together and constitute a relation, then these two elements are the material *vis-à-vis* the form of that relation.[5]

Although Roman Jakobson refers to Husserl's views on meaning and referent (*dinglicher Bezug* or *gegenständliche Beziehung*) (Jakobson, 1921: 92), we may not assume that in general the Russian Formalists were directly familiar with Husserl's writings. They did, however, know the work of Špet, whose phenomenological semiotics and aesthetics were influential in the early 1920s. According to Špet, "structure is a concrete construction, the various parts of which may change as to dimension and even quality, but no part of the whole *in potentia* can be deleted without destruction of the whole" (Špet, 1923: II, 11). The products of the mind and of culture essentially have a structural character. All parts of a structure are potentially effective. All implicit forms in principle can become explicit. The function of the various parts of the structure depends on the context and on the set (*ustanovka, Einstellung*) towards the given structure. The linguistic context of a morpheme has a dynamic character. Likewise, the social and cultural context of an utterance is determined by dynamic laws. A real or imagined object can become an aesthetic object through a specific set or attitude *sui generis* of the observer which aims neither at action nor at logical analysis.

This leads Špet to postulate a third kind of truth, i.e., "poetic truth", which differs from "transcendental or material truth" as well as from "logical truth". Literature deals with fantastic, fictive subject-matter. In the play of poetic forms, the complete emancipation from reality can be attained. But these forms maintain an internal poetic logic, a logic *sui generis,* as well as a meaning (*smysl*), since the emancipation from the familiar situation does not imply an emancipation from meaning (Špet, 1923: II, 66). In fact, Špet gives a rather clear exposition of one of the main characteristics of the literary text, viz. the principle of fictionality, which maintains a claim to truth while defying a direct comparison with reality.

Although Špet did not adhere to the "formal method", and in his *Aesthetic Fragments* (1922–3) never quoted any of the Russian Formalists, his concept of the aesthetic function and of the literary work as a structure was very close to theirs. Later publications by Tynjanov, Ejchenbaum and Jakobson may exemplify this.

Tynjanov's essays "The Literary Fact" (1924a) and "On Literary Evolution" (1927), both reprinted in his book *Archaists and Innovators* (1929), are among the best of the Formalist heritage and have maintained their authority to the present day. As we shall see, both Mukařovský and Lotman took their cue from the views Tynjanov developed in these studies.

Tynjanov defines literature as a "language construction which is experienced as a construction: i.e. literature is a dynamic language construction" (1924a: 407–9). As with Špet, the word "dynamic" here means that the literary text is not an isolated, static fact, but part of a tradition and of a communicative process. Each language construction will gradually lose its effect and become automatized. If the receiver is to experience a language construction as a *construction*, or, as Jakobson phrased it, if the attention of the receiver is to be focussed on the expression, then the constructive factors should be different from those encountered in earlier texts or outside literature. In literature the material must be "deformed" rather than formed. Of course, the deformation can be noticed only against the background of literary and social history. Therefore Tynjanov states that it is unwise to speak of aesthetic qualities in general, as aesthetic qualities are the result of a concrete act of perception within a particular historical context. When a modern reader, with his own perceptional experience, interprets a text from an older period, he may easily take vital and original devices for commonplace constructions, whereas the contemporary of that text would have judged these devices in their relation to previous constructive principles, i.e. in their dynamic function (Tynjanov, 1924a: 411). Here and elsewhere Tynjanov advocates an historicist approach, as in fact all Formalists do, in particular Šklovskij and Jakobson. It also appears that the deformation of the material is considered a necessary (though not a sufficient) condition of the language construction that is to be experienced as a construction and thus to be considered as literature.

Just as, according to Tynjanov, it is impossible to give a static definition of literature, it is also impossible to do the same for the *genre*. The genre is a floating system, which in due course abandons certain devices and attracts others. And, as we all know from literary history, it appears at a certain juncture and may disappear under different conditions. Expressing himself in structuralist terms without, however, using the word "structure", Tynjanov observes that a new genre will be noticed only in confrontation with a traditional genre. He ventures the generalization that each genre moves in the period of its decay from the centre to the periphery of literature, whereas a new phenomenon emerges from the backwoods of literature to take its place at the centre. So the *roman d'aventures* moved to the periphery and turned into boulevard literature, and the position in the centre was filled by the psychological novel, which, says Tynjanov, is now in the process of becoming boulevard literature (Tynjanov, 1924a). Three years later Tynjanov was even more explicit: "The examination of isolated genres is impossible without taking into account the signs of the genre system with which they are in correlation"

(Tynjanov, 1927: 446). The problem of the genre as a shifting or open concept (Weitz, 1972) was already solved by Tynjanov (1924a; 1927). When Wellek (1970) or Lotman (1970) express themselves on the delimitation of genres, they have been inspired by Tynjanov's structuralist approach to literary history. This demonstrates the full significance of his views.

In "On Literary Evolution" Tynjanov elaborated his views on the relation between the literary work and the literary system. In line with Christiansen and the Formalist tradition established by Šklovskij, Tynjanov repeats the view that whether a certain phenomenon in a linguistic text should be considered a literary fact depends on its differential quality *(diferencial'noe kačestvo)* in relation to the literary or extraliterary series: in other words on its function. Therefore, the immanent study of a literary work is a doubtful abstraction and strictly speaking impossible (1927: 441). The literary work must be related to the literary system. But, in addition, the isolated study of the literary system and its evolution, or of the succession of literary systems, is impossible. The literary series *(rjad, Reihe)* is correlated with adjacent cultural, behavioural, and social series which are indirectly, through the intermediary of language, connected with it.

The literary and extraliterary series are mainly correlated at the level of language since in relation to daily life literature has a communicative function. This view was always maintained by Tynjanov. He rejected the Marxist view of the primacy of economic conditions, and considered the literary series as a series *sui generis*. He distrusted "the rectilinear study of the author's psychology and the construction of a causal bridge from the milieu, daily life and class of the author to his works" (1927: 457).

When Tynjanov expressed himself on the relation between literature and the environment of the author, he followed his own structuralist view of literature to its logical conclusions. At the same time, however, he was answering the Marxist challenge which in these years became louder and more vehement. Of all Marxist attacks on the Formalist tenets, Trotsky's *Literature and Revolution* (1924) is the most famous. Of course, Trotsky firmly adheres to dialectical materialism. He asserts that "from the point of view of an objective historical process, art is always a social servant and historically utilitarian" (1924: 168). But on the other hand a certain degree of admiration for Šklovskij and real knowledge of the Formalists' writings emerge from his criticism. His opening statement that the only theory which has opposed

Marxism in the Soviet Union is Formalism, as well as the explicit acknowledgement that a certain part of the research done by the Formalists is useful, can be considered as a tribute to the Formalists. Trotsky quotes some of the most extreme assertions of Šklovskij and Jakobson to conclude that according to them "art has always been the work of self-sufficient pure forms". He criticizes them for having restricted themselves to "an analysis of the etymology and syntax of poems, to the counting of repetitive vowels and consonants, of syllables and epithets" (1924: 162, 163). He incorrectly believes that Šklovskij has embraced the idea of the absolute independence of art from the social environment, and stresses the interrelatedness of art, psychology and social conditions. He criticizes the Formalists for neglecting "the dynamics of development" and restricting themselves to isolated facts.

Significantly, Trotsky does not mention Tynjanov or Ejchenbaum, who paid more attention to "the dynamics of development" than Šklovskij and, moreover, lacked the latter's polemical tone. Whereas Tynjanov in his essay "On Literary Evolution" expressed himself on the issues raised by Trotsky, Ejchenbaum, in 1929, made a final and rather desperate attempt to counter the Marxist criticism, which in the wake of Trotsky's critique grew into a campaign that was to end with the annihilation of the Formalist school. Ejchenbaum acknowledges in his essay "Literary Environment" (1929) that in the past the Formalists had focussed attention primarily on questions of literary technique and that they should rather investigate the relations between the facts of the literary evolution and literary life. He seems to agree fully with Tynjanov in this respect, but goes one step further by demanding a new orientation of literary-sociological studies, which thus far had neglected the problem of the nature of literary-historical facts. Ejchenbaum is prepared to accept the sociology of literature as a useful enterprise, if only the literary sociologists would give up "the metaphysical quest for the prime origin of literary evolution and the literary forms", because "no genetic study, however far it may go, can lead us to the prime origin, as long as the aims envisaged are scientific, and not religious" (1929: 60–1). He goes so far as to quote Engels to enhance his criticism of the crude sociological studies of literature of his day.

Ejchenbaum interprets the difference between the Formalists and the ("vulgar") sociologists as one between hypothetical and axiomatic assertions, or between science and religion. His concept of science is rather modest: science does not explain, but rather establishes the specific properties and relations of the phenomena.[6] Moreover, he does not seem to believe that the hypothesis of a prime origin will be of any use for the present study of literary texts. He holds that "literature [. . .] is not generated by facts belonging to other series and therefore *cannot be reduced* to such facts" (1929: 61). The study of literature has not been emancipated from rendering service to the history of culture, philosophy and psychology, in order to be put to the service of economics.

A year earlier Tynjanov and Jakobson had expressed themselves in a similar way in their famous nine theses. They had severe methodological objections to an examination of the interrelationship between the literary and extraliterary systems that does not take the immanent laws of each system into account (Tynjanov and Jakobson, 1928). In the same theses, they use the word "structure" more or less as a synonym of "system", a term which Tynjanov had till then usually preferred. As the theses were published in a Soviet journal and Jakobson was living in Prague, they can be considered the final summary of the Formalist achievement, as well as one of the initial statements of Czech structuralism.

Ejchenbaum's argument and the theses by Tynjanov and Jakobson are convincing, as the sociologists have still not succeeded in explaining adequately the literary quality of a text on the basis of extra-literary data. The Formalist argument, however, was not judged on its intellectual merit. By 1930 it had become almost impossible for the Formalists to publish their views. Šklovskij, once the admired chairman of *Opojaz*, succumbed to mounting pressures and in 1930 published a self-criticism in which he acknowledged that "in the last analysis, it is the economic process which determines and reorganizes the literary series and the literary system" (Erlich, 1969: 139).

Motif Analysis

By accepting the concept of "structure", the Russian Formalists introduced the new dichotomy of the (organized) structure versus the (unorganized) material, which was to replace the old dichotomy of form and content. The structure of a literary text has both a formal and a semantic aspect. The same applies to the unorganized material. For instance, the rhymes in a real or imagined rhyming dictionary belong to the unorganized material of poetry and have a predominantly formal potential. The words in a (common) lexicon also belong to the unorganized material, but mainly have a semantic potential. Individual philosophies and mythologies or the incidents of real or imagined *fabulae* belong to the unorganized material *vis-à-vis* the literary text in which they have been joined into an organized whole. Šklovskij's concept of the *fabula* as "material for the formation of the plot" or narrative structure (1921: 297) is in full agreement with the structuralist views that were phrased in the later period of Russian Formalism.

In order to avoid confusion, a quite different concept of the *fabula* and its constituent motifs as developed by Vladimir Propp must be mentioned here. Although Propp cannot be considered one of the Russian Formalists (cf. Todorov, 1965a), he was active in the same period and became widely known in Western Europe and America through various translations of his book *Morphology of the Folktale,* originally published in 1928 (Propp, 1928; 1958; 1968; 1970a; 1970b; 1972), and as a result of an elaborate review by Lévi-Strauss (1960) of the English translation. Through the efforts of E. M. Meletinskij, a reprint appeared in the Soviet Union in 1969.

Both Šklovskij and Propp were well acquainted with the work of the great nineteenth-century Russian comparatist and folklorist Veselovskij, but they interpreted his views in different ways. Šklovskij understood Veselovskij's concept of motif ("the most elementary narrative unit") as closely connected with the plot or narrative structure. Propp, however, emphasized the possibility of separating the problem of the motifs from that of the plot (*sjužet*). This was in accordance with Veselovskij, as the latter differed from the later Formalist tradition in that he did not regard the text as a structural whole. By *sjužet,* the Russian Formalists meant the individual narrative structure of a story; we have consistently translated this concept of *sjužet* as "plot". Veselovskij, however, as quoted by Propp, understood *sjužet* to be "a theme, in which the various situations [*položenija*], i.e. motifs, move in and out" (Propp, 1928: 18). He considered the *sjužety* as variables into which new motifs can be inserted. To him the motif is a unit of primary importance, the *sjužet* only the product of a series of motifs. According to Veselovskij, the *sjužet* can be divided into motifs, whereas the motif is an indivisible narrative unit (Propp, 1928: 18).

Propp correctly remarked that from a logical point of view the idea of a most elementary indivisible unit is a rather suspect abstraction. He argued that Veselovskij's motifs as a rule could very well be divided into more fundamental elements. Restricting himself to the study of a limited corpus of Russian fairy-tales, Propp concluded that different motifs may describe similar actions, although the characters and their attributes may differ. For instance, the motifs "A king gives an eagle to a hero; the eagle carries the hero away to another kingdom" and "An old man gives Sučenko a horse; the horse carries Sučenko away to another kingdom" describe a similar action, viz. "The hero acquires a magical agent". The motifs that have a similar action in common are variables of one and the same invariant function. Propp calls these similar actions "functions of the acting characters" (1928: 23).

Whereas there are a great number of motifs, Propp distinguished only thirty-one functions of characters in the material he investigated. This led him to the thesis that the number of functions of characters in the fairy-tale is limited. He also concluded that the order of the functions is always the same, but immediately added that this rule applies only to the fairy-tale in folklore, and not to the literary fairy-tale. In a fairy-tale certain functions can be deleted from the fixed order, and certain functions can be repeated (Propp, 1928: 89). According to Propp, this does not affect the fixed order of the functions. However, in our view it does affect it, as these two "escape clauses" enable us theoretically to apply the law of the fixed order of the functions also to fairy-tales with an inverted order, that is, fairy-tales which begin with function 31 to end with function 1 (deletion of functions 1 to 30; after function 31, the earlier deleted function 30 is repeated; after function 30, the earlier deleted function 29 is repeated, etc.). The inverted order of functions occurs on a more limited scale in the examples given by Propp. In short, the two escape clauses of the deletion and the repetition of functions make the law of the fixed order unfalsifiable (Guépin, 1972).

Although an admirer of Propp, Bremond (1966) explicitly abandoned the thesis of the fixed order. Bremond carried the level of abstraction even further than Propp. From the many possible functions, including those outside the fairy-tale, he abstracted three which generate the most elementary sequence, viz. a function which opens a possibility of action, a function which realizes this possibility, and a function which closes this process with a certain result. All conceivable functions are variables of the invariant functions of this most elementary sequence.

Although Bremond's approach can be defended by postulating that the meaning of a text can be explained only by reference to models outside that text, he has reached a degree of abstraction that so far has been of little avail to the interpretation of literature. Yet his position is characteristic of an interesting trend in the study of literature. Todorov's *Grammaire du Décaméron* (1969), as well as various exercises in generative poetics or the literary text grammar, also belong to this trend which is rather far removed from the main tradition of Russian Formalism (Šklovskij, Jakobson, Tynjanov, Ejchenbaum and others).

The tradition of examining the possible functions of characters in the fashion of Propp and Bremond can be traced back to Veselovskij. As Lotman has explained, Veselovskij defined his concept of motif in semantic terms. According to Veselovskij, motif is the elementary narrative unit which refers to a typical event in the sphere of *daily life* or *social reality* (Lotman, 1972a: 330). The similarities of *action* that Propp recognized in the various functions of characters can also be defined in purely semantic terms. Whereas for Veselovskij the motif and not the *sjužet* or text was of primary importance, Propp's search for the invariants of motifs moved one step further away from the text. Moreover, many authors who took their cue from Propp appeared to have forgotten that his materials, like Veselovskij's, were folklore texts and not literature. Bremond and Todorov are exceptions in this respect, and were well aware of the restrictions of Propp's analysis and their own methods. Todorov explained that the object of his narratological study did not coincide with the literary text, as narration also occurs outside literature (1969: 10). Bremond professed his indebtedness to anthropology and cautioned that the anthropological data can serve only as a frame of reference (1966: 76). Anthropological data can only help to explain the literariness of a particular text indirectly, as the facts of literature do not belong to the level of scientific logic or common sense, which teaches us that the thief must enter the house before he can steal or that prohibition precedes infringement. Indeed, the literary text often violates the laws of common sense and is characterized, in the words of Špet, by a third kind of truth. In Kafka's *Der Prozess* (The Trial) (1925) we read of an infringement, but never learn what law was violated. Lotman sees the trespassing of the established world view of common sense as one of the characteristics of literature: Aeneas and Dante both visit the realm of the dead and return alive (Lotman, 1972a: 338).

Doležel commented on this problem in his study "From Motifemes to Motifs" (1972). In imitation of Alan Dundes, the term "motifemes" is adopted for Propp's "functions of characters". Doležel reduced much of the confusion to the fact that Propp did not clearly distinguish between *fabula* and plot (*sjužet*) and hardly even needed this distinction, since in the fairy-tales which he investigated *fabula* and plot more or less overlapped: they all heeded the chronological order of events, and, for instance, never began with the happy ending. Doležel also convincingly argued that at the various levels of abstraction the search for invariants is useful only *in relation to* variables of the next lower level (i.e. closer to the text). The quest for invariants becomes a useless exercise in abstraction if one loses sight of the variables to which the invariant elements are related. His criticism is in complete agreement with Lévi-Strauss (1960) who, though mistakenly considering Propp as representative of Russian Formalism, correctly observed that Propp's method allows him to arrive at a certain level of abstraction, but does not enable him to find the way back from the abstract to the concrete (Lévi-Strauss, 1960: 23). Doležel concluded that

the structural theory of narrative cannot be reduced to the study of invariants. [. . .] There is no level in the narrative structure which can be described as a "closed system", protected from variation and innovation; on the other hand, there is no structural level which is free from stereotype and repetition. There is no fixed and universal "grammar" of narrative; at the same time, there is no unlimited freedom for the author's idiosyncracy. Every narrative act is simultaneously norm-obeying, norm-creating and norm-destroying (1972: 88).

In taking this position, Doležel (until 1965 in Prague, subsequently teaching in Toronto) manifests his form adherence to the tenets of Czech structuralism, which continued the main tradition of Russian Formalism and forgot about Propp.

Czech Structuralism
Czech structuralism continued the tradition of Russian Formalism, but Russian Formalism is by no means its only source of inspiration. Even if we do not take into account the linguistic structuralism of Mathesius, Jakobson, Trubetzkoy and other members of the Prague Linguistic Circle (1926–48), the origins of Czech structuralism are many and variegated (Cassirer, 1945; Wellek, 1970: 275–304; Günther, 1971b). Apart from work by Czech scholars in aesthetics and philosophy, Christiansen's study of "the structure of the aesthetic object" and "differential experiences" (*Differenzempfindungen*) (1909: 55, 118), which had already influenced Šklovskij (1916b) and Bernštejn (1927), also

inspired the Czechs. Of course, Christiansen cannot be separated from the German tradition of research dealing with the matter of the relation between the whole and its parts which produced the insight of Schelling that "in a true work of art there is no individual beauty, only the whole is beautiful".[7] Finally, in the field of semiotics Husserl, Bühler and Saussure were acknowledged precursors (Mukařovský, 1940: 26–7). Although the origins of Czech structuralism can be traced back to sources which the Russian Formalists also tapped, one must assume that the Czechs had a more direct access to the German tradition. Nevertheless, on various occasions the Czech structuralists have explicitly acknowledged their indebtedness to Russian Formalism. Mukařovský's lecture "On Contemporary Poetics" (1929) is a faithful report on Russian Formalism.

Jan Mukařovský (1891–1975) is one of the foremost Czech structuralists in the field of the study of literature. He elaborated Tynjanov's thesis that the immanent study of the literary text is in principle impossible. More than the Russian Formalists he expressed himself on problems of aesthetics. This led him to define the aesthetic object in a way which was compatible with the major insights of both Russian Formalism and Christiansen (1909).

In a contribution to the Eighth International Congress of Philosophy in Prague, Mukařovský discussed his concept of art as a "semiological fact" (1934). Art is at the same time sign, structure and value he maintains. If it is considered as a sign, two aspects can be distinguished: that of the external symbol or *signifiant* representing a meaning; and that of the meaning represented or *signifié* (Saussure, 1915). The work of art cannot be reduced to its signifying or "material" aspect[8] since the material work of art, or artefact, is a sign that acquires significance only through the act of perception. The object of aesthetics is not the artefact (*signifiant*), but the "aesthetic object" (*signifié*), the "expression and correlate of the artefact in the consciousness of the perceiver" (Mukařovský, 1935: 90).

As the cultural and social background against which the artefact is perceived changes, the interpretation and evaluation of the work of art will change accordingly. In the course of art history, various aesthetic objects have been constructed on the basis of one and the same artefact. The plurality of interpretations which under varying conditions can be attributed to the artefact is to be considered an asset of the work of art. Such a plurality of interpretations is facilitated by "the multiplicity, variety and complexity of the material artefact" (Mukařovský, 1935: 93). Not all the individual interpretations constitute the aesthetic object. The aesthetic object is only what the individual, necessarily subjective interpretations by a certain group of recipients have in common, as far as these interpretations are based on the artefact (Mukařovský, 1934).

Mukařovský regards the work of art as an "autonomous sign" which is characterized solely by its mediating function between the members of the same group. Therefore, the work of art does not necessarily refer to the reality that surrounds us. It must have a meaning that is to be understood by sender and receiver, but need not denote real objects or situations. It may have an indirect or metaphorical meaning in relation to the reality we live in. The work of art "can never be used as an historical or sociological document, unless its documentary value, i.e. the character of its relation to the social context, has been determined" (Mukařovský, 1934: 142). Apart from the autonomous function of the literary work, which is in full agreement with Špet's third kind of truth, or fictionality, Mukařovský argues that the literary work also has a communicative function since it consists of words which express thoughts and feelings and describe situations. He concludes that the individual work of art, as well as the history of the arts, is characterized by a dialectical antinomy between the autonomous function and the communicative function of art. This theme was later pursued with great success by Lotman (1972a). In his short contribution on art as a semiological fact, Mukařovský appeared a full-fledged semiotician claiming that all the humanities study material that consists largely of signs.

In contrast to Roman Ingarden, who will be discussed shortly, Mukařovský studied the literary work primarily as part of a larger communicative and cultural process. His concept of literature is as much tainted by dynamism as is that of Tynjanov whom he often quotes. Like Tynjanov (1924a) and Šklovskij (1916a), he claimed in his seminal study of "Aesthetic Function, Norm and Value as Social Facts" (1935) that the aesthetic potential is not, or at least not completely, inherent in the object. Although "there are certain preconditions in the objective arrangement of an object (which bears the aesthetic function) which facilitate the rise of aesthetic pleasure", Mukařovský maintains that "any object or action, regardless of how it is organized" can acquire an aesthetic function and thus become an object of aesthetic pleasure (1935: 28). Aesthetic evaluation is related to the development of society—in short, to sociological and anthropological data, which form the background against which the evaluation takes place. The aesthetic function has a dynamic character and may vary with the particular conditions under which an object is perceived and with the particular set (*Einstellung*) of the receiver. The aesthetic function, then, is a force or energy, in the form of attention which is focussed on the sign itself (cf. Jakobson, 1921; 1934; 1960; Lotman, 1972a: 277). Mukařovský calls "the concentration of the aesthetic function on the sign itself" a consequence of the autonomy that characterizes the aesthetic phenomena (1938: 48), but one might as well view the latter as a consequence of the former, or assume, in the style of Mukařovský, a dialectical relationship between the focus on the sign itself and the autonomous character of that same sign.

The aesthetic function is the force that creates the aesthetic value, whereas in cases where the aesthetic function does not predominate the question of the aesthetic value will not arise.

In his discussion of the relation between value and norm, Mukařovský firmly adheres to the Formalist tradition, notably in the concept of deviation or deformation. Compliance with an aesthetic norm is no guarantee of aesthetic value. The norm is derived from aesthetic values and is a regulative principle *outside* art. Outside art, aesthetic value depends on fulfilment of the norm. Within art, the prevailing aesthetic norm is to some extent violated, and as a result of apparent aesthetic values a partly or completely new norm is created. Aesthetic value is not a static concept, but a process that evolves against the background of the actual artistic tradition and in relation to the ever-changing cultural and social context.

The dynamism of these concepts of aesthetic function, value and norm is possible only on the basis of a concept of the aesthetic object as an interpreted artefact. Mukařovský's views presuppose that the aesthetic object is not an invariant, but determined by each generation or group of recipients. When Mukařovský finally poses the question whether the aesthetic value has an objective basis, he cannot but conclude that if objective aesthetic value exists at all, it must be sought in the material artefact which, in contradistinction to the aesthetic object, is not subject to change. However, the aesthetic value inherent in the artefact can have only a potential character (cf. Vodička, 1972: 10). Aesthetic values can in fact only be attributed to the aesthetic object, which is a concretization (Ingarden, 1931) or realization (Conrad, see Ingarden, 1931: 354n;

Konstantinović, 1973: 38–51) of the artefact by the receiver. Nevertheless some artefacts are better disposed than others to be concreticized as an aesthetic object.

Mukařovský posits that "the value of an artistic artefact will be greater to the degree that the bundle of extra-aesthetic values which it attracts is greater, and to the degree that it is able to intensify the dynamism of their mutual connection" (1935: 91). This concept of aesthetic value is perhaps not very satisfactory. It was severely criticized by Wellek (1970: 291). Further attempts by Mukařovský to assign a place to the objective aesthetic value do not seem to have solved the question. Apart from "the multiplicity, variety and complexity of the material artefact", which he regards as potential aesthetic assets, he considers the independent aesthetic value of an artefact "higher and more enduring to the extent that the work does not lend itself to literal interpretation from the standpoint of a generally accepted system of values of some period and some milieu" (1935: 93). Here Mukařovský comes close to the concepts of *ambiguity* (Empson, 1930) or *Unbestimmtheitsstelle* (Ingarden, 1931) without mentioning them.

Perhaps Mukařovský would have been wiser to give up the search for the objective aesthetic value entirely, once he had correctly perceived that the aesthetic value of the artefact could have only a potential character. A potential value is only a possible condition of value, not a sufficient condition. Like the so-called "evolutionary value" (*Evolutionswert*), which is determined by the effect of a literary work on the dynamic literary evolution, it is an abstract construction by the literary historian and not the product of a communicative process (Günther, 1971b: 239). Modern value theory views value as a relational concept, a concept that is constituted by the relation between an object and a receiver. Although certain objects are better qualified to be considered as valuable than others, the artefact as an unchangeable notion isolated from any reception can never enter into a relation with a receiver, and therefore its aesthetic value, if it has any, cannot be known.

In the stock-taking article "Structuralism in Aesthetics and in the Study of Literature" (1940), Mukařovský redefined the concept of structure. To the familiar idea that a structure is more than the sum-total of its parts, he adds that "a structural whole *means* each of its parts, and inversely each of these parts means this and no other whole" (1940: 11). A further characteristic of a structure is "its energetic and dynamic character", caused by the fact that each element has a specific function through which it is connected with the whole, and that these functions and their interrelationship are subjected to a process of change. As a result, the structure as a whole is in permanent movement.

It should be emphasized that Mukařovský speaks here of the concept of structure in the study of literature: i.e. a communicative process in which, when enacted, the factors of time and therefore changing conditions play a considerable role. His concept of structure comes close to that of biological organism.

The structure of the aesthetic object is subject to a process of change, but which factors determine this process? To answer this question, Mukařovský subscribes to the position of Tynjanov and Jakobson (1928), who hold that the immanent study of literary history cannot explain the particular pace of literary evolution or the selection of one particular direction where various directions are theoretically possible. The problem of the direction or the dominant direction can be solved only through an analysis of the interrelationship between the literary and other historical series (Tynjanov and Jakobson, 1928). Mukařovský adds that each change in a literary structure finds its motivation outside that particular structure. But the way in which an alien impulse is received and the general effect of that impulse are determined by conditions that are inherent in the literary structure (1940: 19).

The analysis of particular literary texts, rather than the theorization of literature, was the main occupation of the Russian Formalists. In general, this tradition was continued by Mukařovský and other structuralists. Their studies of Mácha and Čapek are famous, but being written in Czech about Czech authors were, for obvious reasons, barely appreciated outside Czechoslovakia. Gradually the need for a subsumption of the various structural studies became more urgent. By 1934 the name "structuralism" was introduced (Wellek, 1970: 276), which Mukařovský, avoiding the terms "theory" and "method", later described as an epistemological "point of view" (Mukařovský, 1940). In Mukařovský's opinion, "theory" means a fixed complex of knowledge, and "method" the unchangeable rules of a scientific procedure. Epistemologically, structuralism merely implies acceptance of the view that the concepts of a given scientific system are interrelated. It does not accept the primacy of the investigated material (the object). In this respect structuralism differs from positivism, says Mukařovský, who in effect criticizes

Ejchenbaum's defence of the hypothetical method quoted earlier (Ejchenbaum, 1926: 3–4). On the other hand, Mukařovský does not assert the primacy of the scientific procedure or method either. Here too the principle of interrelatedness applies. New material may affect the methods of investigation and new methods may uncover new material.

Since Mukařovský does not question his own structuralist point of view or make a serious attempt to test it, it is a value rather than a hypothesis. However, his epistemological reflections never arrived at this conclusion.

After the second World War, possibly pressed by political circumstances, Mukařovský provided his concept of structuralism with a materialist basis. Now the primacy of the investigated material is acknowledged. "Structure", which in 1940 was still a conceptual entity supported by certain properties of the material, now becomes an objective phenomenon belonging to the real world (1947: 7–8). This development in Mukařovský's thinking, which is discussed by Wellek (1970: 275–304), did not result in new contributions to the study of literature.

Although we have restricted our discussion of Czech structuralism to its major spokesman, there were many others who belonged to the Czech school. Bohuslav Havránek, Felix Vodička and others were represented in an anthology edited by Garvin (1964). The contributions of a younger generation were made available only recently in a Western European language (Doležel, 1972; 1973; Grygar, 1969; 1972; and Sus, 1972). Earlier, scholars in the Soviet Union were made more easily acquainted with the products of the later phase of Czech structuralism than their colleagues in the West.

A final remark must be made on the Polish philosopher Roman Ingarden who, in faithful adherence to the teachings of Husserl, designed a theory of the literary work (Ingarden, 1931; 1968; 1969). Both Ingarden and Mukařovský had a deep knowledge of the German philosophical tradition. Both were critics of positivism, Ingarden being most explicit in his rejection of the neo-positivism of Polish logistics (which he detects as early as 1919, cf. Ingarden, 1931: 98n) and of the Vienna Circle (Husserl, 1968: 179–80).

There are more affinities; however, they are less evident (cf. Herta Schmid, 1970). Although the word "structure" appears in Ingarden (1931), it is used in a subdued manner. Ingarden's addiction to phenomenology emerges in every other page of his writings, whereas Mukařovský seldom expresses his preference for the phenomenological method (1940: 12). Mukařovský distinguished between the "material" artefact and the aesthetic object, and devoted most of his energy to studying the latter. Similarly, Ingarden distinguished between the "material" work of art and the aesthetic object *(ästhetischer Gegenstand,* as Ingarden calls it), which is the expression of the work of art in a correct concretization by a competent reader, but he devoted most of his time to investigating the former. Whereas Mukařovský, in the tradition of Šklovskij and Tynjanov, believed in a dynamic concept of literary history, Ingarden mainly studied the literary work in isolation and as a static entity. Mukařovský considers it an advantage that the artefact may give rise to various concretizations; Ingarden (1969: 215) only hesitantly subscribed to that view and at the same time continued to look for the theoretical possibility of the one adequate concretization.

Ingarden hardly ever quoted the Russian Formalists, and probably knew little of their work when he wrote *Das literarische Kunstwerk* (1931), which is the result of research done in 1927–8.[9] Still, one may find concepts and terms in Ingarden's publications which seem to recall the terminology of the Formalists. When he calls "intensified attention" *(geschärfte Aufmerksamkeit)* a precondition of aesthetic appreciation (Ingarden, 1968: 208), one might suspect the echo of Šklovskij (1916a) or Jakobson (1921), only to find a footnote referring to Volkelt (1905). Undoubtedly, the sources of Ingarden, Mukařovský and the Russian Formalists were often the same: notably German philosophy and aesthetics. One should not hasten here to judge their respective originality.

There is one deep chasm that separates Ingarden from Russian Formalism and Czech structuralism, namely his belief in the possibility of detecting the conditions of aesthetic concretization in the material work of art. Mukařovský made a similar attempt when he tried to discover the aesthetic potential in certain properties of the artefact. But in Mukařovský's case the attempt was an unprofitable one, and even an anachronism, if compared to his overriding interest in the dynamic nature of the literary work and the literary system.

Mukařovský's emphasis on the dynamic aspects of the literary work did not represent the final development of structuralism. It seems that Ingarden and Mukařovský were equally biased, though in different ways, in their attempts to solve the problem of the relation between the artefact and the aesthetic object, or the adequate concretization. It occurs to us that the equilibrium between the autonomous and the dynamic approach was restored only in recent publications of Soviet semiotics, notably those of Lotman.

Soviet Semiotics

About 1960, profiting from a general tendency towards relaxation in the realm of culture, the structuralist study of literature in the Soviet Union received a strong impulse from linguists working in the field of cybernetics and information theory, notably those engaged in problems of machine translation. At the same time the works of the Formalists Šklovskij, Ejchenbaum, Tynjanov and Tomaševskij, which for almost three decades had been subjected to severe criticism sanctioned by the Party, were made available again through reprints (cf. Todorov, 1965a: 31–3; Tschižewskij, in Tynjanov, 1929: V). The earlier attacks on the Formalists were now judged to have been inspired by so-called "vulgar sociology".

Restricting ourselves to only one of the many sources that introduced the new line in the discussion of art, we must mention the influential editorial "On the Problem of the Typical in Literature and Art" in the Soviet journal *Kommunist* of December 1955. The editorial warned against a one-sided limitation of "the typical" *(tipičnost')* by making it correspond with the essence of certain social forces, thereby neglecting the specific character of artistic cognition and reflection of the world. Artistic cognition of life has certain elements in common with the approach of the historian, economist or philosopher, but is still different in method. Art is different from science; it operates on another level and with other means. In short, the study of art investigates problems that are not covered by other sciences, and about which other sciences cannot easily judge. Although in this respect Belinskij's century-old formula "art is thinking in images" (rejected by the Formalists) was invoked, the editorial in effect subscribes to the view of Ejchenbaum that literature cannot be reduced to the facts of other cultural or social series (Ejchenbaum, 1929: 61).

From its very inception, semiotics played a central role in modern Soviet structuralism. One of its early publications, the report on a *Symposium on the Structural Study of Sign Systems (Simpozium,* 1962), published by the Institute of Slavonic Studies of the Academy of Sciences in Moscow, opens with a statement about semiotics, describing it as a new science which studies "any sign systems used in human society". Although at times the field of semiotics has been given a wider interpretation including, for instance, animal communication (Sebeok, 1972), the main point here is that the structuralist study of literature in the Soviet Union was firmly based on a discipline which, through its close connection with cybernetics and information theory, also served the sciences.

In Moscow the structural-typological section of the Institute of Slavonic Studies and Balkanistics of the Academy of Sciences is the main centre of structuralist semiotics as applied to linguistics, the study of literature, and culture in general. Vjač. Vs. Ivanov, V. N. Toporov and, until his death in 1974, I. I. Revzin, have been associated with the Institute. They have collaborated with B. A. Uspenskij of the National University of Moscow, whose book on the poetics of composition (1970) has appeared in an English translation (1973), as well as with Ju. I. Levin, the indologist A. M. Pjatigorskij, the medievalist M. B. Mejlach and many others. D. M. Segal also belonged to this group, but recently emigrated to Israel. Their publications are characterized by a keen awareness of the historical context and an amazing erudition, rather than exactness of method. Others like Žolkovskij and Ščeglov, both associated with experiments in machine translation and the semantic study of larger text segments, follow a different approach and attempt to design a generative poetics (*poroždajuščaja poetika*). By the structural description of the literary text, they understand an explanation of its genesis on the basis of the given theme and material by means of various fixed rules. Žolkovskij and Ščeglov necessarily resort to simplification, notably in their concept of theme, and although they aim at scientific exactitude, they tend to neglect the role of the historical context in the process of communication (Günther, 1969; Eimermacher, 1971; Meletinskij and Segal, 1971; Segal, 1974).

More rewarding is the approach of Jurij M. Lotman, who lives in Tartu, Estonia, but works closely with the scholars associated with the Institute of Slavonic Studies in Moscow. Most of their writings have been published in a series from the University of Tartu, called *Works on Sign Systems (Trudy, 1964)*. Although the publications of Ivanov are as valuable as those of Lotman, they are less systematically organized and deal with a wide range of topics, varying from the mythology of the Kets, a small people in Siberia (Ivanov and Toporov, 1962), and the concept of time in twentieth-century literature and film (Ivanov, 1973a), to the defense of the binary opposition (Ivanov, 1973b).

By training a specialist in eighteenth- and early nineteenth-century Russian literature, Lotman published two seminal works (1964; 1970), the first of which has been reprinted in the United States and translated into German (1972b), whereas the second was translated into French, Italian and twice into German.[10] Lotman's work can be considered a continuation of Russian Formalism, but it also has several original aspects. One French reviewer perhaps overstated the case by calling Lotman's insight into the semanticization of formal characteristics a Copernican revolution in the study of literature (Jarry, 1974). We shall compare Lotman's findings with those of the Formalists.

Like the Formalists, Lotman uses the term "device" (_priëm_) and defines it as "a structural element and its function", or "an element that has a function in a structure" (1972a: 157, 200). This, indeed, differs from Šklovskij's concept of device. In a polemical statement, Šklovskij had expressed the view that the literary work is merely the sum-total of its devices (Šklovskij, 1925: 165). This phrase has often been held against the Formalists but, as we have mentioned above, the neglect of the structural organization of the literary work which it exemplifies was already amended in the 1920s, through the influence of Špet, Tynjanov, Bernštejn and others.

Šklovskij's formula also neglects the semantic aspect of literature. If we confine ourselves to the tradition of Russian Formalism and its critical assimilation by Soviet structuralism, it appears that Lotman elaborated on earlier efforts by Brik and Tynjanov and paid full attention to the semantic aspect of literature. He did so on the basis of the semiotic assumption that each signifier must have a meaning. But this does not mean that one can easily distinguish between form and meaning. In this respect Lotman was influenced by M. M. Bachtin, who pointed out that within the domain of culture it is impossible to draw a sharp distinction between expression and meaning (Ivanov, 1973c; Lotman, 1972a: 40). Lotman does not wish to work with an abstract or simplified concept of meaning; neither is he prepared to neglect meaning as a constituent of literature. Instead, he subscribes to Uspenskij's concept of meaning. Relying on Claude Shannon, Uspenskij defined meaning as the range of representations and connotations connected with a certain symbol, or as "the invariant in reversible operations of translation" (Lotman, 1972a: 59;

Uspenskij, 1962: 125). This implies that, in contradistinction to the opinion of Katz (1972), meaning pertains to the surface structure. Lotman uses a concept of meaning that is hard to disentangle from its expression or signifier. He rejects Jakobson's early view that, through the actualization of the phonetic elements, poetic language aims at the destruction of the conventional word meaning in order to reach the ideal of a "transrational language" (*zaumnyj jazyk*). Jakobson believed that when in poetry two synonyms are juxtaposed, the second word is not the carrier of a new meaning (1921). Lotman holds that poetic technique is not restricted to form. He concludes that repetition of semantically equivalent words in poetry has a semantic effect. On similar grounds Revzin (1974) has observed that synonymy does not occur in poetic language. Lotman argues that the poetic or literary effect is achieved by a particularly close relation between the formal and the semantic aspect of the literary text. He believes that certain formal characteristics which have no meaning in ordinary language do acquire a meaning in a literary text. "The signs in art", says Lotman, "are not based on arbitrary convention, but have an iconic, representing character". Iconic signs *(ikoniČeskie znaki)* are constructed according to the principle of an immanent connection between expression and meaning: "The sign is the model of its content." The result is a semanticization of elements that are a-semantic in ordinary language (Lotman, 1972a: 40).

In literature one may distinguish between various forms of iconicity at various levels of the text. In rhyme, for instance, the phonological similarity is only partial, and in effect strengthens both the similarity and the opposition between the words involved. In this way the formal phenomenon of rhyme produces a semantic effect. The signifying function of the rhyme is not arbitrary, as it is determined by the first given rhyming word (cf. Lotman, 1972a: 184–5). Like other semioticians, Lotman relies on Peirce's concept of icon (Peirce, 1958). When Lotman finally reaches the conclusion that "beauty is information" (1972a: 213), it is not a plain denial of the Formalist emphasis on form, but the recognition that artistic form can be interpreted and has a meaning.

Eimermacher (1971: 18) has correctly observed that the Soviet semioticians, including Lotman, do not attempt to pronounce on the social relevance or truth of artistic information. They seem to accept Špet's idea that art is characterized by a "third kind of truth", which has no direct relation with logical or empirical truth. The question of whether the meaning of a sign must *denote* something that belongs to social reality is not raised. In this respect they do not contradict Charles Morris (1964: 67) and Eco (1972: 69–73; 1976: 58–68). Therefore the term "information" in the statement "beauty is information" should be interpreted in the purely technical sense of the degree of organization of a system (Günther, 1969).

The Soviet semioticians were not often explicit in epistemologi-. cal matters, but seem in general to subscribe to Eco's view that the problem of whether a statement is true or false is relevant for the logician but not for the semiotician (Eco, 1972: 73). Linguistic signs have a meaning and provide a model of the world, but the truth value of that model is not examined. There is a remarkable similarity between Lotman's view that language is a "modelling system" (*modelirujuščaja sistema*) and the Sapir-Whorf thesis that "we see and hear and otherwise experience very largely as we do because the language habits of our community predispose certain choices of interpretation" (Sapir, 1949: 162, quoted by Whorf, 1956: 134). The Soviet semioticians were familiar with the writings of Benjamin Lee Whorf (Segal, 1962; Revzina, 1972). Whorf defended the primacy of the language system in our shaping "a model of the universe" (1950) on the basis of the *conviction* that in this respect the language system and not "the objective world" is the primary regulating principle; however, Lotman has avoided expressing such a belief. We must assume that for him the view that language is a modelling system is merely a semiotic *hypothesis*.

The literary text is the product of, at least, two overlapping systems: the linguistic system and the literary system which is superimposed on the linguistic system. Lotman therefore, concludes that literature, as well as art in general, is a "secondary . modelling system" (1972a: 22). The literary system, then, is *supralingual*. The receiver of a linguistic message must know the linguistic code in order to interpret that message. Accordingly, the reader of a literary text must know the literary code in addition to the language in which that text is written. If the receiver does not know the literary code the sender has used, he will in general not be able to interpret the text or even accept the text as being literary. This led Lotman to enunciate the important thesis that "the definition of the artistic text cannot be complete without an additional classification in respect to the relation between sender and receiver" (1972a: 89).

The interaction of the linguistic and the literary system in one and the same text provides that text with a maximum of information. The various elements belong to at least two codes and may be carriers of more than one meaning. Here Lotman pursues earlier observations by Tynjanov (1924b), Brik (1927) and Mukařovský (1934). Moreover, the amount of information can be further increased when the text is subjected to an interaction of two or more subcodes, e.g. those of Realism and Romanticism, the epic and lyrical system, or fictionality and non-fictionality. If a text has been encoded several times, it will seem to us to have an extremely individual or even "unique" character (Lotman, 1972a: 121). What in fact happens in such a case is that, as soon as the reader has become familiar with one code, he will encounter elements that cannot be decoded on the basis of that one code (1972a: 296). The expectation of the reader is thwarted or, in the terminology of the Formalists, "de-automatized". According to Lotman, the interpretation of a text with much entropy (a high degree of unpredictability) will provide much information (a high degree of organization).

In view of this concept of literature, the interpretation of the literary text is not a simple affair, and moreover is related to the knowledge of the code that sender and receiver should ideally have in common. Lotman considers interpretation a kind of translating of information in the literary code into information in the scientific code. It is clear that, if we accept Uspenskij's definition of meaning as the invariant in a reversible process of translation, it will hardly be possible to leave meaning exactly intact as soon as we begin to interpret. One can hardly imagine an interpretation so careful and meticulous that it would enable one to rewrite the interpreted poem on the basis of the interpretation of that poem. Therefore, in principle, interpretation is nothing but approximation (Lotman, 1972a: 107, 121). Moreover, as our knowledge of the codes used in a literary text may be insufficient, and since we may legitimately wish to decode a literary text either against its restricted historical background or in relation to a wider, "mythological" context, it is possible that various interpretations will co-exist without any possibility of deciding which interpretation is the correct one. (In this respect, Lotman is in agreement with Mukařovský rather than Ingarden.) Nevertheless, we have to interpret, i.e. translate information from one code into another, because we have the obligation to relate the various spheres of culture to each other. We must create possibilities for translating the significance of literature into more general terms, if only to be able to defend the value of literary expression or, more modestly, to justify bureaucratic decisions about literary awards.

Lotman's observations on the iconicity of literature and the semanticization of formal characteristics are an important step forward in the study of literature. Although he has perhaps dealt with these problems more elaborately and more systematically than any other author, his thoughts in this respect are not completely original: the concept of iconic sign has been borrowed from Peirce (Peirce, 1958; Greenlee, 1973); and the idea of the semanticization of formal characteristics are an important step by Tynjanov (1924b) and Brik (1927). The semantic effect of rhyme was noticed before, and notably the concepts of irony and paradox in the writings of the New Critics seem to account for the same aspect of semanticization of formal characteristics that do not acquire meaning outside literature (Brooks, 1947).

Lotman's notion of the literary text is ambivalent since he accepts the view that the literary text can be considered a sign that operates in the larger cultural context. In fact, Lotman seems to subscribe to Mukařovský's (1934) view that the literary text has both an autonomous and a communicative character. Although here too Lotman cannot be accorded complete originality, his acknowledgement of a structural relationship between the internal structure of the literary text and the socio-cultural context may be more important for the further development of the study of literature than his detailed comments on the iconic principle. Any so-called autonomous interpretation of a literary text that does not take into account its function in the larger socio-cultural context must fail. This has been made abundantly clear by Lotman, who in fact convincingly elaborated the nine theses of Tynjanov and Jakobson (1928) and the position of Jakobson (1934).

Lotman introduces a semiotic notion of text that includes the linguistic text and the literary text, as well as film, painting or symphony. The text is *explicit,* i.e. it is expressed in definite signs. It is *limited,* i.e. it has a beginning and an end. Finally, it has a *structure* as a result of an internal organization on the syntagmatic level. As a result of these qualities, the signs of a text enter into a relation of opposition to signs and structures outside the text. Often the distinguishing features (the significance) of a text and its constituent signs can be recognized only in relation to other texts and sign systems. Consequently, the absence of an expected element, e.g. the absence of rhyme in a tradition where rhyme is to be expected, may strike the reader as a significant device. Lotman calls the significant absence of a device a negative device or minus-device (*minus-priëm*) (1972a: 82–3). The problem of the minus-device is related to that of *le degré zero* in phonology. Lotman refers to Roland Barthes (1953) in this respect, but could as well have mentioned Šklovskij (1925) or Jakobson (1939). It is clear that the notion of the minus-device is incompatible with a strictly autonomous interpretation of the literary text.

Others have also argued that a literary text cannot be considered autonomous in the strict sense of the word. But the advantage of Lotman's approach is that he introduced the same semiotic method for the analysis of the internal literary structure and the external relations between the text and the socio-cultural context. If this method enables us to overcome the deep chasm that separates the study of the reception of literature (Jauss, 1970), as well as the sociology of literature, from autonomistic interpretations as practised by New Criticism and the *werkimmanente Interpretation* ("intrinsic interpretation"), and to relate to each other the results of these highly divergent approaches, then indeed Lotman's book has introduced a Copernican revolution in the study of literature.

We have seen that Lotman accepts the co-existence of various interpretations without the possibility of deciding which is the correct one; he also abandons the attempt to decide on the correctness of the various possible evaluations. (Lotman does not raise the question of correctness in the sense of the internal consistency of evaluations.) In the study of literary history, Lotman argues, one should distinguish between "the aesthetics of identity" (*estetika toždestva*) and "the aesthetics of opposition" (*estetika protivopostavlenija*). The first is characteristic of folklore, the Middle Ages and Classicism, to which one could add the ancient Asiatic cultures. The aesthetics of opposition is typical of Romanticism, Realism and the Avant-garde. The "aesthetics of identity" presupposes the identity or near-identity of the code of the sender with that of the receiver. The "aesthetics of opposition" comes into play when the codes of sender and receiver differ. Evidently, the functions of a literary text and its devices differ according to whether they will be interpreted in terms of the aesthetics of identity or the aesthetics of opposition. Lotman distinguishes between the two aesthetics by positing that it may be possible to design generative models for texts that heed the norms of the aesthetics of identity; but he doubts whether this will be possible for texts that belong to the aesthetics of opposition. However, the literary text within the aesthetics of opposition is not a text without rules, but one in which some of the rules are designed in the course of its production and discovered during its reception.

The question why the one or the other aesthetics predominates in a particular culture belongs to the typology of cultures and is not further discussed (Lotman, 1972a: 47). We may infer, however, that both aesthetics aim at "intensified perception" (Šklovskij, 1916a), since Lotman holds that art is characterized by a maximum of information, and intensified perception seems to be a precondition of that criterion. Obviously, the question why in certain cultures the aesthetics of identity or the aesthetics of opposition prevails can be answered only if the relation between organization (information) and entropy in other social and cultural series of that same culture is simultaneously examined.

Lotman relates the interpretation and function of a text to a given code and a given value system. Although in practice this will not often be the case, the interpreter should ideally have complete knowledge of the code of the sender. In fact, Lotman has expanded the historical relativism of the Russian Formalists (Šklovskij, 1916a; Jakobson, 1921, 1960; Tynjanov, 1924a) into a cultural relativism. As Lotman presupposes an interrelation between the immanent rules of the literary text and the cultural code to which it belongs, or in which it otherwise functions through translation or tradition, his approach provides a firm framework of reference for comparative literature. Cultural relativism prevents Lotman from expressing an absolute demarcation between literature and non-literature. In fact, he confines himself to the description of the possible conditions of literature, and one necessary condition of literature (the concentration of information), but these cannot be considered sufficient conditions for distinguishing a literary from a non-literary text. The acceptability of a text as a literary text is determined by the code which the receiver uses in decoding it.

Concluding Remarks

If we survey the development of Russian Formalism into structuralism in Czechoslovakia and, in the 1960s, into structuralist semiotics in the Soviet Union, we see both change and continuity. A few final comments on the basic tenets of Soviet semiotics and their relation to earlier positions of Formalism and Czech structuralism may make this clear.

1. We have observed that Lotman's concept of the literary text as conveying a "model of the world" (*model' mira*) did not tempt

him to investigate the truth value of the text. Like Eco, Lotman wishes to keep the problem of truth or falsity outside semiotics. The concept of the text as a model is merely a hypothesis to Lotman, although never explicitly announced as such. The concept of structure has the same status. Here too, a definition by Eco seems relevant to Lotman's concept. Eco defines structure as "a model resulting from various simplifying procedures, which enable one to acquire a unifying view of diverse phenomena".[11] The question of whether a structure indeed exists in the "real world" is not raised by Lotman. Here we detect a remarkable development from the neo-positivist position of Ejchenbaum, claiming the primacy of the investigated material, via the structuralist viewpoint of Mukařovský who posited a dialectical relationship between material and method, to Lotman's apparent recognition of the primacy of the deductive model, at least in the present stage of his research. This development must certainly, in part, be attributed to the influence of Benjamin Lee Whorf.

2. To the Russian Formalists the concept of deviation from the established norm was essential, but it was not always clear whether ordinary language, or the prevalent literary convention, or both were considered as the norm(s) from which new literary works were supposed to deviate. Šklovskij introduced the idea of the "impeding form", which is not necessarily a "difficult" form but is one that is experienced as being difficult. It may be a simple form where the reader is expecting complicated forms. Mukařovský elaborated on the opposition between deviation and norm. Gradually, however, doubts were raised over the status of the norm. Is ordinary usage indeed a norm from which literary language deviates? The correctness of this view has been questioned in American stylistics, and it has been suggested that literary style is rather the product of a selection from various possibilities than a deviation from a preconceived norm (Chatman, 1967). In Soviet semiotics, too, the notion of norm has been stripped of its normative connotations. The introduction of the concept of code and the idea of the succession of different codes, as well as a consequent cultural relativism, resulted in the (structuralist) view that sometimes norms can be considered deviations, whereas deviations from the norm can, under certain conditions, become the norm. In this respect one should recall Mukařovský's· observation that *outside* art aesthetic value is in accordance with the norm, whereas *in* art aesthetic value is the result of breaking the norm. The difference is that in the latter case

aesthetic value is the dominant value, whereas in the former it is not.

Lotman continues this line of thinking, which in fact goes back to the early days of Russian Formalism. But, more than the early Formalist writers, he emphasizes the dialectical relation between the aesthetic function and other functions. By introducing the notion of "aesthetics of identity", Lotman in fact recognizes a reversal of the Formalist position. In his view, art may aim at compliance with the norm, rather than 'deviation from the norm. The aesthetics of identity can only prevail in cultures of a specific type which need (or are told to need) a centripetal force, a focus, rather than the centrifugal, individualizing tendencies of modern art. Lotman's concept of the social function of art is less exclusive than that of the Formalists. His explanation of the aesthetic text as providing a maximum of information emancipates art from being a by-product of culture and restores it to a central position. Even computer engineers should learn from the way information is stored in art (Lotman, 1972a: 42).

3. We have emphasized that Lotman uses the term information in a purely technical sense, i.e. the degree of organization of a system. The difference from Šklovskij's emphasis on intensified perception is clear. To Lotman, art is there not only to be perceived but to be interpreted. Interpretation is a cultural necessity (1972a: 108). Again we see that Lotman provides us with a concept of art that is fully integrated in society. Art is important and indispensable, and not a peripheral phenomenon. The recognition of the central cultural function of art led the Soviet structuralists to explore the semiotics of culture. In doing so they were inspired by the similar research of Mukařovský.

4. Finally, we must mention that the Formalist interest in concrete texts never waned in the writings of the Czech and Soviet structuralists. Like Lévi-Strauss, they hate to devise generalizing abstractions that cannot account for the vital diversity of the text structures. Like the New Critics, their analyses remain close to the tangible qualities of the literary—often highly-valued—texts. One wonders whether this interest in the "living" text is motivated by the urge to counterbalance the notion of the ubiquity of the aesthetic function. In the final analysis, we may distinguish in Russian Formalism, as well as in Czech and Soviet structuralism, an emphasis on the particular not less than on the general. In imitation of Lotman, we must relegate the explanation of that attitude to the study of Russian or European culture as a whole.

This interest in the individual phenomena of literature has not been introduced as a working hypothesis and should be called a value—just as the unexplained belief in the explanatory models of generative poetics is likewise a value rather than a hypothesis.

To the extent that the interests and points of departure in modern Soviet semiotics are not made explicit in hypothetical terms, they are values, i.e. they are "capable of providing for the rationalization" of a scientific procedure (Rescher, 1969: 9). This applies to the rather vague epistemological foundations of Lotman's writings, to the rejection of the normative connotations of the term "norm", to the interest in information rather than perception, and finally to the interest in the concrete text. Far from wanting to argue that the foundations of Soviet structuralism are shallow, we consider the semiotically-based structuralism a very promising approach in the study of literature. Our comments on the vague distinction between values and conviction on the one hand, and hypotheses and their testing on the other—which at times emerges from the structuralist writings as it does from almost all scientific endeavours—merely aim to contribute to a further development of the semiotics of literature.

3

STRUCTURALISM IN FRANCE: CRITICISM, NARRATOLOGY AND TEXT ANALYSIS

Claude Lévi-Strauss confessed his disenchantment with phenomenology and existentialism in his *Tristes tropiques* (1955), where he criticized his teachers for their continual preoccupation with Bergson's *Essai sur les données immédiates de la conscience* (1889), while they did not bother to read Ferdinand de Saussure's *Cours de linguistique générale* (1915). Aside from the question as to whether the reverse situation would have been desirable (the *Cours,* we must remember, was a matter of a collection of lectures published by his pupils), the remark by Lévi-Strauss adequately described the situation in France at the time. Although the classic structuralist texts (Saussure, 1915; Trubetzkoy, 1933; Lévi-Strauss, 1945) were originally written in French, it was also in the French-speaking world that they met with resistance. The structuralist impetus was opposed in the name of factuality and individuality. Factuality, bequeathed by positivism, was represented in literary studies by Gustave Lanson. Lanson is separated from structuralist thought by his aversion to generalizations: "Let us resist the small vanity of using generative formulae" and "Certainty decreases as generality increases" (Lanson, 1910, ed. Peyre 1965: 41, 55). The need for factual certainty rules out the level of abstraction which for structuralism is indispensable.

If individuality becomes the criterion (as was the case in existentialist philosophy), clear limits are set to scientific knowledge. Scientific activity, relying as it must on repetition and generalization, would indeed exclude the irreplaceable individual in his uniqueness. Bergson's irreversible order of temporal sequence—experienced time, which he contrasted with the "spatialized" time of the physicists—supports the primacy of the individual. This concept of time must in principle deny repetition or the return of the same moment—and in so doing must also reject comparability with other moments.

In our opinion, however, it is not primarily Bergson's concept of time that led Lévi-Strauss to make the above-mentioned confrontation between Bergson and Saussure. The *Essai sur les données immédiates de la conscience* suggests a comparison with the *Cours de linguistique générale* in another respect. Both have language as their theme, but from widely diverging points of view and, above all, with different evaluations of the phenomenon. For Bergson the linguistic sign is an obstacle, something which destroys the delicate, fleeting and fragile impressions of the individual consciousness (Bergson, 1889: 99). The stability of language suggests an immutability of impressions, while in reality these impressions are in constant flux. In addition, language has a levelling effect, since the feelings of love or hatred peculiar to each individual must be expressed by all persons by means of the same signs (Bergson, 1889: 126).

The stability of the sign is also recognized by Saussure; in his evaluation of this stability, however, he differs essentially from Bergson. The individual cannot choose the sign himself: it is a matter of a "product inherited from preceding generations" (Saussure, 1959: 71; 1915: 105), and it must be accepted as such. This brings Saussure in the first place to call into doubt the usefulness of the question so zealously pursued in historical linguistics, namely that of the origin of language; thus he begins by excluding the genetic aspect and by devoting himself instead to the relation between signifier *(signifiant)* and signified *(signifié)*. Characteristic of this relation is the absence of a natural correspondence between the signifier and the signified. The arbitrariness and conventionality of the sign in turn influence its stability. It is precisely the arbitrary-conventional nature of language that protects it from sudden and violent changes. The striking "continuity of the sign in time" is again favourable to a synchronic investigation of language.

From this brief contrasting of Bergson and Saussure it becomes clear that the emphasis on individuality which we perceive in Bergson has no equivalent in Saussure. Here existentialism and structuralism decisively go separate ways. Even Sartre, who to some degree relativizes individualism by means of the historical embeddedness of the individual, is not willing to give up the absolute aspect of man: "Far from being relativists, we strongly affirm that man is an absolute" (Sartre, 1948: 15).

Thus at a time when factuality and individualism dominated the French cultural scene, linguistic structuralism postulated that a phoneme cannot be analysed outside a phonological system, and that defining a phoneme means "determining its place in the phonological system" (Trubetzkoy, 1933: 65). Such a definition is only possible "when the structure of this system is taken into consideration".

The starting-point for the phonologist is the phonological system, and from there he proceeds to the individual phoneme. In this manner Trubetzkoy lays a methodological foundation for phonology which declares the independence of this discipline from phonetics. In so doing he can appeal to Saussure but even more to Baudouin de Courtenay, who prepared the way for the separation of the two branches of linguistics. Saussure, however, had not been able to draw the decisive line of separation between the two fields of research, even though he realized that a consideration of phonemes amounted to a study of the "distinguishing, contrasting and relative character of the elements" of which the signifier consists; he also realized that the following can be said of all elements of the linguistic system: "Their most precise characteristic is being what the others are not" (Saussure, 1959: 117; 1915: 162).

On the occasion of the First International Congress of Linguists, held in The Hague in 1928, linguists from various countries were Uable to agree on a basic programme.[1] Especially the linguists from Czechoslovakia represented at this conference considered the questions of literary research to lie within their field of interest (one need only think of Roman Jakobson); in this way the fundamental linguistic problems dealt with in The Hague found a natural entrée into literary discussion. France had no such scholars who straddled the two fields, and the findings in the area of phonology were not passed on to literary studies. Thus the idea did not at first arise there that the concept of the distinct, contrasting and relative character of elements—developed for phonemes—might also be fruitful for literary research or anthropology. The literary work was analysed in relation to its author; or attention was paid to the qualities of a single work. The work was not, however, seen as an element of a system, just as the human individual was not seen as a part of a greater whole, definable in terms of the relative place which he holds. For such a relativistic perspective, such a de-centering of the ego (Bakker, 1973: 30), one was not ready. Meanwhile work in the area of phonology (a more restricted field compared with literature or with philosophy) could of course continue.

As a result of Lévi-Strauss's forced emigration to America, where in 1941 he accepted a position at the New School of Social Research in New York, he came to work with Roman Jakobson. Jakobson taught at the same school, and as a result his influence is plainly evident in the article Lévi-Strauss published in *Word* in 1945, "L'Analyse structurale en linguistique et en anthropologie".[2] The influence of Trubetzkoy, however, comes to expression in this article even more strongly than that of Jakobson. Lévi-Strauss describes the rise of phonology as an independent field within linguistics as a revolution comparable to the rise of nuclear physics. Taking Trubetzkoy's programmatic article of 1933 as his point of departure, he develops his idea of an analogy between phonology and anthropology.

Kinship terms, like phonemes, are elements of meaning; and, like phonemes, these kinship terms derive their meaning only from the position which they occupy in a system. The conclusion is that "although they belong to *another order of reality,* kinship phenomena are *of the same type* as linguistic phenomena" (Lévi-Strauss, 1972: 34).

It must be added that anthropology had reached a stage in its development which was similar to that of linguistics on the eve of the founding of phonology: its new task was seen as promoting synchronic as opposed to diachronic research, which until then had dominated the field. The analogy, inspiring as it was for Lévi-Strauss, did not blind him to its possible dangers. He was well aware that phonology can fulfill the demands of scientific analysis in a threefold manner—"a truly scientific analysis must be real, simplifying, and explanatory" (Lévi-Strauss, 1972: 35)—but that the same cannot be said for anthropology. Instead of moving towards concrete problems, anthropological analysis proceeds in the opposite direction, away from the concrete; the system proves to be more complicated than the observational data, and finally the hypothesis offers no explanation for the phenomenon or the origin of the system. Unlike phonology, anthropology deals with kinship systems at the intersection of two different orders of reality, the system of "terminology" and that of "attitudes". Phonology can be described exclusively in the system of nomenclature; it need not take into account any "attitudes" of psychological or social provenience (Lévi-Strauss, 1972: 37).

In spite of the complicated situation in which, according to Lévi-Strauss, anthropology finds itself, the phonological principle of attributing qualities on the basis of distinctive features—a method in which binary opposition also plays an important role as "discovery procedure"—can be applied in anthropological research.

The initial caution Lévi-Strauss displayed in transferring an epistemological principle and finally a method to another scientific field, met with general approval and was singled out by his critics—by way of contrast with his later development—as exemplary. *Pensée sauvage* (1962) reveals a general swing away from caution towards bold generalizations and towards an extension of structuralism. From the standpoint of linguistics, Lévi-Strauss is judged as "sociologizing" language (Baumann, 1969: 168). From the philosophical-hermeneutic side, suspicion was harboured against the philosophical claims of an explanatory model which had, step by step, proved useful, first in linguistics and later in ethnology (Ricoeur, 1969: 54).

Meanwhile, the more or less explicit protest against facts and individualities as the goal of scientific research—a protest found in the epistemological presuppositions of both linguistic and anthropological structuralism—elicited a lively response among a few representatives of French literary scholarship. The first of these were grouped under the collective name *Nouvelle Critique*. With regard to this "group", however, it must be pointed out that the unity suggested by the collective name should be understood only as a strategic unity and not at all as a methodological one. Their common cause was to polemicize against the traditional literary scholarship of the universities, where descendants of Lanson trod the well-worn paths of "the man and his work" theses. The unity of the *Nouvelle Critique* is described also by Raymond Picard as "in reality less intellectual than polemical" (Picard, 1965: 10). Besides having to deal with structuralism (especially of the anthropological sort), this new criticism had to respond to stimuli from Freud, Marx and, to a lesser degree, also from Nietzsche—with all the consequences and methodological implications which such a diversity of intellectual origins entails. To the extent that the *Nouvelle Critique* is indebted to Freud, it exhibits definite biographical traits. An exact correspondence of life and art is assumed. The psychological structures which are projected on to the *oeuvre* of an author are primary. Raymond Picard, in his apology for traditional academic literary research and his polemic against the *Nouvelle Critique,* criticizes the latter for thoroughly mixing everything together, while the school of Lanson at least treated the man and the work as distinguishable quantities (Picard, 1965: 16). The *Nouvelle Critique* considers the work as a document, sign or symptom, from which it proceeds to make its constructions: "this warehouse in disorder" (Picard, 1965: 121). The facts, the details of the Lansonist method, had indeed been abandoned in favour of the system. "It is a criticism of *totalities,* not of details", states Jean-Pierre Richard, and Picard speaks of the modern criticism as a criticism which deserves the title "totalistic" *(totalitaire)* (Picard, 1965: 107). But in Picard's opinion this approach has not brought anyone closer to the literary work as such. The totality which is studied by such scholars as Richard, Mauron and Weber is "a profound unity [. . .] proper to a psychological or metaphysical biography of the author" (Picard, 1965: 106).

These remarks and similar ones Picard made with reference to the psycho-analytic variants of the *Nouvelle Critique,* to which he devotes one part of his *Nouvelle Critique ou nouvelle imposture* (1965), characterized by Peter Demetz as "a clever and ironic little book in the best tradition of literary polemics".[3] This work, however, primarily represents the public controversy between Raymond Picard, representative of the "old" criticism, and Roland Barthes, representative of the "new".

The confrontation of these two scholars raises the debate to a level which commands attention. For this is not a clash between a traditional biography-oriented Sorbonne positivist and a biased psychoanalyst; instead, the Sorbonne representative is definitely interested in the literary work, and the modern critic proves to be well-versed in linguistic and anthropological structuralism. The latter also asks the basic question regarding the relation of the text to the interpreter.

In this controversy, the year 1965 marks a decisive point for literary scholarship in France.[4] The French publications which play a role in the controversy are: Roland Barthes, "Histoire ou littérature?" and *Sur Racine* (1963); Raymond Picard, *Nouvelle Critique ou nouvelle imposture* (1965); a rebuttal to Picard came in Barthes' *Critique et Vérité* (1966); finally as a cautious reporter but a not impartial discussant of the quarrel: Serge Doubrovsky, *Pourquoi la nouvelle critique: critique et objectivité* (1966).

After this sketch of the conditions which paved the way for structuralism in literary studies, we should consider more closely three characteristic trends in French structuralism. The first trend we shall summarize with the name *structuralist criticism;* under this heading we understand the thought of Roland Barthes as expressed in *Sur Racine,* as well as in his essays "Histoire ou littérature?" (1963: 145–68), "L'Activité structuraliste" (1964a: 213–21), and *Critique et Vérité* (1966). We are aware that Barthes, thanks to his intellectual versatility, unites several possibilities in himself and certainly could also have been included in the second group, that of *structuralist narratology;* nevertheless his earlier impetus has, in our opinion, made the deepest impression, and we shall therefore investigate this earlier aspect in greater detail. The third trend to be dealt with we shall call *linguistic-structuralist text description;* the analysis made by Roman Jakobson and Lévi-Strauss of Baudelaire's "Les chats" (1962) forms the focal point of this variant.

Structuralist Criticism

Barthes' literary research can be traced back, on the one hand, to the anthropological structuralism of Lévi-Strauss and on the other to a concept of perception derived from Merleau-Ponty. The latter component is most clearly apparent in Barthes' criticism, or *critique,* a term which he himself uses by way of contrast with *histoire* or *vérité.* The phenomenological basis serves to justify the "structuralist activity" which Barthes develops in *Sur Racine.*

As soon as literary research does not manifest itself as literary *history,* its goal is the determination of meaning. Barthes conceives of history in the narrow, genetic sense, while the constitution of meaning concerns a relation. In his essay "Histoire ou littérature?", which is filled with binary oppositions, one of the oppositions is "cause" versus "relation". Determining meaning is a matter of decoding a work of art "not as the effect of a cause, but as the *signifier* of the *thing signified"* (Barthes, 1964b: 163). The relation which is then of importance is "the relation of a work and an individual" (Barthes, 1964b: 162), and this relation is in principle characterized by subjectivity. Of course the subjectivity claimed here conceives of the subject as part of a system, i.e. to be classified in certain describable categories of a "world view" *(vision du monde).* The explicit acknowledgement of the "system" as one pole of the relationship ("the franchise of the system") is postulated. So conceived, the opposition history vs. criticism can be subsumed by Barthes under the opposition "objective vs. systematic", in which "systematic", as already explained, is to be understood as theory-bound or system-bound, as "our preconceived idea of psychology or the world" (Barthes, 1964b: 165).

The proximity to Merleau-Ponty on this point can be illustrated by the latter's rejection of every kind of realism: "There is a significance of the perceived which is without equivalent in the universe of understanding, a perceptive milieu which is not yet the objective world" (Merleau-Ponty, 1945: 57–8). With this observation Merleau-Ponty opposes the "hypothesis of constancy" according to which "a square is always a square whether it rests on one of its bases or on one of its points". Merleau-Ponty's phenomenological concept of perception is not, however, a form of introspection (he rejects a return to Bergson's "immediate data of consciousness"), but a question of perspective, of an object/horizon relationship: "I can see an object to the extent that the objects form a system or a world, and that every one of them has others around it at its disposal" (Merleau-Ponty, 1945: 82–3).

The openness of the horizon of meaning or the system-bound constitution of meaning, which in accordance with the phenomenological tradition Barthes represents, had for some time already found acceptance in another part of Europe. The distinction between artefact and aesthetic object forms the basis of Jan Mukařovský's understanding of literary theory, plays a role in the work of Roman Ingarden, and is of great significance in German aesthetics of reception today.[5] Only in a very indirect sense, however, can one speak of a common source, namely, the philosophy of Edmund Husserl. However, the ramifications of literary theory in Czechoslovakia differ so greatly from those in France that independent developments are plausible, especially since Russian Formalism became available for France only relatively late, while it was one of the most important sources of inspiration for the Czechs.

In every reception-oriented hypothesis about literature, which includes Barthes' conception of literature, a loosening of the close ties between language sign and *denotatum* is implicitly or explicitly postulated for the status of literature, and the possibility of transferring the language sign from its original historical context into another—a later—one is assumed. With this transfer, more and more of the potentially denotative aspect of the language sign in literature is lost, and the latitude of general association becomes continually greater. To gauge this latitude one has to examine the literary work in its relation to more comprehensive cultural and communicative processes, as Mukařovský does in the tradition of Tynjanov. Roland Barthes characterizes the latitude of the interpretation of literature as "accessibility" (Barthes, 1964b: IX). This *disponibilité* explains why a literary work can maintain itself "eternally within the field of any critical language;" it is "the very being of literature" (ibid.). Literature is a functional system "of which one term is constant (the work), and the other is variable (the world, the age that consumes this work)" (ibid.). The variable component is the reaction or answer *(réponse)* of the reader, who brings his history, his language, his freedom to the work. History, language and freedom are in perpetual flux; the reaction is infinite, the work as question (challenge) remains, the interpretations fluctuate.

The Czech structuralism of Mukařovský and Vodička came to demand scientific research into the various reactions dependent on the historical context; it made this demand on the basis of its presuppositions, which are similar to those of Roland Barthes.[6] Barthes locates his own answer between reading and scientific analysis, that is, he is not interested in describing various concrete answers but the answer which he himself, due to his participation in a certain "world view", can give. Picard did not see these presuppositions of Barthes clearly enough, and as a result the polemic did not develop in the direction of fundamental questions. The academic critics could have gained more for their own apology if, instead of reacting only to *Sur Racine,* they had in the first place reacted to the fundamental decision which underlies Barthes' interpretation of Racine's work. Repeatedly Picard reproaches Barthes for abstracting from the literary work; but this complaint goes unheeded since Barthes made himself reasonably unassailable on this point: he never denied the "institutionalized subjectivity" of his answer. Thus his foundation is stronger than that of a Weber or even of a Mauron. If Picard, then, had dealt with the problems of an institutionalized subjectivity on a more abstract level, instead of falling back on Racine philology in points of detail, his defense of the Ancienne Critique might have been stronger.

In *Sur Racine* Roland Barthes fully exploited the freedom he had claimed for himself on the theoretical level.

The works of Racine form the basis for the construction of an anthropological system in which relations take the place of individuals. Racine's dramatis personae are

figures that differ from each other not according to their public status but according to their place in the general configuration that keeps them confined; sometimes it is their function that distinguishes them (father opposed to son, for instance), sometimes it is their degree of emancipation with regard to the most regressive figure of their lineage (Barthes, 1964b: 9–10).

Here we find again the kind of thinking characteristic of Lévi-Strauss's anthropological structuralism. Just as the anthropologist had assumed two main categories for the communities of primitive tribes, namely "the relation of desire" and "the relation of authority", so the literary critic Barthes finds that Racine was obsessively caught up in the same categories. Barthes goes on to divide the desire relationship into two opposing forms of love; the content of these forms is less interesting for the purposes of this study, but as a binary oppositional pair they again show Barthes to be a structuralist. The "relation of desire" is, according to Barthes, of lesser significance and derivative; the power relation, on the other hand, is dominant and comprehensive: "the theatre of Racine is not a theatre of love [. . .]; his theatre is a theatre of violence" (Barthes, 1964b: 25), and the only thing that matters is to maintain or gain one's place in a world which is not big enough for two. The world of Racine knows strong and weak. This division does not, however, correspond to the biological division of the sexes; in this world there are "viriloid women" as well as "feminoid men" (Barthes, 1964b: 13).

The binary oppositions, which are aids for constructing structuralist models, become for Barthes the real data of Racine's work. He finds that "Racinian division is rigorously binary, the possible is never anything but the contrary" (Barthes, 1964b: 36).

The bifurcation manifests itself on the most widely varying levels. As a splitting of the ego it becomes apparent in the monologue, but it is most evident in the opposition between dramatis personae. For this character constellation Barthes can substitute the formula "A has complete power over B" (Barthes, 1964b: 24). The power formula is represented most clearly in the continuing struggle between father and son; this struggle is the battle between God and creature. The father is something inevitable, inescapable, "a primordial, irreversible fact" (Barthes, 1964b: 38); and he is that, first of all, not because of blood ties or age or sex, but because of *antériorité:* "what comes after him is descended from him [. . .]. The Father is the Past" (ibid.).

Two opposite substances engage in a similar struggle: light and shadow. Their reciprocal threat, their never settled dispute forms the *tenebroso racinien:* "this great mythic (and theatrical) combat of darkness and light: on one side, night, shadows, ashes, tears, sleep, silence, timid sweetness and continuous presence; on the other, all the objects of stridency: weapons, eagles, fasces, torches, standards, shouts, brilliant garments, linen, purple and gold, steel, the stake, flames and blood" (Barthes, 1964b: 21).

As evidence for his *homo racinianus,* constructed along these and similar lines, Barthes cites a few isolated examples to illustrate his bold generalizations. Picard condemned this kind of argumentation. Barthes, on the other hand, could draw his justification from his essay "L'Activité structuraliste": the structuralist begins with the real object, takes it apart, and puts it together again. The reconstruction, however, is not meant to restore the original object but to bring a new one into existence—a new one which is capable of elucidating "something that remained invisible or, if one prefers, unintelligible in the original object" (Barthes, 1964a: 214). The important thing in making the reconstruction is to display the regularities which govern the functions of an object. In this manner an image *(simulacre)* of the object is gained, but it is a "directed, concerned simulacrum" (ibid.).

Roland Barthes had formulated enough postulates to justify his far-reaching abstractions from the text. Racine's work is form (signifier), to which Barthes must relate a signified if the whole is to be a sign. At this point, however, he takes leave of the given system of language and draws the signified from the anthropological system of Lévi-Strauss. The complication that enters here is of the following kind: that which Roland Barthes borrows from the anthropological system as the signified is, within that system, the signifier. Barthes' method is characterized by an interference of signified and signifier. As a result both systems appear reduced by one dimension; and the pitfalls of a literary structuralism which takes as its precedent a system which is itself derivative (anthropological structuralism, after all, finds its precedent in linguistic structuralism), become clear. Literature, as a system of language, is closer to linguistic than to anthropological structuralism. But as we shall see, the latter, due to the personality of Lévi-Strauss, was more decisive and more inspiring for the French situation than linguistic structuralism. While the linguistic analysis of "Les chats" and similar analyses in its wake caused little stir in France (reactions came mainly from beyond its frontiers), *Sur Racine* triggered off a quarrel. Picard wanted to remain within the one—literary— system and regenerate the original object after dissecting it. Barthes wanted to create a new object, a metatext *(meta-langage),* a new form based on two given forms: the works of Racine and the anthropology of Lévi-Strauss. His "critical" standpoint he made explicit; in this respect he is beyond reproach. As a representative of a reception–oriented point of view in France he deserves our interest; he puts his cards on the table and invites discussion. As a structuralist he confronts literary research with serious methodological problems, the first of which is to clarify the various domains of research and the possible transitions between them.

Structuralist Narratology

Just how influential Lévi-Strauss was in France can be seen in what we have called the second trend in structuralist literary research in France, that of structuralist narratology. It was Lévi-Strauss who in 1960 reviewed *Morphology of the Folktale* by Vladimir Propp; he reviewed the English translation (Propp, 1958) of the original Russian work which had appeared in Leningrad in 1928. Lévi-Strauss presents Propp as a Formalist; and conforming with the prejudice about Russian Formalism prevalent at that time, he criticizes him primarily for over-rating formal aspects, and for adopting the form/content division allegedly characteristic of Russian Formalism. He points out that structuralism, on the other hand, knows of no such dichotomy. His reproach is unwarranted on two grounds: Propp is not a representative of Russian Formalism but only a contemporary of that school; further, the form/content dichotomy is not characteristic of Russian Formalism, and certainly not of Propp.

Aside from the criticisms already mentioned, Lévi-Strauss valued Propp's work highly and in doing so undoubtedly stimulated, in the first place, Algirdas Julien Greimas, Claude Bremond and Tzvetan Todorov; others followed later. What could have brought a structuralist like Lévi-Strauss to see Propp's work as an impetus and a challenge? To begin with there is the material which Propp analysed. The fairy-tales of the Aarne-Thompson collection (Nos. 300–749) belong to a field bordering that of the ethnologist who studies primitive myths. Secondly, there was the growing dissatisfaction within folktale research with the orientation towards origin and development of folkloristic materials. The early voice of Propp, maintaining the primacy of systematic description over genetic research, was most welcome to Lévi-Strauss. Propp maintains: "To discuss genetics, without special elucidation of the problem of description as it is usually treated, is completely useless" (Propp, 1968: 5). It had similarly been the preference for synchrony which had made it possible for Lévi-Strauss to become a follower of Saussure. Thirdly—and this probably constitutes the main reason for the attraction which the structuralists felt for Propp—there was Propp's structuralist credo regarding the relative place of the "function" in plot development:

"An action cannot be defined apart from its place in the course of narration. The meaning which a given function has in the course of action must be considered" (Propp, 1968: 21).

Alan Dundes, the American folklorist who further developed Propp's insights, considers this statement in the *Morphology* as "one of the most revolutionary and important contributions to folklore theory in decades" (Dundes, 1962: 100). With Propp's remark there flashed the idea that folklore research, with its classification of isolated motifs, had been heading in the wrong direction. In the usual classification system according to motifs, two fairy-tales were labelled as two different types if in one case a person and in the other case an animal performed the same action. Repeated observation brought Propp to the hypothesis that in mythical traditions a multiplicity of characters contrasts with a markedly small number of "functions" (a function is understood as an act of a character, defined from the point of view of its significance for the course of the action (Propp, 1968: 21). Propp illustrates this by means of the following example:

1. A king gives an eagle to a hero. The eagle carries the hero away to another kingdom. 2. An old man gives Sučenko a horse. The horse carries Sučenko away to another kingdom. 3. A sorcerer gives Ivan a little boat. The boat takes Ivan to another kingdom. 4. A princess gives Ivan a ring. Young men appearing from out of the ring carry Ivan to another kingdom.

From the preceding example it can be inferred that the actions are the constant elements, whereas the dramatis personae are the variables: "Functions of characters serve as stable, constant elements in a tale, independent of how and by whom they are fulfilled" (Propp, 1968: 21). Propp concludes that not motifs but functions should be considered the basic units of the folktale; different motifs are capable of conveying one and the same action in the sequence of events and can therefore be traced back to smaller units. Opposite the unit which was traditionally smallest (the motif) Propp places his new smallest unit (the function). Motifs are then the variants of one and the same invariant function.

The reasons cited for the affinity which Lévi-Strauss shows for Propp—namely the similarity of research material, the preference for synchrony, the consideration of elements under the aspect of their place in the system—can now be completed by Propp's reference to the search for structural regularities. In the foreword to his work he observes that "it is possible to make an examination of the forms of the tale which will be as exact as the morphology of organic formations" (Propp, 1968: XXV).

The principle that the discovery of regularities is the goal of the ethnologist we find laid down in the introduction to *Anthropologie structurale,* where Lévi-Strauss calls upon anthropologists to discover "the unconscious structure underlying each institution and each custom, in order to obtain a principle of interpretation valid for other institutions and other customs" (Lévi-Strauss, 1972: 21).

Lévi-Strauss maps out the route he wants to follow to attain this goal: "the transition from conscious to unconscious is associated with progression from the specific toward the general" (Lévi-Strauss, 1972: 20–1). This is also the road taken by Propp. A corpus of 100 fairy-tales serves as the foundation for his work; others are used as test material. It should be added that he does not undertake his investigations without theoretical basis. His observations are intended to answer to a given problem: "Since we are studying tales according to the functions of their dramatis personae, the accumulation of material can be suspended as soon as it becomes apparent that the new tales considered present no new functions" (Propp, 1968: 23).

The result of Propp's observations is the following: thirty-one functions can be identified, and in addition the sequence in which they appear is constant.[7] This does not mean that all thirty-one functions can be found in each of the fairy-tales; but it does mean that the absence of some of these functions does not alter the sequence of those present. Fairy-tales with identical functions in the sense we have mentioned belong to one type. Propp mentions three possibilities for the notation of functions: according to sentence, substantive or symbol (the symbol serves for clarity attainable by means of formalization; however, this clarity suffers from the fact that in the various translations the symbols are differently translated).

A fairy-tale is understood to be every story which moves from function A (villainy) by way of intermediate functions to the problem-solving function W (wedding). The seven functions preceding A are to be considered introductory. The function chain A . . . W Propp calls a sequence. Each appearance of an "A" (villainy) indicates a new sequence. A fairy-tale can consist of several sequences. What must be determined, then, is the number of sequences in a text. Since they do not always appear one after the other—it is possible for a sequence to be interrupted by the insertion of a new one—, the analysis is not always a simple matter. It must also be decided whether several sequences can still be treated as one fairy-tale, or whether it is then already a matter of two or more separate tales. Other elements playing a role in the morphology of the fairy-tale besides the sequence-forming functions are the motivations and repetitions of functions as well as the connections between them.

Propp considers intertwined sequences and double or triple functions to be variants and exceptions. This idea, however, was disputed by several scholars, especially by Claude Bremond. Although he was one of the first to adopt Propp's functions as basic units in determining narrative structures, he opposed from the beginning the unilinear chain of elements. He does not conceive of the narrative as "a unilinear chain, but as an interlacing of sequences" (Bremond, 1964: 26). In this connection it must also be mentioned that Bremond does not limit himself to the corpus of Russian fairy-tales. Bremond sees in Propp's analysis precisely the possibility to leave the corpus, no matter how limited, completely out of consideration, and to use Propp's method as a *fil conducteur* in the founding of a general narratology. At this point, however, intertwined sequences as well as double and triple functions, supposedly exceptions, become problematic, because they occur regularly in stories which do not belong to Propp's closed corpus.

All of this is related to Propp's rejection of the distinction between *fabula* and *sjužet* as it was introduced by the Russian Formalists. He was also less in need of this distinction because *fabula* and *sjužet* usually coincide in the "simple forms". But it is precisely when dealing with intertwined sequences and doubled functions that we reach the point at which *fabula* and *sjužet* begin to go separate ways—i.e. where there is deviation from the chronologically final sequence of elements and where components of *sjužet* arrangement make their appearance.

Bremond takes exception to yet another aspect of Propp's theory; and in this respect his criticism agrees with that of Lévi-Strauss and Greimas. Bremond objects most of all to Propp's exclusive concern for syntagmatics, i.e. the succession of actions on the time coordinate. Propp fails to take into consideration the paradigmatic aspect of the logic of action according to which several logical possibilities remain open when a function is inserted (the function "battle", for instance, can entail defeat, victory, victory and defeat, or neither victory nor defeat). In this way logical relationships of cause and effect, means and ends, remain unreflected and can therefore lead to false conclusions. Thus the function "victory" implies "battle" (as a logical postulate); for "battle" to imply "victory", on the other hand, is by no means a requirement of logic but the stereotype of a certain culture (Bremond, 1964: 15).

By this route Bremond comes to differentiate between functions which are necessary by reason of logical postulates and functions which are not. While retaining the "function" as the basic unit, Bremond sets up new units (e.g. three functions forming a sequence) (Bremond, 1964; 1966). This does not happen, however, on the basis of the temporal-final relations in a given corpus, but on the basis of the systematizing of logical possibilities which he discusses in his essay "La logique des possible narratifs" (1966). With this approach Bremond makes a decisive turn away from concrete narrative texts. A *fabula/sjužet* distinction is meaningless in his model since this distinction leads in the direction of the concrete text. By means of his own methodological decision Bremond actually cancels out his main criticism of Propp, since the validity of that criticism depends on a consideration of concrete texts.

Consequently, E. M. Meletinskij, a Russian semiotician standing firmly in the Formalist tradition, criticizes the abstract character of Bremond's model: "Bremond's analysis is very abstract (and for that reason inadequate), because it attempts a general analysis at the expense of a genre-oriented approach [such as Propp's]" (Meletinskij, 1969: 203).

An analysis in terms of genre is, however, of as little interest for Bremond as for Greimas. Both are concerned with a "grammar of the narrative", or, as Bremond formulated it recently, with a "semiotics of the narrative" (Bremond, 1974), in which the logical basis is indispensable: "A model inspired by logic supports this construction and guarantees its validity for every kind of narrative" (Bremond, 1974). In this undertaking Propp's model can be of great help; for by means of the actant model "the semantic universe, which is much too vast to be grasped in its totality, is organized into micro-universes accessible to man" (Greimas, 1966a: 174).

The process of abstraction, which characterizes the French (in contrast to the Russian) variant of Propp's narrative analyses, draws some of its justification from Lévi-Strauss's critique of linear syntagmatics. Meletinskij and Segal state from their Russian perspective: "Propp directed all his attention to the narrative structure of the folktale, to a linear syntagmatics, and not to the logical paradigmatics as Lévi-Strauss did" (Meletinskij and Segal, 1971: 95).

In his myth analyses, Lévi-Strauss was predominantly interested in certain semantic oppositions (raw/cooked, damp/dry), and could therefore leave the linear structure of the narrative out of consideration. His material did not really consist of texts, while texts formed the basis of Propp's work. Meletinskij describes the difference in the following way: "In spite of his most penetrating and detailed thinking regarding a method for a structural analysis of the myth, his concrete examples are not structural analyses of mythical narrative but of mythical thought [. . .]. Lévi-Strauss is essentially interested in mythological logic. Therefore he begins with the myth, combines the functions only vertically, and tries to explain their paradigmatics juxtaposing the mythical variants. His structural model is non-linear" (Meletinskij, 1969: 191).

Greimas conceives of the ideal postulates of a narratology as a combination of the paradigmatics-oriented model of Lévi-Strauss and the syntagmatics-oriented model of Propp. Unlike Propp, Greimas analyses not only fairy-tales but also myths (Greimas, 1963, and especially 1966b). He analysed the myths at first according to the paradigmatic method of Lévi-Strauss, but his later development goes into the direction of the syntagmatic method of Propp. His argument is that the myth as *narrative* has a temporal dimension: "Actions of mythical characters are interrelated with respect to what has happened before and what will happen after" (Greimas, 1966b: 29). He systematizes the function of the narrative with the help of an example from the myth corpus of the Bororo Indians. From there he proceeds to list the roles of the characters, and he deals in particular with role exchanges of the main characters (father and son). Systematically he carries out his analysis of the interrelations between the syntagmatic data of the functions and sequences and the paradigmatic data of roles, role exchange, and the two different forms of the contractual function (the voluntary and the forced contract).

Greimas is concerned in the first place with establishing elementary structures of meaning within a semantic micro-universe. His model takes account of static, non-narrative forms on the one hand, and on the other it is meant to be suited to dynamic, action-bearing processes. Or, as summarized by Bremond: "Having become dynamic the fundamental relations which constitute the taxonomic model (example: gold versus lead) project themselves in operations which have their basis in terms established by the same elementary morphology (telling for example 'how pure gold changed into vile lead')" (Bremond, 1973: 83–4). The regularities of such operations form the syntax of narrative grammar. In this manner Greimas achieved two levels of analysis, the level of "immanent narrative structures" and the level of "the manifestation" (Bremond, 1973: 88).

Bremond, who otherwise thinks very highly of the stringency of Greimas' work, becomes critical at this point. In his opinion Greimas sees the levels in a clearly hierarchical order, in which the "deeper" level of non-temporal, conceptual relations determines the actual meaning of the narrative. The following statement by Greimas supports his suspicion:

We have the right to assume that the a-chronical organisation-model of the contents we find in so very widely differing fields must have a general bearing. Its indifference to the invested contents [. . .] forces us to consider it a metalingual model which is hierarchically superordinated to qualifying or functional models [. . .] (Greimas, 1966a: 233).

The temporal sequence of events, the "surface structure", can in the last analysis add nothing more to the meaning: "on the contrary, it tends to camouflage the play of semiotic constraints, to conceal the meaning" (Bremond, 1973: 89). According to Bremond, a dogmatic tendency creeps into Greimas' analysis. Greimas robs the narrative of its freedom. The narrator cannot choose between various possibilities for continuing his story: "From the network of available trajectories, Greimas selects a combination, possible among many others, and accords to it—but by what right?—the privilege of governing the universe of the narrative" (Bremond, 1973: 99).

Bremond and Greimas differ mainly in their conception of time. As Bremond himself determines, the essence of the story for Greimas lies in the interplay of non-temporal relations which transcend the "becoming" of the narrated events. For Bremond, on the other hand, the essence lies in the "becoming", which implies the possibility of a variable future. Greimas represents a more static, a-historical viewpoint. Although Bremond cannot be called the historian among the French narratologists, one has to concede that he *theoretically* defends the dynamism assumed by the historian.[8] He does this in the name of freedom which disregards the "semiotic constraints" of Greimas: "For us the impression of freedom, truth and beauty, which has always prodded men to arrange narratives, is not an illusion which masks 'the play of semiotic constraints'. If there is a play, it is not one we undergo, it is a play ON the constraints, the liberating experience which exploits and surmounts them" (Bremond, 1973: 101).

Despite this attestation and an alertness to the strengths and weaknesses in the theories of other structuralist narratologists, Bremond blocks his own path to freedom, historicity and personal evaluation by binding himself very closely to logical relations: "A logic of intrigue, an unpleasant task perhaps but also a necessary one, must precede its semiotics. This logic, truly the universal language of the narrative, imposes itself upon us as the first step in a structural analysis of the narrative" (Bremond, 1973: 134).

From abstract logical analysis, the main task of which is to determine which elements imply or exclude each other and which elements can be combined with each other, Bremond has not yet found his way back to the individual manifestation of this logic in individual texts or groups of texts. He has come no farther than to point out a few cultural variants (e.g. that battle should imply victory is a cultural stereotype). The fear which Lévi-Strauss expressed in his review that Propp might not be able to find his way back from the abstract to the concrete would hold true to a much greater degree for Bremond. Propp had not strayed nearly so far from texts. The flexibility of his "sequence", given such emphasis by Bremond, has so far proved to be nothing more than a refinement of Propp's scheme and not yet a "liberating experience". (He had extensively modified Propp's concept of sequence. For Bremond the basic sequence denotes the triadic structure of a process, "potentiality, transition to action, and achievement", with the possibilities "no transition to action, lack of achievement".)

The introduction of roles by Bremond must also be understood as a refinement. On the basis of his role concept, Bremond can define function, at variance with Propp, "not only by an action (which we shall call *process*), but by the position and relation of a person-subject and a process-predicate; or, to adopt a clearer terminology, we shall say that the structure of the narrative rests, not in a sequence of actions, but in the constellation of *roles*" (Bremond, 1973: 133). The major part of his book *Logique du récit* is devoted to a cataloguing of roles which, as he admits, remains incomplete as well as somewhat arbitrary. The thoroughness of Bremond's work, the way in which he values and assimilates studies made by others, and his unpretentiousness all speak in his favour. But unfortunately it seems that he cannot encompass historical diversity, the "becoming", to say nothing of the possibility of explicating the aesthetic value of narrative texts (cf. Scholes, 1974: 96).

One of the few scholars in France who were influenced not only by Propp and Lévi-Strauss but also by Russian Formalism is Tzvetan Todorov, who in 1965 published a number of studies by the Russian Formalists in French translation. Therefore it is not surprising that the distinction between *fabula* and *sjužet,* which generally speaking was not common in French narratology, does play a role in the work of Todorov. As a result Todorov's method presents itself as closer to the text than those of the others. In addition he continually strives to determine the literariness of texts, an undertaking which is familiar to us from Russian Formalism. In his contribution to the special issue of *Communications* (1966), Todorov summarizes a concept apparatus which takes into account the distinction between *fabula* and *sjužet.* In "Les catégories du récit littéraire" he proposes a dichotomy of *histoire* and *discours,* which corresponds to the dichotomy of *"fable"* and *"sujet".* In the section devoted to *histoire* he claims support from Bremond's triadic model on the one hand and from the homology model of Lévi-Strauss on the other; according to the homology model, a narrative is the syntagmatic projection of paradigmatic relations. The logic of action which Todorov postulates along with this model is for him the basis of narratological research, also for precisely those cases in which the congruence of logic and action sequence is disrupted. For deviations are meaningful: "Even if an author does not obey this logic we must be acquainted with it: his disobedience derives all its meaning precisely in relation to the norms which this logic imposes" (Todorov, 1966: 132). Todorov illustrates his general insights with reference to Laclos' *Les liaisons dangereuses.*

Proper to the domain of the *fabula* are also the relations of the characters with each other, which Todorov brings into the triadic scheme of "desire, communication, participation". All other possible relations can be derived from these three general ones with the help of derivation rules. Todorov makes the transition from *fabula* to *sjužet* by referring to the multidimensional time of the *fabula,* as opposed to the time of the *sjužet* which is basically linear. That which can take place simultaneously in the *fabula* must necessarily appear in sequence in the *sjužet* (in the text): "a complex figure is projected on to a straight line" (Todorov, 1966: 139). In this way the natural action sequence is broken even if the author wants to maintain it as exactly as possible. Usually, however, the author strives to change the natural sequence for aesthetic reasons. Besides a specific treatment of time, the narrative point of view also distinguishes the *sjužet* from the *fabula*.

Todorov's essay, which contains a section on aspects of the *sjužet*, leads us to ask whether his statements about the *sjužet* are an integral part of his theoretical discussions. The transition from the *fabula* section, where he developed elements of the logic of action, to the *sjužet* is made in very general terms and restricts itself to linear time and the aesthetic principle as basic concepts. The fact that this transition is not convincing is, in our opinion, characteristic for the difficulty involved in finding a bridge from the abstract level of the logic of the *fabula*, developed by individual researchers as a more or less rigorous and tightly reasoned field, to the more concrete level of *sjužet* arrangement. If this bridging is not eventually achieved, however, the danger that the logical postulates become autonomous, independent of textual data, is great.

In his *Grammaire du Décameron* (1969) Todorov drops the *sjužet* as a goal of research. Instead, he deals with the syntactical level of narrative *(fabula)*, which he distinguishes along with the semantic and the verbal (stylistic-rhetorical) levels. This puts him in direct proximity to Propp. In addition, the fact that Todorov in this case starts from a certain material, the novellas of Boccaccio, shows his kinship with Propp. Nevertheless Todorov works with an eye to general narratological laws which go beyond the material—a perspective which was unfamiliar to Propp. In this study Todorov relies heavily on the triad. On various levels he develops triadic schemes, with the result that we gain some insight into the weaknesses peculiar to triadic models, namely that there usually proves to be some disparity between one element of the triad and the other two. Bremond, who devotes one chapter of his *Logique du récit* to Todorov's study, points out such discrepancies without however casting doubt on the triad itself, as he too thinks largely in triadic terms. In the scheme "proper noun, adjective, verb", for instance, the adjective as a more descriptive-qualifying element is dropped from the narrative syntax because it lacks the dynamic potency to carry the action forward: " 'God is omnipotent' is an attributive proposition that narrates nothing; 'God created the heavens and the earth' is a minimal narrative, but a complete narrative" (Bremond, 1973: 112). In Propp the adjective is classed with the attributes and plays no role in the function. Its qualifying aspect offers, in our opinion, room for evaluations of characters and actions, evaluations which fall outside the scope of the French narratologists.

The three verbs which form the lexicon of actions in Todorov show up a similar inconsistency: "to modify, to sin, to punish" fall into two groups because only "to modify" has a general action-advancing function; the verbs "to sin" and "to punish" lack generality and semantic neutrality. "To punish" proves the least adequate since it is by no means certain that a punishment must always follow a sin. In the *Decameron,* for instance, this is not at all the rule.

Due to his closeness to the text, Todorov, the French structuralist with roots in the East European tradition, does not succumb to the constraints of the logical system (as is the case, most prominently perhaps, with Greimas), nor does he enter a domain of abstractions from which there appears to be no easy way back to the literary facts (as Bremond does).

Historicity and evaluative reaction—proclaimed by Barthes as the basis of all encounters with literature—play no role in the narratological variant of French structuralism. In the endeavour to make the logical-anthropological universe intelligible and to trace it back to general schemes, there is no place for the historical individuality of a text and its reader.

The third trend in French structuralism, exemplified in the analysis which Jakobson and Lévi-Strauss made of Baudelaire's sonnet "Les chats", can certainly not be accused of abstracting too far from the text.

Linguistic-Structuralist Text Description

The central position of Lévi-Strauss in the extension of the structuralist method to French literary research also becomes evident in the field of structuralist text description. Not only did Lévi-Strauss collaborate with Jakobson in analysing "Les chats", but the first publication of this analysis, which appeared in *L'Homme: Revue française d'anthropologie* (1962), was also introduced and defended by him. In the meantime the inclusion of this essay in anthologies of literary studies has freed it from its anthropological ambiance.

In his foreword Lévi-Strauss first attempts to counter the reader's astonishment at finding the analysis of a poem in an anthropological journal by pointing out the analogous problematics of the linguist and the ethnologist. This idea is familiar to us from his *Anthropologie structurale*. In this respect nothing new is developed in *L'Homme;* rather, it might be ascertained that here the analogy argument is less convincing. Lévi-Strauss tells us that the linguist discovers structures in literary works which are surprisingly analogous to those which the ethnologist finds in his analysis of myths, and that, on the other hand, strong aesthetic feelings are evoked in ethnologists by the myths, which are at the same time works of art. The distinction between myth and poem should of course not be denied, but the contrast between the two should be understood as a structural principle, as proof that they belong to the same category.

If one proceeds from the assumption that the theoretical framework of the analysis is determined by Jakobson's concept of the poetic function as projecting "the principle of equivalence from the axis of selection into the axis of combination" (Jakobson 1960: 358), then the analogy maintained by Lévi-Strauss is not very convincing. As he says himself in the foreword, myth can "in principle be interpreted only on the semantic level". Equivalences on the combination axis are therefore hardly relevant—in myth only the contiguity relation dominates on this axis.

Our preceding critical remarks concern only the attempt to legitimize by means of analogy the publication of a poetic analysis in a journal which was devoted neither to literature nor to linguistics; they are in no way directed against the analysis as representative of one variant of the structuralist method.

A comparison with the two forms of French structuralist scholarship which we have already discussed yields the following outline of the variant under consideration:
1. The basis is not anthropological but linguistic structuralism.
2. No search is made for a system of rules on a higher level of abstraction; rather a functional principle (the equivalence principle) is demonstrated.
3. The equivalence principle of Jakobson is built into a hierarchy of hypotheses. The list of the six communicative functions precedes it. In the case of poetic communication the principal accent lies on the sign carrier ("focus on the message for its own sake").
4. The equivalence principle is presented as a necessary but not sufficient condition of the poetic function.
5. Nothing is stated about the disposition of the reader, which is only implied. The implicit presupposition is the evidently

universal value which man attributes to order (information) in contrast to disorder (entropy). Equivalence relations of many kinds, all of which can be demonstrated in a text, display a high degree of order.

6. An analysis undertaken on the basis of equivalence relations is subject to intersubjective testing.

In this way the claim "one can speak truly about Baudelaire" is contrasted with Barthes' dictum "one cannot speak truly about Racine". How far this claim to truth extends and where its possible limits lie will be discussed in the following pages.

One limit lies in the isolation of the sign carrier within the communication system. Jakobson starts from this system when he lists the various language functions, but then, on the grounds of his description of the poetic function, he omits the relations which exist between the message and the sender, the receiver and extra-linguistic reality; he concentrates on the message and its internal relations. The linguistic levels which are compatible with this degree of concentration and isolation readily offer themselves to analysis by this method. For instance, the equivalence relations in a selected corpus can definitely be constructed on the phonological and the syntactic level, and in a manner which is both exhaustive and falsifiable. As to the semantic level, however, complications will present themselves: to the extent that not only a lexical meaning (central meaning, core of meaning [Schmidt, 1969]) must be postulated for a word but also a constitution of meaning in the context, the isolation of the sign carrier proves problematic, and the analysis on this level is to be methodologically less rigorous. Semantic features as such do not elude description, and with the help of a lexicon rather exact analyses can be made. Contextual and situational data are, however, capable of changing the semantic features of a word in a specific text.

"Les chats" offers examples for such contextual influences at the point where the features "inanimate, animate" and "masculine, feminine" become decisive for the *interpretation* (hypothesis about the interrelationship of meaning) and where either equivalence relations (intratextual influence) or cultural tradition (extratextual influence) have an effect on the final constitution of meaning of a word. Since the meaning in both cases is constituted in deviation from the listed lexical features, semantics would have to be able to account for the deviations and transitions if genuine methodological strictness is desired. But semantics cannot at present accomplish this task.

As a result of Jakobson's formulation of the poetic function, precisely those features of a word which are not laid down in a lexicon now make their appearance. Equivalences on the combination axis contribute to the activation of "marginal" meanings which play a substantial role in, for instance, metaphors. The equivalences on the combination level make selections possible which are not admissable in a non-artistic text (Lotman, 1972a: 123). The poetic principle does not mean merely a strengthening or doubling of a previous, primary selection. Often a meaning is constituted only by means of combination; a selection is made and experienced as meaningful which in non-artistic language would be considered a defective selection. We are confronted with this phenomenon especially in modern hermetic poetry. The analysis of a difficult modern text would probably have brought Jakobson and Lévi-Strauss to accept semanticizing on the basis of combinations. This might have lessened the discrepancy which shows up in the Baudelaire analysis with respect to the criteria of exactness and susceptibility to testing between the lists of phonological and syntactic identity relations on the one hand and semantic relations on the other. The studies of Ursula Oomen (1973), which are based on transformational grammar and accordingly assign a favoured position to syntax, indicate a possible direction here for further research.

Jakobson and Lévi-Strauss do not make a total survey of the influence of the combination of equivalences on the field of semantics. Neither in theory, nor in the analysis of the poem do they allow for the possibility of a hierarchical ordering of equivalences; and only by taking such a hierarchy into account would it be possible to come to grips with the field of semantics, which today is still resistant to exact description. In the analysis of Jakobson and Lévi-Strauss high-sounding and far-reaching statements are made about semantic aspects. With regard to method, however, these statements are vulnerable. This weakness takes on all the more significance if the theoretical foundation of poetic analysis does not allow for an *interpretation* (in the sense we described above). The formulation of the equivalence principle offers the possibility of demonstrating the poetic function as exemplified in Baudelaire's "Les chats". In consequence, the study under consideration, restricted by the limits set by theory, can only have the character of an *analysis,* and, as such, is of exemplary value. Within the limits of an analysis a cataloguing, as exhaustive as possible, of relations fully satisfies the theoretical demands; and if this cataloguing had been accompanied by a more elaborate account of observations and a supplementary hypothesis, it would in addition have disclosed the structure of the particular Baudelaire text.

For example, further observations could have been made on the distribution of equivalence classes. The fact that two differently defined equivalence classes have the same distribution in a text contributes, according to Roland Posner, to the structuring of the text: "For the more text levels that can, independently of each other, be correlated with the segmentation, the more relevant that segmentation is for the text structure" (Posner, 1972: 218). Posner offers as an example the word *"fin"* from Baudelaire's poem. This word is a member of five equivalence classes, namely the classes A-E. (It is (A) an adjective, (B) of masculine gender, (C) at the end of a line; it has (D) masculine cadence, and (E) rhymes with a homonym—Posner limits himself to formal categories; he does not mention lexical data.) From this summation of structural features he infers a high degree of necessity (irreplaceability) of the text segment in question: "The more different vertical equivalence classes comprise a text level and the more intersections raise this level from the rest of the text, the more significant this level is in the text as a whole" (Posner, 1972: 219).

In this way Posner draws the conclusion from Jakobson's implicit assumption of the high value of order and brings into the discussion a value hypothesis which enables him—in contrast to Jakobson and Lévi-Strauss—to hierarchize and evaluate the observations about equivalence relations. This broadening of the theoretical foundation of the poetic function is, in our opinion, necessary, if only to distinguish combinations in non-literary texts (e.g. advertising) from those in literary texts. It is also needed to check the accumulation of the smallest imaginable identity relations in a text. The idea underlying Lotman's concept of interference is also basic for Posner. A multiplicity of interferences determines the individuality and the value of a text: "The more regularities overlap at a given point of the structure, the more individual the text appears to be" (Lotman, 1972a: 121).

In 1968 Nicolas Ruwet posed the question whether the equivalence principle as such is sufficient to produce a poetic-aesthetic effect since this principle is realized in other texts as well. He refers to Samuel R. Levin and his theory of "coupling" (in which equivalence is present on at least two different levels) in order to find some clue for a distinctive feature of poetic texts. In his own analyses he tried to introduce the hierarchization which is lacking in Jakobson and Lévi-Strauss by pointing out that syntactical equivalences form the basis of phonological and semantic equivalences. Although he shows the relevance of this hierarchy, his method—in the analysis of "Je te donne ces vers" (1971)—is still very close to that of Jakobson and Lévi-Strauss.

Jakobson's formulation of the poetic function includes no basis for a hierarchy of equivalences: strictly, he could not leave the stage of cataloguing. Nevertheless his analysis contains evaluations of equivalence relations (e.g. with respect to the two parts of the second quatrain) which in fact presuppose a review of the distribution of equivalences as made by Posner. The transition from cataloguing to the reconstruction of a hierarchy of equivalences can be achieved by means of a supplementary hypothesis, with no detriment to the precision of the analysis, as becomes clear in the cases of Levin, Ruwet and Posner.

The transition from analysis to interpretation presents itself as substantially more complicated. Jakobson and Lévi-Strauss did not, however, want to abandon interpretation altogether, either because they were dissatisfied with mere cataloguing or because they felt the poem to have value. But since Jakobson's theory does not account for interpretation, their results in this area are good mainly for eliciting criticism.

Often without indicating in any falsifiable way just how the phonological and syntactic levels might exert influence on the semantic level, Jakobson and Lévi-Strauss jump from phonological and syntactic equivalence observations to the boldest claims regarding meaning (e.g. "The effacement of /r/ as before /l/ eloquently evokes the transition from the empirical cat to its phantastical transfigurations" (Jakobson and Lévi-Strauss, in Lane, 1970: 211)). Unfortunately a semantic foundation for this contrast is lacking; neither can it be provided since it would contradict the professed reduction of the communication system to the sign carrier. A similar cancelling out of the chosen methodological position appears when the concept of dynamic transition is used to defend the more highly evaluated fourth level of organization (with the distych).

If, on the other hand, the relations to extra-linguistic reality—to sender and receiver—are included in the theoretical postulates, then a time factor, indispensable for semantic observations, can be introduced into the "spatial" structural model of Jakobson. Indeed, Jakobson's research has been characterized by a spatial concept of structure.[9] In his analyses, the internal relations of the poem as a whole (i.e. after completion of the reading process) are investigated, and thereby separated from the linear time sequence.

Michael Riffaterre, who criticized the method of Jakobson and Lévi-Strauss and countered their analysis of "Les chats" with an interpretation of his own, includes the time factor in both of its aspects. In the first place it plays a role in the reading process. Riffaterre uses the concept "contrast experience" in the constitution of the poetic structure by the reader: "Each point of the text that holds up the superreader is tentatively considered a component of the poetic structure" (Riffaterre 1966: 204).[10] Contrasts arise when the expectations of a reader with respect to repetitive structures prove wrong and predictability is lessened. Without rejecting the equivalence principle (Riffaterre in fact needs it for constituting expectation patterns), he makes it dependent on the perception of the reader during the temporal sequence of the reading process. When a contrast experience takes place, it is capable, according to Riffaterre, of influencing retroactively the meanings in the text which have already been perceived. After completion of the reading process this influence manifests itself most clearly: "Then the total of all data and knowledge of the ending surges back to modify what we perceived at the beginning" (Riffaterre, 1966: 221).

Besides this time factor which is bound up with the process of reading, Riffaterre's interpretation is marked by the factor of time which appears in the tradition of cultural history and in the literary tradition in particular. When Riffaterre determines that Baudelaire's poem includes literary allusions, clichés and irony, he cannot get by without this aspect of time. Equivalence relations cannot in this case replace knowledge about older linguistic usage and familiarity with older literature. Of irony he says: "It is in the whole second quatrain, that irony is amplified. Jakobson and Lévi-Strauss are blinded by irrelevant parallelisms and do not see this" (Riffaterre, 1966: 210). The expression *"horreur des ténèbres"* which Riffaterre considers a cliché (not in the negative sense) to the cultivated reader, and which he regards as an allusion to Racine and Delille, derives from this knowledge of the literary tradition and leads to a meaning which differs completely from the one set forth by Jakobson and Lévi-Strauss. Jakobson's "powers of darkness", which are connected with "the grisly task of *coursiers funèbres*" (in Lane, 1970: 213) appear in Riffaterre, with historical background taken into account, as "an asylum for the secret life, a privileged abode for meditation, a sanctuary" (Riffaterre, 1966: 212).

In this discrepancy the difference between the two theoretical foundations becomes most tangible: on the one hand isolation of the sign carrier, on the other the inclusion of the reader and his code whereby the temporal element is implied. It is hardly surprising that in describing the theme on a level which abstracts extensively from the poetic text, Jakobson and Lévi-Strauss on the one side and Riffaterre on the other arrive at opposite conclusions. The symbol of *"androgyne"* is rejected by Riffaterre in favour of *"contemplation"*. This is done with the help of references to the lexical interrelationships in the text, which the two structuralists lose sight of in their search for grammatical equivalences, and by including meaning changes which came about in the course of time: "French, significantly, shifted from *la* to *le sphinx* during the eighteenth century" (Riffaterre, 1966: 226).

Riffaterre considers Jakobson and Lévi-Strauss's analysis of "Les chats" successful to the extent that is presents a convincing demonstration of the extraordinary concatenation by which the parts of speech are held together (Riffaterre, 1966: 195). But—and here his focus on the reader is again unmistakable—he has reservations about equivalences which elude perceptibility even though they are possible in a purely theoretical sense. Divisions three and four as set forth by Jakobson and Lévi-Strauss are, in his opinion, exemplary in this lack of perceptibility. (At question is the chiastic form which connects the first quartet with the second terzet and the second quartet with the first terzet, as well as the transition structure which allows lines 7 and 8 to be read as a distych located between two sextets.) The stress on language form, which is required for poetic effect, must at least be "visible", otherwise it is irrelevant. Working from such a standpoint Riffaterre has to reject the two divisions already mentioned above: "Divisions three and four, especially the last, make use of constituents that cannot possibly be perceived by the reader; these constituents must therefore remain alien to the poetic structure, which is supposed to emphasize the form of the message, to make it more visible, more compelling" (ibid.). The same is true for the connection which Jakobson and Lévi-Strauss claim to find between line 4 and line 12. Riffaterre, however, observes that *"comme eux sont frileux"* of line 4 is visibly homologous to *"comme eux sédentaires"* (also line 4), thus making the connection with line 12 appear irrelevant.

Crucial for Riffaterre, who thoroughly agrees with the equivalence principle, is the contact between the text and the reader; this contact has the final say about the acceptability of equivalence observations and their aesthetic necessity. Concerning the equivalence principle, the difference between Jakobson/Lévi-Strauss and Riffaterre can be described as follows: the former collect as many potential equivalence relations as possible, while Riffaterre wants to consider only realized equivalence relations. In that way Riffaterre found his solution to the problem of hierarchization.

As we have already indicated, Nicolas Ruwet also voiced his objection to the immense number of equivalence relations which are possible within the framework of Jakobson's theory: "It systematically and, in a sense, blindly registers the greatest possible number of equivalence relations at every level taken separately" (Ruwet, 1968: 61).[11] Moreover Ruwet takes a moderate position regarding those aspects which can be accounted for by means of linguistic analysis. He warns against overestimating the elements of a work of art that can technically be described, and excludes *"connaissance du monde"* from the linguist's domain of competence.

We have gone to considerable detail in discussing the criticism directed against Jakobson and Lévi-Strauss's applied method. This seemed to us all the more justifiable since the three critics we discussed—Riffaterre, Ruwet, Posner—adhere to the structuralist tradition. Consequently their statements about the weaknesses and limits of the method are markedly constructive. Even Riffaterre, who of the three scholars mentioned is the farthest removed from Jakobson, does not reject the equivalence principle. Jakobson's linguistic method (and we may free him for a moment from his partnership with Lévi-Strauss) offers a beginning which until now has been the most promising of its kind. One possibility for developing this approach may take place within the framework of the communication model which allows for additional relations. This is the case in the semiotic variants of structuralism of, for example, Lotman. But the same is also true of a reception-oriented literary research to the extent that it counts the testable analysis of the sign carrier among its tasks.

Summing up, the development of Jakobson's theory must, in our opinion, be attempted along the following lines. First in a systematization of equivalence relations based on a hierarchical order: "An adequate assessment of equivalence relations must leave room for the possibility that a few but important equivalence classes that have the same extension may be of greater influence for the segmentation of the text than the co-presence of many but trivial segmentations" (Posner, 1972: 221).

Once it is possible to evaluate equivalence relations, one can defend the semanticizing of grammatical categories and in so doing take one more step in the direction of interpretation—i.e. towards establishing the context of meaning. Lotman's theory points in this direction: "Since everything that is noticed in an artistic text as being undeniably meaningful is felt to contain certain semantic information, the striking grammatical elements are also necessarily semanticized" (Lotman, 1972a: 233).

Finally, Jakobson's spatial concept of structure would have to be broadened to include and describe the time factor; it would then be possible to perceive and describe changes. Such changes might have to do with semantic features, but they might also concern participation in a genre and a period. Aided by the time factor, the interpreter would be able to evaluate the absence of features—or in a special case the absence of equivalence relations—as meaningful (Lotman's , minus-device). By including the recipient code, Riffaterre supplies the presuppositions for the evolutionary aspect. Important elements of meaning such as irony or parody become available in this way. A concept of structure with the temporal component we find in Mukařovský.[12]

Literary scholarship in France received the impetus of structuralism and assimilated it on its own terms. The international orientation, initially lacking, is being realized more and more. Possibilities for international scope lie in the common basis displayed by linguistic structuralism and Russian Formalism. Similarly, in its reflection on the receiver French structuralism follows an international line of research. Structuralist narratology and linguistic structural analysis have, as opposed to Barthes' variant, the advantage that they are on the way to developing a metalanguage, while the "meta-text" of Roland Barthes is a variation of object language.

We have not dealt with the Marxist variants of French structuralism. The connection between Marxism and structuralism in France can, in our opinion, be treated more fruitfully within a study of Marxist literary theory.

4

MARXIST THEORIES OF LITERATURE

Marxism is a philosophy of contradictions, and any attempt to explain Marxist theory in a rational way will encounter apparent inconsistencies. The belief in the primacy of material conditions and the simultaneous effort to emphasize the human role in changing these conditions is one of the most characteristic contradictions of Marxism. How can materialism and heroic revolt be considered as compatible?

If one were to accept that this contradiction can be solved by resorting to the dialectical method, a new problem arises, namely the question whether any criticism of the dialectical method is possible at all. Different from Russian Formalism or French structuralism, Marxist literary theories have a basis in a normative philosophy with explicit ideas about epistemological questions. Marxist theory cannot accept any criticism on a purely empirical basis. On the other hand, the criticism of Marxist theory on the basis of norms derived from that same theory cannot be considered satisfactory either. For instance, criticism of the Chinese interpretation of Marxist theories on the basis of the original writings by Marx and Engels, or criticism of Marx and Engels on the basis of criteria derived from neo-Marxism will necessarily remain limited in scope. The very basis of Marxist thought, common to the original Marxist philosophy and its various offsprings, would escape a critical assessment in this way.

We have decided to analyse Marxist literary theory from a metatheoretical point of view, in spite of the fact that Marxist theorists deny that such a point of view is at all possible. The non-attractive alternative is acceptance or rejection of Marxist theory on non-scientific grounds. On the other hand, we do not claim that our metatheoretical position gives us access to any superior wisdom. If we analyse Marxist theories in terms alien to these theories, we are only relating one system of thought to another system of thought. Of course, our own framework of reference can also be subjected to analysis and criticism by scholars who for one reason or another may prefer another epistemological position (perhaps that of Marxism).

Any 'analysis, any attribution of meaning and value occurs within the limits of certain rules. If one is prepared to explain what the guiding rules are (and adheres to them), any analysis and assessment is valid. The rules which we will respect in our analysis are those of precision, explicitness, falsifiability, the distinction between theory and practice (or between metalanguage and object language), and the distinction between observed facts and attributed values. These conventions belong to the tradition of critical rationalism. It is our firm conviction that this tradition, of which Karl R. Popper (1969b; 1972a) is one of the main representatives, has been extremely productive and has yielded results, also in the field of literary theory, which have withstood the test of severe criticism. Though Marxist scholars reject various tenets of the Popperian tradition, they take it seriously, as may appear from the highly interesting volume *Der Positivismusstreit* (Adorno, 1969), to which we will return below.

Marx, Engels and Lenin

It cannot be our aim to present here a systematic survey of Marxist thought. But if we were to restrict ourselves to the Marxist pronouncements on *literature,* we would probably fail to see the relation of literature to society, to historical development, and to the materialist conditions which serve as its basis. Marxism refuses to consider phenomena in isolation, and therefore it can be characterized as holistic. In this it resembles structuralism; but structuralism still allows the scholar to restrict his field of research for practical reasons, whereas Marxism is less inclined to mitigate its holistic claims. Another basic postulate of Marxism is the primacy of matter over thought. This, in fact, separates Marx and Engels from Hegel. All three have embraced the dialectic method. But Hegel conceives the dialectic merely as a movement of *thought,* whereas the founders of Marxism suggest that dialectical relationships exist both in *thought and nature.*

Dialectical materialism, which explains the development of the world as dialectical, is hard to understand unless we take into account that it implies a certain dynamism and describes a process of development from a lower to a higher stage. Here it may help to recall the original meaning of the word "dialectic", which is derived from a Greek verb meaning "to carry on a discussion". Statement (thesis) and counterstatement (antithesis) may give rise to a certain conclusion (synthesis). Under favourable conditions the conclusion can be considered as belonging to a higher level.

The conclusion, of course, may serve again as the starting point or first statement in a new discussion.

Marx and Engels applied the dialectic principle mainly to the sphere of social development. They believed that the class struggle between the bourgeoisie and the proletariat would lead inevitably to the overthrow of capitalism, thus promoting the cause of social progress. It was in his later years that Engels took up the study of natural science in order to elaborate the idea that "amidst the welter of innumerable changes taking place in nature the same dialectical laws of motion are in operation as those which in history govern the apparent fortuitousness of events."[1] Engels tried to show that the dialectic principle is at work throughout nature or reality.

The omnipresence of the dialectic principle has been emphasized also in recent Soviet philosophy, which views the dialectic as "the theory of the most general laws of the development of nature, society and thought" (Rozental' and Judin, 1963: 124).

Besides dialectical materialism, which aims to establish the objective necessary laws governing the whole of reality, the Marxist philosophers have distinguished historical materialism. Historical materialism is the extension of the tenets of dialectical materialism to the study of social life and social development. The laws of historical materialism are complicated by the human factor. Marxism is not purely deterministic. There is a margin of free will and individual convictions, which accounts for the difference between dialectical and historical materialism. It is clear that literature, which Marxist critics view primarily as ideology, must be studied within the terms of historical materialism.

The effect of Marx's materialist conception of history is often hard to discover in his pronouncements on literature, especially his earlier statements which appear more representative of an educated young German in the 1840s, well versed in classical literature, than of an iconoclastic revolutionary. In general his literary assessment is based on 1. the criterion of economic determinism, which is concerned with the question whether a literary work represents advanced or regressive developments in the economic basis; 2. the criterion of verisimilitude, which is in full accordance with the literary code of his days; and 3. the criterion of personal preferences, such as for the writings of Aeschylus, Shakespeare and Goethe, which belong to the literary canon of his time. Although one might expect that the first criterion is the most important from the Marxist point of view, later Marxist authors (with the exception of the defenders of *Proletkul't* and Chinese critics during the Cultural Revolution) have rather consistently upheld the last two Marxian criteria as well.

In his "Foreword" (1859) to *Zur Kritik der Politischen Ökonomie* Marx expressed most clearly how he saw the relation between the economic basis and the superstructure (including literature):

The mode of production of material life determines altogether the social, political, and intellectual life process. It is not the consciousness of men that determines their being, but on the contrary their social being, that determines their consciousness. At a certain stage of their development the material forces of production in society come into conflict with the existing relations of production or, to mention the legal expression, the property relations within which they have been at work. From conditions for the development of the forces of production these proprietary relations become their fetters. Then a period of social revolution begins. With a change in the economic basis the entire immense superstructure is transformed with greater or less speed.[2]

This is a concise statement of Marx's economic determinism which, in spite of its imprecision, has always remained in the background of later Marxist explanations of the relation between ideological superstructure and economic basis, or literature and the economic structure of society.

The quoted statement is imprecise because, as a result of changes in the economic basis, alterations in the superstructure will follow *sooner* or *later*. Apparently, certain expected changes in the superstructure may trail behind. This produces an epistemological complication which in some cases makes it impossible to refute the Marxist thesis of economic determinism. If, for instance, the expected changes in the superstructure have not occurred (say, the rise of a splendid socialist literature in a socialist society), the Marxist theorist may claim that such changes are merely delayed for one reason or another. Therefore, in principle the Marxist thesis of economic determinism cannot be falsified.

In the same year Marx and Engels applied their concept of economic determinism in their criticism of Ferdinand Lassalle's *Franz von Sickingen* (1859), a play about a rebellious knight in the Peasants' War of early sixteenth-century Germany. In a letter of March 6, 1859, Lassalle asked Marx and Engels to comment on the text of his tragedy. Marx and Engels considered Lassalle, the future founder of the first German workers' party, as a possible political ally. Their criticism is kindly phrased but rather severe (cf. Demetz, 1967: 107–16). First, in their separate letters to Lassalle, they display the criticism of men of literary taste. Marx regards the main character as rather shallow and gives the much-quoted advice that he should have taken Shakespeare rather than Schiller as an example to follow.[3] Engels too makes a positive reference to Shakespearean vividness, and hopes that in the future Lassalle may succeed in expressing his message through the action of his characters rather than in abstract discussions.

There are, however, two other issues at stake which are related to economic determinism. It is Marx who questions whether the choice of the historical Franz von Sickingen (1481–1523) as a tragic hero is correct. Marx rejects Sickingen as a reactionary, who failed "because he as knight and representative of a disappearing class rebelled against the existing order" (Marx and Engels, 1967: I, 180). Engels adds that Lassalle had neglected the non-official plebeian and peasant elements in the Peasants' movement. Lassalle's lengthy answer to Marx and Engels of May 27, 1859, which appears in many anthologies of Marxist literary criticism, is revealing. He clearly sees that Marx and Engels had wanted him to write about more progressive events in German history and not about a reactionary knight who, in accordance with the laws of historical development, was doomed to fail. But Lassalle retorts that the historical Sickingen was less reactionary than Marx believed, and that there is no historical basis for assuming that the lower classes during the Peasants' War were politically more advanced than Sickingen: "In the last instance the idea of a Peasants' War was not less reactionary than the plans of Sickingen" (Marx and Engels, 1967: I, 192). Lassalle accuses Marx and Engels of defending a deterministic view of German history: this concept of history, which destroys the possibility of individual decisions and action, "provides no basis for practical revolutionary action or the represented dramatical action".[4]

From a literary point of view things become even more interesting when, apart from the political assessment of the historical Sickingen, Lassalle claims that *his* Sickingen cannot be measured with the yardstick of the historian but is a product of poetical treatment. Lassalle asks the rhetorical question: "Has not the poet the right to idealize his hero and to attribute a higher consciousness to him? Is Schiller's Wallenstein the historical figure? Is Homer's Achilles the real one?" (Marx and Engels, 1967: I, 200). Lassalle finds support for his view with Engels, who had conceded in his letter to him that he did not wish to deny Lassalle the right to conceive Sickingen and Hutten in such a way *as if* they had intended to emancipate the peasants. Lassalle emphasizes the right of the poet to idealize his material. In short, he stresses the fictional nature of literature. Marx did not comment on Lassalle's answer and only scathingly protested at the length of his letter. Nevertheless, the Aristotelian idea that literature may deviate from a depiction of historical truth, and may idealize reality instead, remained one of the constitutive concepts of Marxist literary theory.

Marx's comment on Lassalle's play can hardly be regarded as a piece of literary criticism. The main thrust of his remarks concerns the interpretation of historical facts. Similarly, his commentary on Eugène Sue's *Les mystères de Paris* (1842–3)—a highly popular serialized novel about the Parisian underworld and upper class, persecuted innocence, rescue and salvation—was motivated not by literary interest but by the opportunity to strike a blow at his philosophical opponents, the Young Hegelians Bruno, Edgar and Egbert Bauer (Marx and Engels, 1968: II, 64–142). The three brothers Bauer had accepted a review of *Les mystères de Paris* in their monthly *Allgemeine Literatur Zeitung*. Author of the review was Szeliga, pen-name of Franz Zychlin von Zychlinski (1816–1900), a Prussian officer. Marx's criticism deals with the confused and far-fetched Hegelian interpretation of *Les mystères de Paris*, rather than with the novel itself. His abhorrence of the unwarranted, idealist interpretation of the French novel becomes all too evident, as well as his inclination towards the application of the criterion of truthfulness, which in Marx's narrow interpretation is nothing more than fidelity to social reality. As Peter Demetz (1967: 102–7) has shown, from his criticism of a far-fetched philosophical interpretation Marx gradually turns to a sociological criticism of Sue's novel, thus making his own preconceived idea of social reality into a yardstick of literary quality. This aspect of Marx's criticism, which was characteristic of nineteenth-century positivism, contradicts the Aristotelian concept of literature as representing an idealized and more universal image of reality, which was defended by Lassalle and apparently accepted by Engels. It seems that from the very beginning Marxist literary theory was built on contradictory strains, which later Marxist philosophers had little trouble in reconciling with the help of the dialectic method.

In addition to the criteria of economic determinism and verisimilitude, Marx upheld his own literary preferences which largely coincide with the literary canon of his days. In this respect his observations on ancient Greek art are interesting. In 1857, two years before *Zur Kritik der Politischen Ökonomie* appeared, Marx drafted an "Introduction" to that book, which was published posthumously by Karl Kautsky in 1903 and even then did not immediately receive much attention in Marxist writings. In fact, it stretches the point that has also been made in the "Foreword" (1859), viz. that changes in the superstructure will follow *sooner* or *later* as a result of changes in the economic basis. In the manuscript of the "Introduction" (1857), Marx departs from the deterministic concept that developments in the superstructure, notably in the realm of aesthetics, must necessarily follow from changes in the economic basis. He emphasizes that there may be an unbalanced development of artistic and material production.[5] Intrigued by the fact that in antiquity Greek art had reached "unsurpassable" heights when social and economic development were still low, Marx concluded that periods of great artistic momentum do not necessarily correspond to a high development of the material basis.[6] His main problem is to understand how the art of an archaic society can radiate "eternal charm" *(ewiger Reiz)* and give pleasure to people in the industrial age. His explanation is psychological, rather than materialist, as he relates the admiration for Greek art to a nostalgia towards the historical youth of the human race.[7]

Although this explanation cannot be considered materialistic and the draft "Introduction" was published only posthumously, the theory of the unbalanced development of artistic and material production has become a lasting tenet of Marxist literary theory, serving now as an escape clause through which the assimilation of the great classical writers was to be justified, now as an embarrassing argument in the hands of dissident writers in socialist states who protested against the excessive claims of Socialist Realism. For if Marx's theory of unbalanced development is applied to modern times, it follows that a socialist society does not necessarily give rise to a superior literature.

Friedrich Engels has contributed two important documents to the corpus of Marxist writings on literature. On November 26, 1885, he wrote a letter to Minna Kautsky on the occasion of the publication of her novel *Die· Alten und die Neuen* (1884). In this letter two problems of a more general nature are raised. The first is that of the relation between literature and political commitment or "tendentiousness" *(Tendenz)*. Engels disapproves of the obvious political bias in Minna Kautsky's novel. Although he is in no way opposed to "tendentious literature" *(Tendenzpoesie)* as such and counts Aeschylus, Aristophanes, Dante, Cervantes and Schiller among the best *Tendenz* writers, he also believes "that the *Tendenz* has to be evident from the situation and action, and should not be explicitly explained; the poet is not obliged to present the reader with the historical, future solution of the social conflicts described by him."[8] Engels' critical attitude towards obvious political bias in literature is part of his bequest to the tradition of Marxist criticism. It appears that his position can be held against the very essence of Socialist Realism which, according to the Soviet definition of 1934, is expected to represent "a truthful, historically concrete representation of reality in its revolutionary development" (quoted by Swayze, 1962: 113). It would seem to be impossible to present reality in its revolutionary development without indicating "the future solution of social conflicts" described by the writer. In fact, a Chinese critic who during the Hundred Flowers period attempted to escape from the political restrictions of Socialist Realism, tried to support his argument by referring to Engels'· position on *Tendenz* literature (Fokkema, 1965: 130–2). One may conclude that Engels' reserves *vis-à-vis* literature with an obvious political bias is the source of another contradiction in Marxist literary theory.

The other problem raised in the letter to Minna Kautsky is that of the typical. From German idealism Engels borrows the view that every character in a novel should be "a type, but at the same time also a particular individual, a 'this one', as old Hegel expresses himself."[9] But on the basis of which criteria should the typical properties of a character be selected? In his letter of early April 1888 to Margaret Harkness, who had sent him her novel *City Girl* (1887), Engels holds that the selection of typical characteristics should be compatible with the requirement of realism. In this letter, written in English, Engels coined the famous phrase: "Realism, to my mind, implies, besides truth of detail, the truthful reproduction of typical characters under typical circumstances" (Marx and Engels, 1953: 122). In his comment on *Franz von Sickingen* the word "realistic" had appeared as the opposite of abstract and ideal, and as a characteristic of Shakespeare's drama (Marx and Engels, 1967: I, 186). Almost thirty years later Engels uses the term in a similar way. Realism means fidelity to historical truth. Miss Harkness should have devoted more attention to the rebellious protest of the proletariat against exploitation, because that protest had manifested itself as an historical fact. Again Engels rejects the idea of a *Tendenzroman,* and rather points to Balzac who in *La comédie humaine* has given "a most wonderfully realistic history of French 'Society' " (Marx and Engels, 1953: 122). It appears that Engels relates his concept of type to that kind of literature which later Marxist criticism was to call "critical realism". Unlike Demetz, we believe that Engels saw the typical as "a model representation of experience" rather than "an ideal image" (Demetz, 1967: 137–8). The assumption that Engels should be considered a precursor of Socialist Realist criticism is indeed hard to substantiate.

The kind of realism Engels advocates may even lead to results that contradict the political opinions of the writer. Balzac is a case in point, as he, despite his sympathy for the nobility, wrote with unconcealed admiration about the republican heroes of Cloître Saint-Merry, the men who, according to Engels, in the 1830s represented the masses of the people and in fact were his own political opponents. Engels calls this "one of the greatest triumphs of Realism". His theory of a possible discrepancy between the political views of the writer and the meaning of his work has been a significant contribution to Marxist literary theory. In 1858 N. A. Dobroljubov had defended a similar view in relation to Gogol, who "unconsciously, simply with artistic intuition" came very close to the point of view of the people (Dobroljubov, 1961: 213). However, Engels does not seem to have known Dobroljubov's critical writings although he had heard about his work and respected his political views (Marx and Engels, 1967: I, 598–9). But, when phrasing his opinion of Balzac, Engels may have been familiar with a similar judgement of Zola on Balzac, published in 1881 and 1882 (Wellek 1955–65: IV, 18).

In Marxist criticism usually both Engels and Dobroljubov are quoted as the authors of the theory of the possible discrepancy between the writer's world view and the meaning of his work. The theory has heavy implications. Like the thesis of the unbalanced development of material and artistic production it has helped to assimilate the classical writers into the corpus of permitted reading matter. Moreover this theory of Engels and Dobroljubov is incompatible with a quick judgement of literary works on the basis of the author's biography or political intentions. It turns the attention of the critic to the literary text, and as such disavows what the New Critics have called "the intentional fallacy".

Like Marx, Lenin admired great art and was plagued by the problem how to reconcile it with revolution. Between 1908 and 1911 Lenin wrote five articles on the occasion of the eightieth birthday and the death of Lev Tolstoy. Although repeatedly admitting that Tolstoy's works "rank among the greatest in world literature" (Lenin, 1967: 29, 48, 53), he at the same time equates Tolstoy's point of view with "that of the patriarchical, naïve peasant". He detests in Tolstoy "the landlord obsessed with Christ", "the jaded, hysterical sniveller", "the crackpot preaching of submission", and the defender of clericalism (Lenin, 1967: 55, 29). Lenin is evidently worried by the political effect of Tolstoy's writings. But from the literary point of view he attributes lasting value to Tolstoy's work. Quite in accordance with Marx's thesis of the unbalanced development of material and artistic production, and Engels' theory of the discrepancy between world view and work (but without referring to them), Lenin posits that "Tolstoy [. . .] produced artistic works which will always be appreciated and read by the masses, once they have created human conditions of life for themselves after overthrowing the yoke of the landlords and capitalists" (Lenin, 1967: 48). It is clear that Lenin is opposed to cutting all ties with great literature, which induces him to justify his admiration for great art as far as possible in political terms.

Lenin's approach to justifying his appreciation of great art is that of historical relativism or historicism, which in free imitation of Friedrich Meinecke (1936) we have defined earlier as the attempt to interpret and evaluate the historical phenomena of a certain age in relation to the other phenomena (including the norms) of that age. As historical materialism stipulates that the superstructure evolves as a result of specific historical changes in the economic basis, the development of the superstructure cannot be disconnected from its material basis. In principle, changes in the superstructure are supposed not to run ahead of changes in the economic basis, although, according to later Marxist thinking, certain developments in the superstructure may be considered to be conducive to further changes in the economic basis. This has been exemplified by the institution of ideological campaigns or "cultural revolutions" in socialist states. However, in the last resort the development of "social consciousness" or culture is governed by material production (Wetter, 1966: 240). Therefore, the possibilities of literature of a certain period are in principle restricted by its historical, material conditions. It is in this sense that historical materialism allows of a certain degree of historicism.

The historicist argument of historical materialism is that the merit of a writer should be measured against the background of the socio-economic conditions of his time, rather than with the yardstick of the modern revolutionary movement. Or in Lenin's own words, "the contradictions in Tolstoy's views must be appraised not from the standpoint of the present-day working-class movement and present-day socialism (such an appraisal is, of course, needed, but it is not enough), but from the standpoint of protest against advancing capitalism, against the ruining of the masses, who are being dispossessed of their land—a protest which had to arise from the patriarchal Russian countryside" (Lenin, 1967: 30). It appears from this quotation that Tolstoy should be judged both from the point of view of his contemporaries and from the standpoint of "present-day socialism". Thus two different yardsticks can be used: the historicist standard in order to assess Tolstoy's historical role and to save him as an important writer, and the political standard in order to judge his work in relation to the political expediency of the day. Any contradiction between the two norms obviously requires a dialectical solution, with the possibility that under certain political conditions the first norm is emphasized rather than the second, or the other way round. In a similar way many years later Mao Tse-tung (1942) comes to differentiate between "the artistic criterion" and "the political criterion". Since Lenin rejects any abstract " 'eternal' principles of morality" (Lenin, 1967: 59), Mao denies the existence of "an abstract and absolutely unchangeable artistic criterion". The artistic judgement of literary works of past ages by the proletariat depends largely on the question whether or not these works "had any progressive significance historically" (Mao Tse-tung, 1942: 89). Here, too, it is the historicist argument that must save great literature.

Lenin's judgement of great literature is based on both an historicist and a straight political norm. The historical materialist can never indulge completely in historical relativism because political expediency may require a different attitude. A more general reason why the historical materialist cannot identify himself completely with the historicist approach is that (according to Marxist theory) historical materialism, with neglect of its nineteenth-century origin, must be considered as objective truth which itself can not be subjected to a relativist judgement.

However, apart from the historicist and political criteria, one must infer that Lenin, like Mao Tse-tung,[10] is aware of a straight artistic criterion, on the basis of which certain works of art must be appreciated from an aesthetic point of view, although they may have diverted the recipients from revolutionary action. Artistic intuition claims its toll, when Lenin in a conversation with Maksim

Gorky calls Beethoven's *Appassionata* sonata "amazing, superhuman music", adding that it affects his nerves and makes him want to say sweet nothings and to pat the heads of people, whereas "today we mustn't pat anyone on the head or we'll get our hand bitten off" (Lenin, 1967: 247). It is possibly a similar experience that prevented Marx from reasoning away the contradictions in the theory of the unbalanced development of material and artistic production.

Perhaps more important than Lenin's pronouncements on Tolstoy and Beethoven is his article "Party Organization and Party Literature" (Lenin, 1967: 22–8). Written in late 1905, it deals with a new situation resulting from the disappearance of the distinction between the legal and the illegal press in Russia (Simmons, 1961). Previously the illegal Party press could easily be controlled and kept inviolate. But when writers of all kinds had legal access to the press, Lenin was worried about possible bourgeois influence on the Party press by writers who, holding leftist or even outspoken Christian ideas, were not members of the Social Democratic Party or did not want to submit to Party discipline. This was the occasion for Lenin's statement.

Later interpreters have stretched the original purport of the article at least in two ways. First, they have overlooked the fact that Lenin only speaks of Party control over Party publications, and not of any Party or state control over non-Party publications. Although Lenin's article has been used to justify state censorship in communist nations over non-Party publications, it provides no basis for such a justification. Secondly, the difference between political and literary publications has been blurred. In fact, Lenin meant writing in general rather than creative literature. E. J. Simmons (1961: 82) has correctly observed that the Russian equivalent of belles-lettres, i.e. *chudožestvennaja literatura,* does not occur even once in Lenin's "Party Organization and Party Literature". To mention only one example of an interpretation which sustains the view that Lenin aimed his remarks at creative literature and cleared the way for censorship also outside the realm of Party publications, one may refer to the report of A. A. Surkov to the Second Congress of Soviet Writers, published in *Literaturnaja gazeta* of December 16, 1954. Surkov says of Lenin's "Party Organization and Party Literature": "These words of Lenin, which have now been confirmed in practice by the entire development of our literature, assume—given the common *direction* through the application of the method of Socialist

Realism—the possibility of the existence of various *currents,* of creative competition between them, and of broad discussions of the advantages of this or that current." Although Lenin of course did not say anything about an obligatory or standard literary method, not to mention Socialist Realism, Surkov implies that there will only be freedom to discuss literary issues in so far as such discussion takes place within the framework of the official method of Socialist Realism. Surkov's interpretation is in flagrant contradiction to Krupskaja's view that "Party Organization and Party Literature" is not concerned with literary works (Eimermacher, 1972: 44).

It is far-fetched indeed to suggest that Lenin laid the basis for state censorship in an article which deplores the situation in "literary work, which has been defiled by the Asiatic censorship" (Lenin, 1967: 24). One is bound to conclude that the one-sided propaganda for Socialist Realism in the socialist states and the institution of censorship of creative literature deviating from that official method cannot be justified by references to Marx or Engels, or Lenin's pre-revolutionary pronouncements on literature. In fact, censorship is not the logical consequence of historical materialism, because changes in the economic basis must sooner or later, but inevitably produce changes in the superstructure. Theoretically, censorship can be applied only temporarily and for tactical reasons. In practice, it has appeared that "temporarily" may be a fairly long stretch of time.

Theory and Practice after the October Revolution

The introduction of a socialist economic structure after the October Revolution created a new situation, in the field of Marxist literary criticism as elsewhere. From a Marxist point of view, the cultural situation in the Soviet Union and other socialist states is completely different from that in Western Europe or North America. As convinced Marxists, the Soviet leaders were expected to believe that the new economic basis would sooner or later produce a new culture. But they could not know *when* that new culture would come into being and to what extent its creation could be furthered by political or other means. Another question was what attitude should be taken towards the old or bourgeois culture. These questions divided the Soviet leaders for about a dozen years, until in the early 1930s the problem was temporarily shelved, although not solved. When in 1934 Socialist Realism was announced as the highest form of literature, older literature was in principle relegated to a secondary position. The recurrent references to Socialist Realist works *avant la lettre,* such as Gorky's *Mat'* (Mother, 1906), Serafimovič's *Železnij potok* (The Iron Flood, 1924), Gladkov's *Cement* (Cement, 1925), and Fadeev's *Razgrom* (The Nineteen, 1927) served to substantiate the view that the construction of a new culture was well under way. Moreover, the concept of Socialist Realism served as a guiding principle in official literary criticism and was supposed to further the literary expression of the new society.

Although the notion of Socialist Realism was a compromise, it was not the natural and self-evident outcome of a long discussion on theoretical matters among the Soviet leaders. In the first years after the October Revolution, there was a definite trend to abstain from Party interference in the sphere of culture, or at least, to restrict Party decisions in matters of culture to a minimum, and to wait patiently for the revolutionary literature of high quality that the writers were expected to produce. In the meantime one continued to read older literature of which millions of volumes were printed in cheap editions. This line was represented by A. K. Voronskij, from 1921 until 1927 editor of the journal *Krasnaja nov'* (Red virgin soil), and at a higher level and more hesitantly by A. V. Lunačarskij, head of the People's Commissariat for Education during the 1920s, by Leon Trotsky, one of the main theoreticians of the CPSU in the early 1920s but expelled from the Party in 1927, and to some extent also by Lenin, who however died in 1924 (cf. Maguire, 1968).

In the first issue of *Krasnaja nov'* Lunačarskij expressed his appreciation of Marx's position, as recollected by Franz Mehring, that those people who did not understand the significance of classical art for the proletariat were "incurable idiots" (Eimermacher, 1972: 96). Lenin also stressed the principle of cultural continuity. In a draft resolution of 1920 he implied that proletarian culture is "not the invention of a new [. . .] culture, but the development of the best examples, traditions and results of the existing cultures from the position of the Marxist world view . . ." (ibid.: 81). Perhaps Lenin's own literary preferences may have played a role here. He had no appreciation whatever of Majakovskij's Futurist verse, although it was well received by audiences of workers when recited by the author. But the other Soviet leaders, including Trotsky, also felt in general that the writers who wished to ignore the accomplishments of bourgeois culture, such as *Proletkul't* (a group of proletarian writers advocating the construction of a proletarian culture) and the communist Futurists supporting the review *Lef,* had little to offer that could compete in quality with older or non-Marxist literature. Whereas Homer, Shakespeare, Balzac and the great Russian Realists remained among the permitted reading matter (ibid.: 261–2), Voronskij complained that censorship of modern literature was too strict. He could accept only one criterion for censorship, viz. if a literary work were counter-revolutionary. The censors, however, should not interfere with the artistic evaluation of a work and, in principle, the writer should be free to describe the dark sides of Soviet life. The censors should not consider "the representation of life in the manner of Gogol, Saltykov-Ščedrin or Chekhov as an attack on the revolution" (ibid.: 20). This attitude, shared by Viktor Šklovskij and backed by Lunačarskij (ibid.: 300, 262), opened the way for such writers as Zamjatin, Pil'njak and Bulgakov to continue publishing during the 1920s. Lunačarskij and Voronskij in general emphasized the cognitive value of literary works, which were believed to convey information one would never find in statistical surveys. They urged the writers to write the truth, and nothing but the truth, even if it would contradict the expectations of the Party (ibid.: 265–7).

The writers centred around the banner of *Proletkul't* were of a different opinion. Their aim was to create a proletarian culture without the help of other classes. Shakespeare and Molière had fulfilled their historical mission, and were only of historical interest to the proletariat (ibid.: 133). But the proletarian writers seldom plainly rejected the cultural heritage. Kirillov's appeal to burn Raphael in the name of the future and to destroy the museums is an exception. Conveyed in a poem (of 1917), it is a late echo of similar Futurist views.[11] In a conference resolution of 1925 the proletarian writers claimed that "the destruction of all kinds and shades of bourgeois and petty-bourgeois literature had become necessary," but this conclusion was somewhat mitigated by simultaneous lip-service to the Leninist programme of critical assimilation of classical and bourgeois art and culture (ibid.: 278–9).

Proletkul't attempted to reach its goal by means of budgetary allocations, censorship and defamation campaigns. They believed that far too much support was given to writers such as Boris Pil'njak, who openly said that he was not a communist and did not intend to write as a communist, or Il'ja Erenburg, who by this time had completed his satirical novel *Julio Jurenito* (1922) (ibid.: 199–200).

In 1924 a protagonist of *Lef*, N. Čužak, explained most clearly what he hated in the still prevailing cultural policy which allowed such writers as Pil'njak and Erenburg to publish and Voronskij to articulate his views on literature. The Party should check all that kills the will to act and to gain a decisive victory. Everything that contradicted good taste or the enjoyment of life should be eliminated. Any writer should know exactly what he wanted to say and what effect he wished to reach with his writing. No talk about inspiration or the mystique of "artistic creation" should be allowed. But the theory that literature has mainly cognitive value should also be rejected. In Čužak's view, the basic task of class literature was to train—first of all among the young people—the will to participate in the construction and victory of socialism (ibid.: 168–72).

There were various reasons why the Party was hesitant to side with *Proletkul't* in its quarrel with the other writers. In the early 1920s *Proletkul't* was not supported by any of the major writers. Further, it seemed politically unwise to regiment cultural life too strictly at a moment when the political and economic situation was far from stable. Finally, the problems of the young Soviet state were so vast that literary issues were mainly left to the second echelon, which implied that no clear directives were issued by the Party centre. Trotsky tried to justify the attitude of the Party in cultural matters as follows:

Art must make its own way and by its own means. The Marxist methods are not the same as the artistic. The Party leads the proletariat but not the historic processes of history. There are domains in which the Party leads, directly and imperatively. There are domains in which it only cooperates. There are, finally, domains in which it only orientates itself. The domain of art is not one in which the Party is called upon to command. It can and must protect and help it, but it can only lead it indirectly (Trotsky, 1924: 218).

One of the most important reasons why the Party did not unconditionally side with *Proletkul't* was the claim of *Proletkul't* that it could direct the whole field of literature without interference from the Party centre. Although nearly all members of *Proletkul't* organizations, such as the Russian Association of Proletarian Writers (RAPP), were Party members, the Party still feared that the *Proletkul't* organizations would assume a position independent from the Party. However, the Soviet leaders gradually became impatient with the situation in literature when they saw that the non-Marxist writers did not automatically turn

into supporters of the regime. As a result, the position of *Proletkul't*
became stronger. This did not, however, lead to a complete victory for *Proletkul't*.
When in 1930 RAPP had absorbed almost all other writers'
organizations, it could be held responsible for the poor shape of
Soviet literature. RAPP had reached its monopoly position by
vehement criticism, defamation and intimidation of competitive
organizations and individual writers, of which the attacks on Boris
Pil'njak and Evgenij Zamjatin from 1929 onwards were the most
notorious. As a result of the action by RAPP against dissident
writers, the major authors were silenced. More or less supported
by Maksim Gorky, they lodged complaints with Stalin, who
urged the Central Committee to dissolve the organizations of
proletarian writers and unite "all writers who support the
programme of the Soviet power and try to participate in the
construction of socialism" in one Writers' Union (Eimermacher,
1972: 434).

At the First Soviet Writers' Congress (1934), Socialist Realism
was accepted as the guiding principle in literary creation. In the
Statutes of the Writers' Union it was described as follows:

Socialist Realism, the basic method of Soviet literature and literary
criticism, demands of the artist truthful, historically concrete
representation of reality in its revolutionary development. At the same
time, truthfulness and historical concreteness of artistic representation of
reality must be combined with the task of ideological remoulding and
education of the working people in the spirit of socialism (Swayze, 1962:
113).

The formula was evidently a compromise, and contained a
number of contradictions. It was intended to loosen some of the
severe political restrictions that *Proletkul't* had wanted to introduce
in literature, but the official definition of Socialist Realism
maintained the demand that propaganda be made for the political
ideals of socialism. Describing reality in its revolutionary
development in fact meant to portray that which could be
considered as reality as well as that which was not yet reality. From
the very beginning the concept had to be extensively explained,
and the explanations were contradictory. In an address to the
Writers' Congress, Maksim Gorky—whom A. A. Ždanov, in
view of Gorky's distrust of *Proletkul't*, praised with unmistakable
irony as "the great proletarian author"—elaborated on the power
of the word, on literature as "exorcism" and "incantation"
(Problems of Soviet Literature 1935: 15, 29). Nikolaj Bucharin,
however, believed that Socialist Realism "is the enemy of

everything supernatural, mystic and all other-worldly idealism" (ibid.: 251). Bucharin emphasized the realist component of Socialist Realism, whereas Gorky and Ždanov stressed the romanticist component. The one saw the writer primarily as an observer, the others rather like a preacher or propagandist. Although in later years in different situations different answers have been given as to the required emphasis on the one or the other function of the writer, the claim that the Soviet writer must participate through his work in propaganda for the socialist way of life has never been dropped.

The First Soviet Writers' Congress took a less rigid view of classical and bourgeois literature than *Proletkul't*. With a reference to Stalin's dictum that the writers should be engineers of human souls, Ždanov, speaking in his capacity of secretary of the Central Committee of the CPSU, explained that "the critical assimilation of the literary heritage of all epochs" represented a task which should be fulfilled without fail (ibid.: 22). Gorky expressed a positive opinion of "Griboedov, Gogol, and so on, down to Chekhov and Bunin". He called the critic Vissarion Belinskij one of the most talented and honest Russian men. But he rejected Dostoevskys's *Memoirs from Underground,* as well as Proust and Céline. Karl Radek criticized Joyce, who had portrayed "a heap of dung, crawling with worms", and counselled the writers to learn from Tolstoy and Balzac rather than from Joyce (ibid.: 153, 182). In this way the writers were urged to write about the splendid future of communism in terms borrowed from the nineteenth century! Many years later Abram Terc (pseudonym of A. D. Sinjavskij) rightly concluded that the concept of Socialist Realism suffered from eclecticism (Terc, 1957).

Why are the modern Soviet writers not allowed to experiment with new and unfamiliar forms? In principle the Party must at all times have access to the whole field of literature. Complex forms and their corresponding meanings, however progressive they may be, will detract from the accessibility of the literary text and therefore incommode the required inspection by the Party. The communist writer is allowed and even encouraged to dream, but his dreams should remain within the confines of Marxist logic and comprehensible to the Party censors. The history of *Proletkul't* has shown clearly that ultimately no authority other than the Party is entitled to decide whether a literary work is harmful or advantageous to the cause of the revolution. Different from Trotsky's rather tolerant position in literary matters, the Stalinist

Party believed that it could not delegate its powers, or literary life in general, to a few intelligent critics or writers. The Party claimed that at all times it should be able to discuss literary works in ideological terms, and it therefore continued to talk about literature in the nineteenth-century fashion as consisting of content and form that are separable.[12]

From the early 1930s the Soviet writers were expected to accept the final guidance of the Party. They had to respect the principle of "party spirit" *(partijnost')*, i.e. they must adopt the standpoint of the Party and remain loyal to its continually changing policies. Party spirit also came to serve as a criterion in the judging of contemporary literary works. Similarly, the term "popular nature" *(narodnost')*, which in 1836 Belinskij (1953–9: I, 283) used to characterize Gogol's stories, described the progressive, "folk" character of older literature and also served as a standard in Soviet literary criticism. Marxist critics consider the communist Party spirit as the highest level of "popular nature" (Ovsjannikov, 1973: 395).

Attributing the principle of party spirit in literary matters to Lenin (though without much foundation), A. A. Ždanov carried it to its extreme consequences. His influence on early post-war literary life was as extravagant as it was detrimental. In 1946 he urged the Central Committee to censure Michail Zoščenko and Anna Achmatova, which initiated an extremely strict regime in literary life.[13] Ždanov died as early as 1948, but it was only after the death of Stalin in 1953 that a cultural thaw set in.

One of the indications of that thaw was a change in the definition of Socialist Realism. The Second Congress of the Soviet Writers' Union (December 1954) acknowledged that the demand to combine the truthful expression of reality in its revolutionary development with the task of ideological education of the working people should be considered redundant, as any truthful expression of reality should be expected to further ideological education. The definition of Socialist Realism was simplified as follows: "Socialist Realism demands of the writer truthful representation of reality in its revolutionary development" (Swayze, 1962: 114). In spite of the emendation, the main contradiction in the requirement to describe present and future at the same time was maintained.

The editorial "On the Problem of the Typical in Literature and Art" in *Kommunist* of December 1955 also contributed to the general relaxation in the realm of culture. We have mentioned in chapter 2 that it raised the problem of "the typical" *(tipičnost')*. The editorial criticized the view that the problem of the typical is always a political problem. Merely rephrasing ideas that had been expressed before,[14] G. M. Malenkov had pronounced in this way as late as 1952 (Erlich, 1955: 414; Swayze, 1962: 81, 133).

The editorial is divided into three sections, dealing respectively with the typical, party spirit and exaggeration as a means of typification. It states that the meaning of typification lies in the use of "clear, concrete and affective, aesthetically impressive images which not only influence man's reason, but also his emotions". Thus it is wrong to restrict the concept of the typical by making it correspond with the essence of certain social forces. Artistic cognition of life has certain elements in common with science, but is still different from it. It is determined by its own laws, of which typification *(tipizacija)* is a basic one. Different from science, "art reflects the laws that govern reality in images, i.e. in concrete and affective forms which embody the general in the particular."

The editorial admits that typification is always connected with the world outlook of the artist, but it regards as wrong the endeavour to find expression of a party standpoint in everything typical regardless of the time and conditions in which the artist worked. Here the danger of vulgarization threatens. For it is possible that the "objective" significance of a work contradicts the political views of the author. In this context the well-known example of Balzac is mentioned. Not all artists possess the necessary party spirit, but their work may still be worth reading. Nevertheless, the communist party spirit is "the highest expression of class character in world outlook". Party spirit is "the basic ideological principle of the artistic method of socialist literature".

Finally, the editorial censures the mistake of many dogmatists who understand the method of "exaggeration" in a superficial way. They forget that the uncommon in realistic art can become typical only if it carries "germs of the new with the potential of mass character" in them, or if it is connected with regular, not accidental phenomena of life. This sort of error in the application of the device of exaggeration has been the origin of needless and unwarranted embellishment *(lakirovka)*.

As usual in Marxist writings, the editorial deals with the genetic aspects of literature and with its effect on the reader. It hardly discusses any characteristics of the literary text. It recognizes the literary use of aesthetic images which may influence the emotions, but significantly does not explain to what extent these aesthetic images elude political judgement. The principal message of the editorial seemed to be that in the past political censorship had been too severe. On the other hand, the basic Marxist tenet that in the last resort everything is political, and in principle should be subjected to a political judgement, was not revoked. On balance, the cultural thaw introduced a *less explicit* Marxism than had been usual in the Ždanovist period. This enlarged the area in which discussion was possible. The issues of the 1920s were rediscovered, not only Russian Formalism but also the views of Lunačarskij and Voronskij, some of whose statements and articles were reprinted.

The Marxist critics who avoided the structuralist approach focussed their attention on the origin and function of literature. In explaining the genesis of literature, the editorial in *Kommunist* of December 1955 had referred to Belinskij's formula, "art is thinking in images". In doing so, it had caused a concept with Romanticist and idealist connotations to be introduced into the genetic explanation of literature, which was otherwise supposed to be materialist.[15] This can be exemplified by the following historical expatiation, which aims to demonstrate that Belinskij's theory of art was characterized by the concepts of unconscious creation and an almost mystical contemplation of truth. It is all the more necessary to examine briefly the heritage of nineteenth-century Russian literary criticism (including also N. A. Dobroljubov and N. G. Černyševskij), since, together with Marxist thought, it has provided basic concepts to Soviet literary theory.

First one should recall Belinskij's view of the creative act mentioned in an essay on Gogol of 1836: "The power of creation is a great gift of nature. The creative act in the soul of the creator is a great secret. The moment of the creation is a moment of sacrosanctity. The creative act is purposeless with a purpose, unconscious in consciousness, free in dependence." According to Belinskij, the nature of the creative act implies that the artist should be left completely free in the choice of his subject-matter. He concludes his essay by saying: "Can the subject-matter add something to the value of the [literary] work? [. . .]. Let Mr. Gogol describe those things which his inspiration orders him to describe, and may he shrink from describing the stuff that is urged upon him by his own will or by the critics" (Belinskij, 1953–9: I, 285, 307). Secondly, in the same essay he explains his concept of the typical: "One of the most significant characteristics of creative originality," Belinskij says, "consists in the typification *(tipizm)* [. . .]. In the works of a true talent every person is a type and every type is, for the reader, a known unknown." In one instance he calls a famous literary character in one of Gogol's stories "a symbol, a mystical myth, [. . .] a caftan made so amazingly well that it fits the shoulders of a thousand people" (I, 295–7). The type as explained by Belinskij is the immediate result of the impulse of inspiration. He described art as "the immediate contemplation of truth, or thinking in images" (IV, 585), which is reminiscent of Hegel and A. W. Schlegel.[16]

Belinskij's thinking has also been popular in early Russian Marxism. Discussing the reception of art, the outstanding Russian Marxist critic G. V. Plechanov took a position which harks back to the Romanticist tradition. He has praise for Kant's postulate of the disinterested enjoyment of beauty, and expects the writer to speak the language of images, rather than the language of logic. He adds that "the useful will be judged by reason; the beautiful by contemplation. The domain of the first is calculation; that of the second the instinct." And with a clear reminder of Hegel and Belinskij he adds that "the most important feature of aesthetic enjoyment is its immediacy."[17] As a corollary of this position and in full agreement with Belinskij, Plechanov distrusted any attempt to make writers disseminate political propaganda (Demetz, 1967: 189–98).

As one of the leaders of the Mensheviks, Plechanov was arrested immediately after the October Revolution and died in prison in 1918. His early critical writings, however, remained a topic of literary polemics in the 1920s. Lunačarskij and Voronskij emphasized that the relation between a literary work and the economic basis was of an indirect and circumstantial nature. Art is in no way a simple reflection of reality, Lunačarskij wrote in 1924. The writer is not only an observer, but also a preacher, and can give immediate expression to his thought and feelings. In his defence of literature, Lunačarskij attributes to Krupskaja the idea that the masses also prefer "to think in images" (Eimermacher, 1972: 262, 265). In the same year I. Vardin, a spokesman of *Proletkul't,* branded Voronskij as a non–Bolshevik critic who still upheld traditional ideas from Belinskij's days (ibid.: 201). As late as 1932, Plechanov's views on logical thinking and thinking in images were criticized in *Pravda* as leading to "the reactionary theory of immediate impressions" (ibid.: 429).

One sees that the acceptance or rejection of Belinskij's concept of the creative act has a heavy bearing on various issues in Marxist literary policy. Acceptance means in fact that the writer must remain free to select his subject-matter, and that one cannot expect him to propagate prescribed ideas in his work. Any censorship would be out of bounds. When they restored Belinskij as a permitted source of literary theory, the Soviet leaders avoided making these consequences explicit. When necessary, they have resorted to other strains in the nineteenth-century Russian critical tradition to support the claim that the writer should deal with prescribed subject-matter and be a propagandist of socialist ideals. Both N. A. Dobroljubov and N. G. Černyševskij could provide the required support. Whereas Dobroljubov to some extent still embraced the Romanticist concept of the creative act, both admit that form and content can be discussed separately and accept their own preconceived knowledge of social reality as a standard whereby to judge a literary work. Advocating a strictly materialist theory of reflection, Černyševskij in a book review of 1856 asked the rhetorical question whether one would admire Raphael so much if he had painted only arabesques, birds and flowers (Černyševskij, 1950: 230). A few years later Dobroljubov observed: "We will never agree that a poet wearing out his talent in an exemplary depiction of leaves and brooklets can have the same significance as the one who with equal force of his talent is able to represent, for instance, the phenomena of social life" (Dobroljubov, 1961: 262). Recently the Soviet critic Moissej Kagan expressed himself in a similar way and declared that the value of a literary work depends immediately upon the character of the theme.[18]

Nevertheless, it is quite understandable that the Chinese Marxists, unrestricted by the need to preserve the Russian critical heritage, discarded the whole gamut of critical writings by the Russian revolutionary democrats, including even Černyševskij. In 1966 and 1967 Belinskij, Dobroljubov and Černyševskij, as well as Chou Yang, the Chinese theorist and politician who had popularized their views in China, were criticized as representatives of bourgeois idealism.[19]

But even today, the defenders of Socialist Realism in the Soviet Union rely in part on a heritage of Romanticist concepts of inspiration, immediate impression and unconscious creation. This is another instance which shows the eclectic nature of Soviet literary theory, which accounts for its many contradictions. According to recent Soviet literary theory, the creative act is both conscious and unconscious. The literary work is the result of both subjective creativity and the reflection of objective reality

(Guljaev, 1970: 128; cf. Fizer, 1963). The writer is requested to describe reality realistically and to make socialist propaganda at the same time; he is both observer and preacher. He is to respect the political principle of party spirit and the aesthetic principle of the typical. His work is socially determined as well as the result of individual efforts (Ovsjannikov, 1973: 247). The Marxist theoreticians assume a dialectical relationship between the opposite terms in these various contradictions. One textbook carries the argument so far as to postulate "a dialectical relationship between party spirit and artistic talent", since the truthful expression of reality is assumedly connected with the interpretation of the world "in the light of the most advanced, Marxist-Leninist world view" (Guljaev, 1970: 128). These conclusions are acceptable only if one accepts the underlying assumption that Marxism-Leninism is identical with truth or the only and guaranteed way to truth.

But how could the original Marxist economic determinism gradually turn into a vague and unfalsifiable eclecticism? Whenever in some practical situation any law of dialectical or historical materialism did not apply or convince, the Marxist theoreticians in the Soviet Union have tried to adjust themselves, not by rejecting the Marxist law in question, but by condoning exceptions to that law. In this way, the theory of economic determinism was invalidated, although this invalidation was never officially acknowledged as such.[20]

Practice and, as Morton Blóomfield (1972a) has suggested, political expediency became the judge of truth. Indeed, whenever the changing political moment determined the truth value of a Marxist position, the easy road of eclecticism could no longer be avoided.

The Chinese Reception of Marxist Literary Theories

Marxist thought was introduced into China only in the twentieth century, and no serious attention was paid to Marxist literary theory before the May Fourth Movement (1919). Aimed at the political and cultural emancipation of China from the fetters of Confucianist traditionalism, the May Fourth Movement opened the way to the study of European thought, including Marxism. The 1920s were characterized by a rapid proliferation of literary movements and journals covering the full range from *l'art pour l'art* to plain Marxist utilitarianism. Many Chinese writers were convinced that literature should serve the revolution, but apart from uncertainty about the character of the revolution there was a protracted debate over the degree to which literature could maintain its literary characteristics in that subservient position. In 1928 Lu Hsün, the most influential critic of his day, expressed the dilemma of the leftist writers as follows: "Though all literature is propaganda, not all propaganda is literature; just as all flowers have colour (I count white as a colour), but not all coloured things are flowers. In addition to catchwords, slogans, notices, telegrams and textbooks, the revolution needs literature—just because it is literature."[21] Although a true revolutionary, Lu Hsün remained first and foremost a writer, who always defended the particular nature of literary expression and the freedom it needed. When Mao Tse-tung expressed himself on literary theory in 1942, he was influenced rather by a more rigid current of leftist thought, as represented by the Marxists Ch'ü Ch'iu-pai and Chou Yang.

One striking difference between Chinese and Soviet Marxist criticism is that the former is much less entangled in efforts to assimilate European literature from the Renaissance down to the pre-revolutionary Russian classics. It appears that in general Maoist literary criticism can be applied more consistently and more rigorously, as the European heritage means evidently less to the Chinese than to the Russians. This enables the Chinese leaders to apply certain Marxist principles, or what they consider to be Marxist principles, in an uncompromising way. In particular they have tended in recent years to strip Marxist literary theory of its eclecticism, hardly aware of their being eclectic themselves in doing so. Since the Cultural Revolution, the Maoist critics have rejected Marx's criterion of verisimilitude,[22] as well as his personal admiration for the European classics, whereas they have given full emphasis to his criterion of economic determinism and the "Leninist" principle of party spirit.

During the Great Leap Forward, the Chinese made a similar attempt to avoid eclecticism in their critique of the ambivalent concept of Socialist Realism. In China, Socialist Realism had been cherished as an ideal between 1953 and 1958.[23] But when certain Chinese writers during the Hundred Flowers period had attempted to deprive the concept of its ideological content by replacing it with the phrase "realism of the socialist epoch", [24] the official Chinese theoreticians coined the concept of "the combination of revolutionary realism and revolutionary romanticism" to supersede the ambiguous Soviet formula.[25] The new concept emphasized the revolutionary goals of literature and detracted from the claim of truthful representation. The Chinese theorists plainly sided with Gorky's romanticist attitude as well as the Ždanovist emphasis on the political function of literature. This was clearly pronounced in one of the articles explaining the new Chinese formula:

Another opinion is that the combination of revolutionary realism and revolutionary romanticism is an enrichment and development of Socialist Realism. Most comrades acknowledge that this enrichment and development become manifest in the emphasis on revolutionary romanticism, and although according to the explanations of Gorky and Ždanov this revolutionary romanticism was an organic part of Socialist Realism, later it did not receive satisfactory attention either in practice or in theory.[26]

The last sentence conveys a critical attitude *vis-à-vis* recent developments in Soviet literary theory and practice. Therefore, the introduction by the Chinese of the new literary concept can also be interpreted as an attempt to emancipate Chinese Marxist literary theory from Soviet patronage. Significantly, a conference address by Chou Yang, who as a vice-director of the Propaganda Department of the Central Committee was supervising literary life between 1949 and 1966, was entitled: "Establish *China's own* Marxist literary theory and criticism."[27]

Suspicious of eclecticism, the Chinese critics hardly ever made any reference to Marx's theory of the unbalanced development of artistic and material production, which contradicts the materialist law of economic determinism. One of the few exceptions is an article by Chou Lai-hsiang, who concludes that either the theory must be considered as not universally valid or as applicable also to the socialist epoch.[28] Both conclusions were embarrassing: the first because it detracted from Marx's thesis, the second because it would justify dissident literature. Chou Lai-hsiang decided that Marx's thesis no longer applied, and attributed to Mao Tse-tung the phrasing of the new law of "the parallel development of cultural, artistic and material production in the socialist epoch." Although we definitely see here an attempt to straighten Marxist literary theory, for some reason or another the issue did not receive much attention in later Chinese criticism.

More attention was paid to the possibility of a discrepancy between the writer's world view and the meaning of his work, as formulated by Engels and Dobroljubov. For instance, the theory was invoked during the discussions on the interpretation of the eighteenth-century novel *Dream of the Red Chamber (Hung lou meng)* in 1954. As in the Soviet Union, the theory served to make the assimilation of the classical work of the cultural heritage possible. The theory was recurrently referred to, and during the first fifteen years of the People's Republic the main works of the Chinese tradition were reprinted and accessible to the public. Characteristically, however, during the Cultural Revolution and coinciding with an extremely vehement repudiation of almost all traditional literature, an attempt was made to eliminate this theory as it made possible an escape from economic determinism. Cheng Chi-ch'iao and T'an P'ei-sheng, the critics who tried to eliminate Engels' discrepancy theory from Maoist criticism,[29] also rejected the idea of unconscious creation, as well as the distinction between logical thinking and "thinking in images" (as defended by Belinskij, Plechanov, Lunačarskij and, in China, by Ch'en Yung). Cheng Chi-ch'iao moreover criticized the Soviet view, expressed in "On the Problem of the Typical in Literature and Art" (1955), that the typical is not always the result of party spirit. The Chinese critics had detected an idealist strain in all these positions, and correctly so. They paved the way for a non-eclectic materialist conception of literature, but they failed to have their ideas definitely accepted by the Chinese political leaders, who have avoided a clear decision on Engels' discrepancy theory, which in spite of its idealist origins, is certainly appropriate to justify the assimilation of older literature. Very recent developments have shown that to some extent Chinese classical literature has been made accessible again to the reading public. This would imply that Engels' theory of the possible discrepancy between the writer's world view and the meaning of his work is badly needed to justify this development. Perhaps in the near future also other "idealist" notions such as the difference between party spirit and the typical, the unconscious character of the creative act, and the concept of "thinking in images" will be restored as respectable elements of Chinese Marxist literary theory. Whether or not this will happen, cannot be predicted with certainty.

Let us, after these general observations, examine the few sources of Marxist literary theory which, at present anyway, are valid in China. The prevailing current of contemporary Chinese criticism has been determined by Mao Tse-tung's "Talks at the Yenan Forum on Literature and Art" (1942). If we consider the years from 1949 until Mao's death in 1976 as one period, Maoist literary theory is the mainstream and the only school of thought which survived the vicissitudes of the political tide. Mao's "Yenan Talks" were conceived in wartime, when literature was naturally supposed to support the war effort. The view that literature is a "weapon" was hardly qualified in later years, although conditions changed considerably. Five later pronouncements by Mao Tse-tung on literature were published in the *Red Flag* of May 27, 1967.[30] The oldest of these dates from 1944 and the most recent from 1964. In 1944, with due emphasis on subject-matter, Mao expressed his doubts about the traditional Chinese opera, in particular *Pi shang liang shan* (Driven to Join the Liangshan Rebels), which stages "lords and ladies and their pampered sons and daughters" and "presents the people as though they were dirt". In a criticism of the film *The Life of Wu Hsün* (1951), Mao advocated the application of historical-materialist explanations in literature and art. Three years later, in a letter to the Politburo, he addressed himself to the current discussions of the eighteenth-century novel *Dream of the Red Chamber*; on that occasion he condemned "the Hu Shih school of bourgeois idealism". The two other pronouncements by Mao, of 1963 and 1964, deal almost exclusively with political matters. All these statements are completely in line with the position taken in the "Yenan Talks". This also applies to Mao's most recent—and his shortest—statement on literature, which was published in *People's Daily (Jen-min jih-pao)* of December 16, 1971: "I hope that more and better works will be produced." Here too an aspect of Maoist literary theory is being emphasized which was announced in the "Yenan Talks", namely the idea that a socialist society cannot do without literature.

Apart from Mao Tse-tung himself, his wife Chiang Ch'ing contributed to Maoist literary theory. In 1964 she took an uncompromising position concerning the traditional Peking opera in a short speech which was not published at the time but appeared only in 1967.[31] More important, and in fact the most important Maoist document on literature since the "Yenan Talks", is the "Summary of the Forum on the Work in Literature and Art in the Armed Forces with which Comrade Lin Piao Entrusted Comrade Chiang Ch'ing" of February 1966.[32] Mao Tse-tung is said to have revised the text three times before its publication and this may prove to be a guarantee against the "Summary" (or, at least, the ideas expressed in it) being outlawed, in spite of the fact that both Lin Piao and Chiang Ch'ing were ostracized. As we will see, the "Summary" is a quite faithful repetition of views expressed in the "Yenan Talks".

During the Cultural Revolution Chiang Ch'ing made occasional pronouncements on literary and theatrical matters. On

November 28, 1966, she launched a desperate attack on Western culture:

Capitalism has a history of several centuries. Nevertheless, it has only a pitiful number of 'classics'. Some works modelled after the 'classics' have been created, but these are stereotyped and no longer appeal to the people. [. . .] On the other hand, there are some things that really flood the market, such as rock-'n'-roll, jazz, striptease, impressionism, symbolism, abstractionism, fauvism, modernism—there is no end to them—all of which are intended to poison and paralyse the minds of the people. In short, there is decadence and obscenity to poison and paralyse the minds of the people.

After its publication in *People's Daily* of December 4, 1966, her disparaging view of art, which equalled or even surpassed Ždanov's pronouncements in vehemence, has not been reprinted. This justifies doubts as to whether its unqualified one-sidedness is still considered appropriate.

In his "Yenan Talks" Mao Tse-tung rephrased the main concepts of Marxist and Soviet literary theory. Like the Soviet Marxist theorists, Mao does not attempt to define fiction, poetry or drama, or to analyse the function of plot construction, rhyme or dialogue. We know from Mao's own performance as a poet that he is aware of the difference between poetic forms, such as *lü-shih* (stanzas of eight lines, each of seven characters) and *tz'u* (a metrical form of which the length of each line, rhyme and tonal pattern are determined by the traditional "tune" which the poet chooses), but these distinctions are not part of the Maoist literary theory. In the late 1950s there was a lively discussion in the literary journals about poetic devices (touching on such questions as the function of rhyme and metre) which did not conflict with the official views on literature, for the simple reason that neither Mao nor any of his close associates ever expressed themselves on these matters. For the same reason, novelists were free to experiment with plot construction, although they usually remained on the safe side and did not go beyond models that had been established by Mao Tun, Pa Chin, Lao She and others in the 1930s or by early Soviet writers such as A. A. Fadeev, whose *Razgrom* (The Nineteen, 1927) was mentioned in the "Yenan Talks" as an example to be followed. In the "Yenan Talks" Mao Tse-tung says very little about drama, but this gap was filled two years later with his comment alluded to above, on the subject-matter of the traditional opera.

Subject-matter is also one of Mao Tse-tung's main concerns in the "Yenan Talks", as well as in recent criticisms.[33] A characteristic feature of Maoist literary theory is that subject-matter can very well be considered in isolation, separate from its formal expression. The historical explanation that in this way Mao was continuing an old, largely Confucian tradition and that moreover his "Yenan Talks" were primarily meant as a moralist response to moralist criticism by "rightist" authors (Ting Ling, Hsiao Chün and others) is not relevant here. Mao can pay almost exclusive attention to subject-matter, since in full accordance with Marxist literary theory his assumption is that form and content can be separated. Mao's view on the relation between form and content appears from the following statement: "[. . .] Nor do we refuse to utilize the literary and artistic forms of the past, but in our hands these old forms, remoulded and infused with new content, also become something revolutionary in the service of the people" (1942: 76).

According to Mao, the class struggle and the anti-Japanese war may serve as subject-matter. Anti-national, anti-scientific and anti-communist views should not be represented. The "Summary" supports the view that the fullest attention should be given "to the themes of socialist revolution and socialist construction", and is even more specific in the claim that literary works should be created about three particular military campaigns. Of course, the "Summary" addressed itself primarily to the military, but in·a country where the people are constantly reminded to learn from the army and the army from the people, the hint to deal with military themes should not be interpreted as being restricted to military men.

Further restrictions about the proper subject-matter are to be found in Mao Tse-tung's comments in the "Yenan Talks" on "the theory of human nature", "the love of humanity", etc. Mao's position is that "there is no human nature above classes" and "there has been no [. . .] all-inclusive love of humanity since humanity was divided into classes" (1942: 90–1). The basis of these statements is the belief that the class struggle is the all-pervading force in human life. The idea of the class struggle as the primordial factor in human life is rooted in the conviction that "Marxism-Leninism-Mao Tse-tung Thought" has provided the final answers to all human problems. That conviction has a number of consequences. It means, for instance, that Marxist political solutions are in principle always correct. A society where the Communist Party has come to power has no serious flaws. Therefore, Mao Tse-tung explains, the writers should portray mainly the bright side of socialist construction. If shortcomings or negative characters are described, they should only "serve as a contrast to bring out the brightness of the whole picture". As the Soviet political leaders had distrusted the satirical prose of Zamjatin and Zoščenko, Mao Tse-tung determined that Lu Hsün's style of the "satirical essay" *(tsa-wen)* should not be imitated (1942: 91–2).

Implicit in the "Yenan Talks" is the idea that all human problems have in principle been solved by Marx, Engels, Lenin and Mao Tse-tung. As a result of the heavy reliance on one particular ideology, Mao's literary theory in fact provides no justification for experiment. With the exception of the small margin which is the result of a more or less daring interpretation of Party directives, it must be clear to a Chinese writer what his message should be. There is no urge to doubt established solutions that have been sanctioned by the Party or Chairman Mao, or to discover alternative solutions by creating imaginary worlds which considerably depart from the Marxist mould. The stiffening effect of an accepted, once-and-for-all ideology can be seen also in the language of the literary texts. Not only is the solution to all problems known in principle, but the phrasing of that solution also leaves little leeway. In the 1967 version of the modern Peking opera *Raid on the White Tiger Regiment,* 3 per cent of the text consists of quotations from Mao Tse-tung's works and his name is mentioned twenty-five times. This particular text is an extreme example of the way the Maoist literary theory was to lead. Even if certain texts do not contain direct quotations from Mao, the writers are still held to abide by the phraseology that can be found in his works.

The exclusiveness of Maoist ideology and the infallibility of its wording prevent the Chinese writers from probing into the relation between sign and concept, or between word and reality. In fact all propaganda work in China, of which literature is often considered a part, is directed towards spreading the belief that words and concepts are one and that things do exist in reality if words only say so often enough. It is clear that the conception of poetry as a means to refine communication and to prevent language from being polluted is incompatible with the acceptance of the Maoist ideology.

Maoist ideology has a direct bearing on contemporary Chinese literature. But neither in theory nor in practice is literature completely equated with propaganda. Mao Tse-tung is aware of the fact that "the people are not satisfied with life alone and demand literature and art as well." He also mentions the reason why: "Because, while both are beautiful, life as reflected in works of literature and art can and ought to be on a higher plane, more intense, more concentrated, more typical, nearer the ideal, and therefore more universal than actual everyday life" (1942: 82). In spite of the attempts to do away with eclecticism, recent Chinese literature still seems to be a compromise between political and artistic demands.

The overriding end value of Maoist literary theory is the advancement of the revolutionary struggle. Or, as Mao Tse-tung said in the "Yenan Talks", the Chinese writers must ensure that revolutionary literature provides "better help to other revolutionary work in facilitating the overthrow of our national enemy and the accomplishment of the task of national liberation" (ibid.). This normative statement suggests how literature may function in social life. The end value implicit in the statement ("literature should serve the political struggle") does not seem to have a specific literary character. Within the framework of Maoist ideology the same norm could be applied to intellectual work in general, industrial production, or leisure. All these "should serve the political struggle." Although this main value is not exclusively applicable to literature, it does determine Maoist literary theory which in that way becomes part of a larger ideological system. It should not be considered exceptional that the justification of a literary value system exceeds the literary context. In general, all literary evaluation is determined by the relation between the valued object and the valuing subject who, consciously or not, takes the social context into account.

One may object that the end value of literary production was formulated by Mao Tse-tung in a war situation, and does not warrant far-reaching conclusions. However, as was mentioned earlier, the views expressed in the "Yenan Talks" have never been negated or superseded by later statements, although the circumstances under which Mao Tse-tung made his speeches in 1942 have certainly changed. It appears from the "Summary" that the struggle is now mainly against "bourgeois idealism", "modern revisionism" and pacifism. The subservience of literature to the political struggle has remained the same.

The political struggle that is referred to here is largely determined by the Marxist-Leninist and Maoist ideology and by the Communist Party. Maoist literary theory implies, as Mao has said, adherence to the principle of party spirit,[34] which, as in the Soviet context, means that the writers and critics in their work have to side with the Party and, in practice, are obliged to follow the Party's directives. This principle accounts for the dynamics of Maoist literary criticism and can explain many of the ups and downs in the reception of classical and contemporary Chinese literature, as well as foreign literature. Due to changing circumstances and in connection with other political developments, the directives of the Party are subject to change. Therefore, literary works which seemed in accordance with the Party line in the early 1960s were liable to be outlawed during the Cultural Revolution when another policy prevailed, and may be restored to the body of permitted reading matter again if that would suit the Party. The recently revitalized interest in classical poetry, triggered off by the publication of Kuo Mo-jo's book on Li T'ai-po and Tu Fu in November 1971, may illustrate this. Studies of Li T'ai-po and Tu Fu were as normal in the early 1960s as they were impossible during the Cultural Revolution. The official evaluation of modern literature may show a similar curve.

The imminent or open disapproval of certain texts by the Party can be by-passed by rewriting. A standard example of a book that was subjected to repeated rewriting is *The Song of Ouyang Hai* by Chin Ching-mai. The Chinese editions of 1965 and 1966 favourably mentioned the political ideas of Liu Shao-ch'i, which necessitated rather excessive rewriting. Fragments of the last edition published in 1967 made mention of Lin Piao, then Vice-Chairman of the Communist Party and after September 1971 in disgrace. If only for that reason, the novel must be revised again before it can be republished.[35] Also in the Soviet Union authors have been compelled to rewrite their books, but the principle of rewriting has been applied more consistently in contemporary Chinese literature. The texts of the various new Peking operas on modern themes have been repeatedly rewritten and published with the date of the new text added, but *without any reference to the earlier editions*. In this way, literary history is being rewritten as well. The Chinese critics are not in any way allowed to respect the past; even less than their Soviet colleagues may they indulge in historicist considerations. Therefore, we may conclude that in China the primordial norm of party spirit has produced the principle of *permanent revision* or the *non-finality of the literary text* as an instrumental value which very much determines contemporary Chinese literature. Whereas Chinese criticism speaks repeatedly of party spirit, the principle of the non-finality of the literary text is hardly made explicit.

There are more instrumental values. Since literature should serve the political struggle, Mao Tse-tung logically calls himself a "utilitarian". The concept of literature as a weapon in the revolutionary struggle leads to the demand that the weapon should be appropriate and forceful. Hence Mao Tse-tung's defence of artistic criteria—which, however, remain subordinate to the political norms. The latter make censorship necessary and, as in the Soviet Union, the idea of ideological supervision has decided the question of the relation between form and content in favour of their separability. Soviet and Chinese Marxists apparently agree that the structuralist concept of form and content as aspects of an organized whole (which implies the conviction that certain small changes in the text may destroy the work of art) might bolster resistance to political censorship. The concept of structural unity provides the text with an unassailability that is anathema to Marxist literary theory.

There are other, more specific norms in Maoist literary theory. As to genres, there is a preference for folksongs (characterized by standard imagination), reportage (which suppresses the fictional aspect) and the modern Chinese opera (which relies heavily on extra-literary devices such as music, dance and acrobatics). The whole system of Maoist literary theory and much recent literary practice show a strong preference for those texts which can easily be tested with political norms. Finally, the advancement of the political struggle dictates a firm choice in favour of "popularization", to the neglect of the "elevation" or improvement of artistic standards.

The concepts and values of Maoist literary theory cannot be fully understood if the historical context is neglected. Mao's literary theory was a reaction to both traditional (Confucian, Taoist, Buddhist) concepts of literature and the confusing intrusion of Western influences (Naturalism, Symbolism, Expressionism, the stream-of-consciousness novel, Socialist Realism). In his "Yenan Talks" Mao Tse-tung offered a relief from the depressing multitude of new movements and ideas which, often in a simplified or distorted way, confronted the intellectuals of modern China. Mao's choice was largely the Soviet model as interpreted by theorists such as Ch'ü Ch'iu-pai and Chou Yang. It was not Mao's intention to write a complete poetics, but to provide a unity of focus. The incompleteness of the "Yenan Talks" left some margin for creative freedom. Only gradually did it appear that essential constituents of literary creation were fettered. During the first twenty-odd years of the existence of the People's Republic, Chinese cultural policy led to ever more neglect of the forms and function of literary imagination. Mao Tse-tung's encouraging words of December 1971 give some hope that this trend has been reversed. During the Cultural Revolution—or, to be more exact, in the years 1967–71—the national press was unable to recommend a newly-published or reprinted novel or any volume of poetry by one single poet. In fact, the literary scene was utterly barren. If the observation in the "Yenan Talks" that the people demand literature is still valid, something must be done to satisfy that demand.

There is a plain political reason for encouraging literary production. As Lu Hsün observed, literature is needed as propaganda. But prose that is devoid of fiction and verse that consists of straight political admonitions are too easily recognized as propaganda. Literature loses its exceptional value as a means of propaganda as soon as it loses most or all of its specific literary character. Oddly enough, this political consideration may finally save a residue of the Chinese literary potential. The publication of several novels since 1972, renewed attention to the problem of the "typical", and the hesitant acknowledgement that literature should not be equated with politics confirm that possibility.[36]

Lukács and Neo-Marxist Criticism

A survey of neo-Marxist literary criticism cannot neglect Georg Lukács, although in the greater part of his publications he can by no means be called a neo-Marxist. The label "neo-Marxism" is used by non-Marxists rather than by the neo-Marxists themselves, which makes it difficult to agree on a definition of the term. For the present purpose we shall use it to distinguish between those theoreticians who base themselves unconditionally on the writings of Marx, Engels and Lenin—accepting at the same time the leading role of the Communist Party in matters of culture and science—and those others who, while often relying on Marx and Engels, do not interpret their writings in a dogmatic way, or accept the absolute supremacy of the Communist Party in problems of culture and science.

In this sense Th.W. Adorno, Walter Benjamin and Lucien Goldmann, as well as Jacques Leenhardt and Fredric Jameson are neo-Marxists, but Lukács is not. It is necessary to make a distinction between those who accept the Marxist canon as definite truth and those who regard it merely as a source of inspiration, particularly in the study of Marxist literary criticism. The distinction should prevent us from considering high quality criticism based on an unorthodox Marxism as a tribute to Marxism rather than a defeat for it. It might appear that the more interesting criticism comes from writers who depart from the orthodox canon. In a discussion of recent Marxist criticism we are on the safe, orthodox side if we first try to establish the position of Lukács, who as a Marxist in his writings never explicitly criticized Marx, Engels or Lenin, or the CPSU, except in a single case in which the CPSU first had criticized itself (Lukács 1963–75: IV, 459). However, Lukács' *Die Eigenart des Ästhetischen* (The Particular Nature of the Aesthetic, 1963) stands somewhat apart from his earlier work, since it expounds a Marxist aesthetics that is founded also on sources other than Marxian ones.

It is impossible and also unnecessary to discuss here the complete works of Lukács. The writings of his pre-Marxist period such as *Die Seele und die Formen* (1911) and *Die Theorie des Romans* (1916) are, as Lukács has explicitly admitted with regard to the latter, exponents of the *"geisteswissenschaftliche Methode"* (Lukács 1962: 6–7). In 1938 he disqualified *Die Theorie des Romans* as "a reactionary work throughout, full of idealistic mysticism, mistaken in all its interpretations of the historical development".[37]

Lukács, who joined the Communist Party in 1918 and after a brief visit to Moscow (1930–1) emigrated to the Soviet Union in 1933, cooperates here with M. A. Lifschitz in his search for a Marxian aesthetics. Thus begins his orthodox period which lasts from the early 1930s to about 1956. (In 1944 he returned to Budapest.) The main contributions of this period are his studies of nineteenth-century Realism, his selective essays on the new Soviet literature and Socialist Realism, and his attempts to emphasize the Realist aspects of twentieth-century literature, e.g. in the work of Thomas Mann, at the expense of other trends, such as those of Expressionism and Surrealism, as well as the narrative prose of Kafka, Joyce, Döblin and Dos Passos. The assumption that Lukács too easily submitted to the current cultural policies of the Soviet Union should perhaps be qualified; indeed, he clearly threw the weight of his influence into the scale of a cultural policy that stood for the continuity of the literary tradition. One may deplore the fact that he never defended the avant-garde, but he had success in taking sides with those who were critical of the illusory ideals of *Proletkul't*. Among others (not all of them good company), Lukács was instrumental in defining a cultural policy that in Eastern

Europe prevented a break with the rich nineteenth-century literary tradition. Goethe, Balzac, Dickens, Gogol, Tolstoy and Dostoevsky belong to the permitted reading matter in the Soviet Union, partly as a result of Lukács' efforts. The significance of this may appear from a comparison with China, where this is no longer the case. Aided by a keen political intuition, Lukács made use of any opportunity to broaden the margins of freedom. Within two years of the publication of Solzhenitsyn's *One Day in the Life of Ivan Denisovich* (1962), Lukács wrote a very favourable review. *Die Eigenart des Ästhetischen* is a similar case. Indeed, ever since the editorial "On the Problem of the Typical" (1955) had appeared in *Kommunist,* emphasizing the difference between the aesthetic and political effects of literature,[38] it has again been possible in the communist countries to discuss the particular nature of aesthetic texts. Yet in *Die Eigenart des Ästhetischen,* Lukács made the broadest possible use of the opportunity.

In the following pages we shall restrict ourselves mainly to two pivotal topics: the debate on Expressionism and Realism, and the problems related to political commitment and the principle of party spirit.

The debate on Expressionism and Realism, which was mainly carried on in the German review *Das Wort,* published in Moscow between 1936 and 1939, is generally believed to have been started by Lukács in his article " 'Grösse und Verfall' des Expressionismus", which was published in *Internationale Literatur* in 1934.[39] It has a revealing motto from Lenin: "[. . .] that which is inessential, apparent and superficial most often disappears, and does not take root like the 'essence'."[40] Lenin's saying induced Lukács to formulate his main point: Expressionism had succeeded only in describing the surface of phenomena, while Realism had access to the essence of the historical development. After several German writers such as Klaus Mann, Herwarth Walden and Ernst Bloch had rejected Lukács' position, Lukács published his well-known essay "Es geht um den Realismus" (1938) in *Das Wort* (Lukács 1963–75: IV, 313–44).

In that article Lukács mainly criticizes Ernst Bloch, whom he otherwise respects as a fellow-Marxist. Bloch had doubted Lukács' view of reality as a coherent totality. If that view were correct, Bloch concluded, then the Expressionist devices of disruption, interpolation and montage would be an "empty play" (ibid.: IV, 315). Here Bloch too relied on Marxist thinking. He accepted that literature, as part of the superstructure, should reflect the true nature of reality (the economic basis). However, he differed from Lukács on the nature of reality. He considered Lukács' conception of reality as a coherent totality to be a remnant of classical idealism, and countered that, particularly under the capitalist system, "perhaps a real reality can also be interruption".[41] Bloch believed that Surrealism may serve as an example here. "Surrealism", wrote Bloch "consists of montage. [. . .] It is the description of the confusion of an experienced reality [*Erlebniswirklichkeit*] with broken spheres and caesuras."[42]

Lukács introduces a new element by reformulating the problem as follows. Do the capitalist system and the bourgeois society in their unity of economy and ideology objectively, *independently from consciousness,* form a coherent totality? (ibid.: IV, 316).

Bloch had based his defense of Expressionism on a conscious experience of reality *(Erlebniswirklichkeit)*. Lukács refers to a reality independent of consciousness. As experience cannot serve as an argument to support his position, Lukács must appeal to the authority of Marx, who had written that the conditions of production in *every* society (i.e. also the capitalist society) form a whole (ibid.: IV, 316). According to Lukács, this should settle the dispute, at least among Marxists such as Bloch and himself. In this way, the difference had been reduced to a different interpretation of the social and economic reality. Lukács' polemic manoeuvre derives straight from Marx who, in his criticism of *Les mystères de Paris,* also used his own interpretation of reality as a yardstick to judge literary quality. Lukács does not discuss the quality of the work of Joyce or Dos Passos, or of Expressionist literature, but rather the characteristics of the reality they supposedly reflect. The discussion is seriously hampered by branding experience as superficial and Marxist theory as revealing the essence. "Every Marxist knows that the immediate reflection in the minds of the people of the basic economic categories of capitalism is always distorted."[43] Lukács holds against Bloch that he pays attention only to superficialities, to the fragments of reality, whereas the basis of his own holistic argument consists of rather dogmatic references to Marx and Lenin, and suffers—to use the phrase of Guillén (1971: 444)—from "abstractionism".

According to Lukács, the Naturalist, Symbolist, Expressionist and Surrealist writers made the mistake of reflecting reality as it immediately appeared to them (ibid.: IV, 321). They overemphasized the isolated moments of the capitalist system, its crisis and disorder. But they did not dig for a deeper "essence", for the coherence between their experiences and the "real life of society", nor for the "hidden causes" of their experiences (ibid.: IV, 322). For the reflection of the whole of reality one should turn to great Realists, such as Gorky and Heinrich Mann, who have been able to produce literary types of lasting value (Klim Samgin, Professor Unrat), types with "lasting characteristics [. . .], which, as tendencies of the objective development of society, or even of humanity, will be effective over a long period."[44] The Realistic writers who succeed in creating such types are the real avant-garde. The tendencies of social development are described in their budding *(im Keim)*. Therefore, the question whether a writer has seen things correctly can only be judged from hindsight.

Finally, Lukács refers to the range of the reading public as an argument in defense of Realism. Realism is popular *(volkstümlich)* and complies with the criterion of *Volkstümlichkeit* or, in Russian, *narodnost'* (the latter term recalls the early Romanticist essays by Belinskij.) Lukács is aware that the word, particularly in German, is loaded with adverse connotations, which induced Brecht to make a number of sarcastic observations in his diary (Brecht 1968: XIX, 323–4). To Lukács, the popular nature of literature means continuing the cultural tradition. Popular literature is diametrically opposed to avant-garde literature. To Lukács the total rejection of the past is equal to anarchy. He could easily find a quotation from Lenin to support that view (Lukács 1963–75: IV, 339).

Clearly the Realism of Romain Rolland and of Heinrich and Thomas Mann exemplify literary continuity more convincingly than Joyce or other representatives of the avant-garde, in particular to uneducated readers. The avant-garde can be approached only through a very narrow gate. The man in the street *("der Mann aus dem Volke")* has easier access to Realist authors, and this, says Lukács, is of political significance. The political interest of Realism appears from the necessity to create a popular front. Lukács' defence of Realism cannot be disconnected from the Soviet-supported popular front policy.

Lukács expressed himself in favour of a literature that could provide answers to questions by the reader, answers to questions posed by life itself. Therefore the answers should be recognizable and clear. In fact, Lukács argues—to use Lotman's terminology—for an aesthetics of identity, rather than an aesthetics of opposition. From a Marxist point of view, this is quite understandable because, since Marx, the interpretation of the world in principle has been known. In other words, the orthodox Marxist has no need for new codes.

It is this consequence of Marxist literary theory—in our view an inevitable one—that went against the grains with many creative writers. Bertolt Brecht may serve as an example. In 1938 he wrote in his diary regarding the Expressionism debate: "No Realist will be content to repeat forever what one already knows; that would not indicate a living relation with reality."[45] Brecht shunned the petrification to which Lukács' position might lead, and preferred a less rigid and less orthodox point of view. He opted for the possibility of an unobstructed literary evolution:

> Do not proclaim with the face of infallibility the one and only possible way to describe a room, do not excommunicate the montage, do not put the interior monologue on the index! Do not beat the young people with the old names! Do not take the attitude of permitting technical development in the arts up to 1900, and from then onwards no more![46]

The differences between Brecht and Lukács went back at least as far as 1932, when Lukács in his essay "Reportage oder Gestaltung?" rejected Brecht's argument for a non-Aristotelian drama, including his concept of alienation *(Verfremdung)*. In this article Lukács had suggested that Brecht's theatrical convictions were incompatible with the teachings of Marx and Engels (Lukács 1963–75: IV, 58–60). Moreover, their differences had a lasting effect: Brecht's plays were never performed in the Soviet Union during his lifetime (Rühle 1960b: 48).

Brecht considered himself involved in the Expressionism debate when Lukács attacked the technique of the montage in the work of Dos Passos. Brecht notes that he himself is not prepared to abandon that technique. He observes that Lukács' thinking is dictated by the past. He sees in Lukács' essays an inclination to capitulation, utopianism, idealism, artistic enjoyment *(Kunstgenuss)* and escapism.[47] He concludes from Lukács' criticism of Dos Passos and his preference for Balzac a penchant for the idyllic, but, as Brecht warns, the assimilation of the cultural legacy is not a peaceful process (Brecht 1968: XIX, 317). Indeed, from a revolutionary point of view one could very well argue so. Brecht is opposed to a dogmatic interpretation of the Marxist canon. Clearly alluding to Lukács, Brecht writes that one should not worry too much when critics condemn the avant-garde as formalist on the basis of quotations from the Marxist classics in which the word 'form' occurs (ibid.: XIX, 308). Brecht obviously questions the authority of Marx and Engels on current literary issues.

Brecht did not stand alone. Anna Seghers too, in her famous letters to Lukács (reprinted in Lukács' collected works), expressed her reservations about the use of isolated quotations, which she compares to a magic broom (Lukács 1963–75: IV, 365). She also questioned the mirror metaphor used by Lukács, defended Dos Passos, and pointed out that Lukács' great examples, Romain Rolland and Thomas Mann, grew up under quite different circumstances from the so-called decadent writers criticized by him. In a later discussion of the Expressionism debate, Jürgen Rühle correctly observed that the later work of Thomas Mann is characterized by "reflections, essayistic features and irony" to such an extent that it cannot simply be brought under the heading of Realism. Contradictory times produce contradictory literature, writes Rühle (1960a: 245). (On similar grounds, but without referring to Lukács, Harry Levin (1966) included the later work of Thomas Mann in his period concept of Modernism.)

Lukács, however, remained undisturbed under the wealth of counter-arguments. His orthodox argument is based on a distinction between appearance and essence, between experienced reality *(Erlebniswirklichkeit)* and objective reality, between superficial explanations and "hidden causes". But how to check and discuss "hidden causes"? The crucial point in the Marxist criticism of literature is always the prevailing interpretation of Marxist theory, which may differ with the temperament or erudition of the interpreter and which is also largely determined by the opportunities of the political moment. The current interpretation of the Marxist canon determines which "hidden causes" must be uncovered. It draws the line between subjective experience and objective reality.

Lukács is fully aware of the significance of the political situation for his own work. His important essay "Die Gegenwarts-bedeutung des kritischen Realismus", which was published in Hamburg under the title *Wider den missverstandenen Realismus* (1958), is clearly a product of the destalinization process. In a foreword Lukács explains that he always was opposed to the term "revolutionary romanticism", but that he can only now criticize it openly (Lukács 1963–75: IV, 459). He calls this criticism merely "verbally new", although in fact his argument against "revolutionary romanticism" is of more than "verbal" significance against the background of the canonization of the term in China in the same year. Lukács' rejection of "revolutionary romanticism" is the corollary of his idiosyncratic interpretation of

Socialist Realism, which in his view should be close to critical realism.

Lukács' defence of Thomas Mann and rejection of Kafka is arbitrary to the extent that his position is politically motivated. Because in 1957 communist propaganda harped on the anti-war theme, Lukács concluded that the choice was no longer one between capitalism and socialism (ibid.: IV, 550). Soviet peace propaganda enabled Lukács to differentiate between the products of bourgeois society. Lukács opted for Thomas Mann, as he leads away from *Angst,* at the expense of Kafka who supposedly leads towards it. Simply on the basis of his style Kafka could be considered a Realist, but he halts before "the blind and panic *Angst"*. Kafka attributes a nihilistic significance to the world, the (realistic) description of which he allegorizes in a transcendental way (ibid.: IV, 498, 534). The realistic details of his work are interchangeable. In Thomas Mann's fiction they are not; there everything has its fixed place. The non-interchangeability of the details in Mann's work is assumed to be based on the belief in a final, immanent significance and meaning of the world *("eine Jetzthinnige immanente Vernünftigkeit, Sinnhaftigkeit der Welt")* (ibid.: IV, 496). It is this belief in an immanent purpose that is shared by the Marxists.

Lukács considers much of Thomas Mann's political views naive or even reactionary, but he declares as applicable to Mann, Engels' theory of the possible discrepancy between the writer's political convictions and the significance of his work. His novels are acceptable because he "instinctively" organizes the phenomena of life in a correct way. Mann's fiction takes part in "the triumph of Realism", as do the novels of Conrad, Hemingway and Steinbeck.

The updating of critical realism, motivated by Russian peace propaganda, was detrimental to Socialist Realism. As was mentioned above, Lukács had already argued in 1938 that Realist authors must create types that show the budding tendencies of social development. Usually this kind of prefiguration of the future is reserved for Socialist Realism. Lukács' definition of Realism empties Socialist Realism of its particular meaning. The differences between critical and Socialist Realism were elaborated in the last part of "Die Gegenwartsbedeutung des kritischen Realismus". Socialist Realism is characterized by the "concreteness of the socialist perspective". It describes the people who attempt to build a socialist and communist future, and whose psychology and morale reflect that future. Critical realism, on the other hand, focusses on the protest against the capitalist system (ibid.: IV, 554).

Lukács emphasizes that two factors have spoilt the case for Socialist Realism: the sectarianism of *Proletkul't* and the propaganda for revolutionary romanticism coinciding with Stalin's personality cult (ibid.: IV, 563, 599). Revolutionary romanticism is as objectionable as Naturalism. The first relies too much on revolutionary zeal, the second too little. Revolutionary romanticism neglects the necessary stages of social development, confuses future and present, and ends, says Lukács, in a schematization and vulgarization of the current socialist reality. The answer to the "sectarian schematization of the Stalin period" should be a close alliance between critical and Socialist Realism (ibid.: IV, 602).

Lukács is even more explicit in his review of *One Day in the Life of Ivan Denisovich*. He observes that even in the socialist nations Socialist Realism has become a term of abuse. The central problem now is the critical review of the Stalin period. If Socialist Realism is again to reach the level of the 1920s, it must again become realistic. Too often it had remained at the stage of doing no more than commenting on Party resolutions. One should appreciate Lukács' assessment of Solzhenitsyn's novella, which he surprisingly called a milestone in the history of Socialist Realism. But his review of *Ivan Denisovich* is not an argument for unrestricted freedom. Lukács knows too well that all Soviet literature is bound to provide "illustrations" of the Marxist canon, if it is to be condoned by the orthodox Marxists. As long as absolute validity is being attributed to the writings of Marx and Engels—and that, officially, is the situation in the communist countries—any innovation must remain within the bounds of the Marxist truth. Literature, then, will mainly be an "illustration" of that truth. However convinced Lukács was of the adverse consequences of the Stalinist dictatorship, he avoided examining the social and ideological conditions of that dictatorship and, in a rather un-Marxian way, identified the Stalinist malaise with the personality of Stalin.

In spite of his criticism of Socialist Realism (in particular its romanticist component), to most Western-Europeans Lukács was and remained a major spokesman for Marxist orthodoxy. In a review of *Wider den missverstandenen Realismus*, first published in 1958, Theodor W. Adorno attacks Lukács severely and personally[48]. He condemns his repeated attempts to adjust to the directives of the Soviet bureaucracy, which had degraded philosophy to a power instrument. Adorno considers as being dogmatic Lukács' rejection of all non-Realist modern literature. He regards his aesthetics as out-of-date and his reliance on the pronouncements of Marx and Engels as doubtful.

The crucial point in Adorno's argument is his analysis of Lukács concept of art, as explained in the latter's book *Über die Besonderheit als Kategorie der Ästhetik* (On Particularity as a Category of Aesthetics), most of which had been published in the *Deutsche Zeitschrift für Philosophie* by 1956.[49] Lukács discussed, among other things, the difference between art and science, but in a way that was unacceptable to Adorno. Lukács finds that art and science have much in common. Both reflect the same reality, and, in this reflection, both aim at universal validity, at "totality". They differ insofar as science searches for abstract, general laws, whereas art creates "perceptual, symbolic images of something particular that organically comprises and sublates both general and individual aspects [. . .], and aims at a universal empathy."[50] The generalization at which art aims includes a sublation *(Aufhebung)* of the individual to the level of the particular (or the typical), as well as a concretion of the general which also takes place at the level of the particular.

This concept of art, which was later elaborated in *Die Eigenart des Ästhetischen*, differs from modern aesthetics in that Lukács explicitly defended the primacy of the semantic content. He criticizes Kant for having attempted to free art completely from any conceptualization *(Begrifflichkeit* or *Gedanklichkeit)*, and Hegel for his insufficient criticism of Kant in this respect (Lukács, 1963–75: X, 714). Conceptualization is inherently present in art, although it is sublated to the level of the particular. The primacy of the "content" is evident. According to Lukács, the content determines the form; any influence of the form on the content is of secondary importance.

Adorno objects to this view. He agrees with Lukács that art is a form of knowing, but he disapproves of the reduction of the dialectical unity of art and science to a simple identity, as if works of art from their own perspective would only anticipate what is to be covered later by the social sciences. On the contrary, the gap between art and science cannot be bridged that easily. "Art does not convey knowledge about reality because it photographically or 'perspectively' represents reality, but because, on the basis of its autonomous nature, it expresses those things that are concealed by the empirical forms of knowledge."[51] Art is "knowledge *sui generis"*, because it affects the empirical data. It connects reality with the subjective intention, which results in "objective significance".[52]

Adorno comes close to Lotman's concept of the semanticization of formal features. According to Adorno, it is the construction that may overcome the accidental aspects of the individual. The interior monologue was necessary as, in an atomistic world, man is controlled by alienation. In the great works of the avant-garde the interior monologue is only *seemingly* subjective. Likewise, from Beckett's subjectivist drama all historical elements are seemingly eliminated; in fact, his work is in an objective way polemical (Adorno, 1958–74: II, 166).

Although one may be tempted to side with Adorno in this dispute, some reservations should be stated. Adorno's reference to things that are concealed by the empirical knowledge of reality but known by means of artistic intuition comes close to Bloch's concept of experienced reality *(Erlebniswirklichkeit)*. Lukács' concept of knowledge, however, exceeds the concept of empirical knowledge. The things that escape empirical verification may be covered by Lukács' concept of knowledge, and therefore Adorno's claim that art may convey a kind of knowledge *sui generis*—correct as it is, in our view—does not really affect Lukács' position. Another point is his interpretation of the interior monologue or Beckett's drama. It appears that Adorno is as clever as Lukács at juggling with the opposition of essence versus appearance. As long as his interpretation is not couched in a theory of interpretation or related to a specific literary or cultural code, it remains as arbitrary as that of Lukács. Further, one may detect a doctrinaire attitude in Adorno's position, where he claims that art may make things "objectively significant" *(objektiv sinnvoll)*. Can such a thing as an objective significance of the world or of history exist? Here Adorno's view comes close to that of Lukács and other Marxists who would answer the question in the affirmative. The argument that Lukács is a dogmatist is also applicable to Adorno. His dogmatic attitude appears also from the value he attaches to his own quotations from Marx. Indeed, as Adorno suggests, Lukács' career can be characterized as "forced atonement", but it is somewhat strange to see that the critic subscribes, without compulsion, to a similar Marxist world interpretation, uses the same dialectical method as his despised opponent, also juggles with essence and appearance (though with different results) and, like all

Marxists, discovers an objective sense in a postulated world which escapes empirical examination.

Yet Adorno and Lukács differ on important points. Adorno stresses the particular epistemological function of art, and defends the autonomous character of literature. Perhaps Adorno and Lukács differ most where the concept of the political commitment of literature is at stake. In *Über die Besonderheit als Kategorie der Ästhetik* Lukács emphasized the role of conceptualization in art, which enabled him to accommodate the concept of party spirit *(Parteilichkeit* or, in Russian, *partijnost')*. Conceptualization *(Gedanklichkeit)* in literature appears as a concrete factor of life, within the setting of concrete situations with concrete people, as part of the struggles, victories and defeats of men. The representation of reality in art implies a partisan view of the historical conflicts of the time in which the artist lives.[53] The selection of the represented segment of reality and the attitude of the author towards his material *(Stoff)* reveal his party spirit. Both that selection and the author's attitude towards his material belong to the range of content and can be judged from an extraliterary point of view. According to Lukács, the originality of literary works derives from the "correct position, as far as the content is concerned, in relation to the great problems of the time".[54] The question whether a position is "correct" or not, cannot be answered on the basis of the text alone but is ultimately judged from an extraliterary point of view, viz. that of the current interpretation of Marxism. In 1932 Lukács had described literature as "a product and weapon of the class struggle" (Lukács, 1963–75: IV, 24). In 1956, the wording has changed, but the principle of party spirit is still based on the acceptance of the correct Marxist world interpretation, and therefore basically an extraliterary affair.

In an essay originally published under the title "Engagement oder künstlerische Autonomie" (1962), Adorno presents a quite different approach to the persuasive function of literature (Adorno, 1958–74: III, 109–36). Literature, including texts that express a political commitment, cannot be reduced to a justification of one political view. Adorno rejects the old concept of *Tendenz* literature; his concept of political commitment leaves the ambiguity of the literary text intact in principle. As in his criticism of Lukács, Adorno now objects to Sartre's emphasis on communicative meaning. Again he seems to argue for the semanticization of formal features. Words do not mean the same in a literary text as outside literature. The hermetic literature of the avant-garde, whatever the communicative meaning of the words may be, resists attempts at political manipulation, since it cannot easily be assimilated by the accepted cultural system. The difficult form is a more effective protest against the established system than any plain political message. "The emphasis on the autonomous work is itself rather of a social and political nature", wrote Adorno,[55] and this position does not imply a rejection of the autonomy of the literary work, notably that of the avant-garde, as naive readers may have believed; on the contrary, Adorno expresses here his firm belief in the subversive nature of abstruse, avant-garde art. Or, as he phrased it in his unfinished, posthumously published *Ästhetische Theorie* (1970), "the a-social aspect of art contains an expressed negation of a particular society."[56]

Political censorship, which is quite compatible with Lukács' concept of party spirit, is impossible from Adorno's point of view (which moreover has serious implications for the interpretation of literature). As to the question of censorship, Adorno is diametrically opposed to the views of Lukács and of the Soviet bureaucracy. Of all Marxist baggage it is primarily the dialectical method that characterizes Adorno's criticism. His dialectics, his postulate of an objective sense in a world that escapes empirical examination, and his many references to Marx and Engels are generally held to be sufficient for him to be considered a neo-Marxist, although it is clear that his Marxism and that of, say, Mao Tse-tung are worlds apart and with quite different implications for the study of literature.

As appeared from *Die Eigenart des Ästhetischen,* Lukács remained unsusceptible to Adorno's objections. He repeated and expanded the argument of *Über die Besonderheit als Kategorie der Ästhetik.* Systematically he explains the similarities and differences between ordinary thinking, science and art. They all reflect reality, i.e. a reality that exists independently of man's consciousness. In contradiction to science, the reflection of reality in art is anthropomorphic. It derives from the world of man and is directed towards it.

Another difference between the scientific and the artistic reflection of reality is the evocative character of art. In evoking the emotions and passions of life, the work of art uses certain techniques such as rhythm and symmetry (Lukács, 1963–75: XI, 283 and 298). In view of the anthropomorphic nature of art, the artistic evocation is first of all geared towards the inner life of man.

It extends his experience of life and gives shape to his own image of himself and of the world he lives in. In this context Lukács recalls the effect of the Aristotelian catharsis, as well as the principle of party spirit. Now, the principle of party spirit is qualified by the aesthetic concept of "the suspension of the immediate practical interest" (ibid.: XI, 655).

In order to fuse the general and the individual in the particular, art reflects reality by means of types. Again there is a difference between the artistic and the scientific typification. Science, says Lukács, aims at the reduction of types and abstracts from the individual and the particular in order to approach a maximum degree of generalization. Artistic types, on the other hand, remain closely related to the individual: "the type is conceived in such a way that the unity with the individual in which it appears in life, is not dissolved, but on the contrary deepened"[57] (cf. Parkinson, 1970: 109–47).

The similarities with the aesthetics of German idealism, even with its Russian interpreter Vissarion Belinskij, are obvious. But Lukács departs from that tradition by postulating that art and science reflect the same objective reality. We have already discussed Adorno's objections to this postulate. Contrary to Klaus Völker (1969: 147), we believe that Lukács is firmly on the side of Marx. Parkinson (1970: 139) has correctly observed that, like Marx, Lukács has consistently defended the position of philosophical realism. But in other respects too Lukács defends the Marxist analysis of the world. Discussions with Lukács are not simply discussions about the qualities of things or the characteristics of reality; they are concerned as much with explanations of the Marxist writings, which he has invested with infallible truth. It is this—and not his philosophical realism—which has elicited the objections of Brecht, Anna Seghers, Adorno and many others. Nevertheless Lukács' *Die Eigenart des Ästhetischen* is characterized by a conciliatory tone. He clearly emphasizes the continuity in European aesthetics, which begins with Aristotle rather than with Marx or Hegel.

As with Lukács, the recurrent theme in the criticism of Walter Benjamin and Lucien Goldmann is the relation between objective reality and art, or, more generally, basis and superstructure. It is the merit of Walter Benjamin that he described the material basis of artistic production in a rather sophisticated way in his essay "Das Kunstwerk im Zeitalter seiner technischen Reproduzierbarkeit" (The Work of Art in the Age of its Technical Reproducibility,

1936). The basic idea of this study is that every period has its own devices for the reproduction of art, but that the modern reproduction by technical means has totally changed the traditional image of art. The technical reproduction of a work of art, however adequate it may be, destroys anyway "the here and now of the original" (1936: 14). At this point Benjamin introduces his concept of "aura", the distinctive atmosphere surrounding the original work, which he defines as "a peculiar web of space and time: the unique appearance of a distance, however short that distance may be".[58] The technique of reproduction loosens the reproduced form from the tradition to which the original work belongs, and ignores its genuineness and aura. So far, Benjamin's argument is strictly historicist. His conclusion, however, is firmly in the Marxist tradition: "As soon as the criterion of authenticity no longer applies to the production of art, the whole function of art has been transformed *(umgewälzt)*. In place of its ritualistic basis another practice appears; henceforth it is based on politics."[59] The autonomous nature of art has disappeared with the disappearance of its ritualistic basis. As far as literature is concerned, Benjamin mentions Dada as a programme that capitalizes on the new function of art. The Dadaists aim to destroy the aura of their products which they brand as *re*production while using the means of production. In fact, this positive attitude of Benjamin towards the avant-garde is quite incompatible with Lukács' defence of cultural traditions. Benjamin sides with Brecht and Adorno when he expresses his reservations *vis-à-vis* the conventional devices of artistic creation. He attaches a political value to the work of the Dadaists, as "revolutionary content" in traditional forms is too readily assimilated by the capitalist society (cf. Helga Gallas, 1969: 149). It is in this way that Benjamin's claim that art should be political is to be understood (1936: 51).

This position was almost a matter of course for writers living in Germany in the 1930s or familiar with the fascist *Kulturpolitik*. But the political situation of the 1930s can no longer be an excuse for the naivety and exaggerations inherent in Benjamin's argument. He certainly makes the mistake of taking the new developments in art and the reproduction of art in an absolute way. From hindsight we know now that records did not replace live musical performances but complemented them. The film did not replace the stage play. Reportage did not mean the death of the novel, nor did Dada signal the end of other artistic traditions. Benjamin is clearly myopic in his judgement of Soviet literature as "the expression into words of work itself".[60]

In our opinion, Benjamin has been overestimated as a critic of literature; however, his influence has been enormous. Ernst Fischer (1971), for instance, copies his ideas and imitates his style. Adorno often leans on Benjamin's authority, but also feels the necessity to qualify his crude ideas on art in the technical age (Adorno, 1970: 322–6). Thousands of students have read his essays as part of the Marxist canon. Indeed, Benjamin at times entrenches himself in Marxist jargon. On other occasions—which may account for his popularity among students of literature—he seems almost to forget his professed Marxism and indulges in erudite analyses of cultural history, such as his essays on Baudelaire, which can hardly be called Marxist except for a dubious play with the opposition between essence and appearance.[61]

Apparently, references to Marx and Engels cannot guarantee acceptance of an argument, even among Marxists. Obviously Benjamin considers the work of Baudelaire as representative of the Second Empire. *Les fleurs du mal* are the last lyrical work of which the influence was felt throughout Europe (Benjamin, 1969: 161). Brecht countered this position with a series of sarcastic observations on Baudelaire, culminating in the view that "he in no way expresses his epoch, not even ten years of it."[62]

Quite another tradition of neo-Marxist thinking came to the fore in the work of Lucien Goldmann. After his great work *Le dieu caché* (Goldmann, 1955) in which he analysed the relation between seventeenth-century French literature (Pascal, Racine) and the ideology of Jansenism, he turned to the problem of the relation between the literary text and social and economic reality—in fact, the old problem of basis and superstructure. The difference from older expositions of the same problem is that his investigations are based on the hypothesis of a direct relation between economic structures and literary phenomena, i.e. without the intermediation of the collective consciousness (Goldmann, 1964: 30). Although Goldmann does not uncritically accept the Marxist canon, he firmly bases his theory on Marx's observations on the fetishism of merchandise. Goldmann argues that Marx has foreseen that in market economies, i.e. societies with a predominant economic activity, "collective consciousness gradually loses all active reality, and tends to become a simple reflection of the economic life and, finally, to disappear."[63]

Goldmann's hypothesis indeed introduces a new element in the discussion of the relation between literary phenomena and the economic basis. But he does more. He is aware of recent developments in narratology. He uses the concept of structure ("the whole of the relations between the various elements of the content" (1964: 30n)), and has a keen eye for the formal aspects of literature. One may suspect that he can exclude the intermediation of the collective consciousness only because he is able to invest the formal features of narrative constructions with meaning.

Certainly, Goldmann works in the Marxist tradition, from which he selects his sources carefully and eclectically. He relies heavily on Lukács, but often on material, such as *Die Theorie des Romans*, which Lukács himself has discounted as a product of the *geisteswissenschaftliche Methode*. Goldmann specifies his more general hypothesis, and suggests that there is a "homology between the structure of the classical novel and the structure of exchange in the free economy".[64] For example, the *nouveau roman* is characterized by dissolution of the character and, consequently, by increase in the autonomy of objects. This development can be explained by the reification *(Verdinglichung)* which is the result of the unrestricted growth of the free market economy, its trusts and monopolies, capital investments and government intervention. Here he assumes a direct relation between the economic system and the forms of literature (Goldmann, 1964: 187–9). As Peter Demetz (1970: 30) has observed, Goldmann, in accordance with earlier Marxist criticism, conceives of art as reflecting social reality.

Goldmann inspired Jacques Leenhardt (1973) to analyse Robbe-Grillet's *La jalousie* in a similar way. But Leenhardt has more fully assimilated the writings of structuralists such as Roland Barthes, Jean Ricardou and Roman Jakobson. As a result of his careful analysis of the text, his attempt to establish analogies between the text structure and the socio-economic basis of France in the 1950s distinguishes itself from other, more general studies in the field of the sociology of literature (Levin L. Schücking, 1923; Leo Lowenthal, 1957; or Robert Escarpit, 1970). But it is legitimate to question whether the Marxist framework, including the dialectical method, is an asset or rather a liability to Leenhardt. Although at many points his analysis is convincing, one may wonder whether his theory of a close analogy between the socio-economic structure and the structure of literary phenomena can explain the difference between *La jalousie* and *L'Année dernière à Marienbad,* as Leenhardt seems to believe (1973: 30). One may doubt even more whether his theory would be applicable to the fiction of Julio Cortázar or John Barth, and all those who come under the ill-coined heading of Post-Modernism (Hassan, 1975). Their work is an elation of the subjectivist spirit—in the disguise of anonymity—and can be related to reification only by way of the introduction of a false collective consciousness.

Within the Marxist tradition, the question whether a particular consciousness is true or false cannot be decided by empirical means. It is highly dependent on the class position of the people whose consciousness is discussed, as well as on the current teleological interpretation of their social conditions. Here we are back where we were at the beginning of this chapter. If one does not subscribe to the Marxist teleology and its paraphernalia (the correct interpretation of the political situation by the correct Party), one simply cannot decide whether a particular consciousness is true or false. The discussion between the Marxists Bloch and Lukács on the question whether Expressionism and Surrealism reflected a true or a false consciousness provides a convincing example. It cannot be stated clearly enough that in the Soviet Union this particular issue was decided in favour of Lukács, only because his position was supported by the guardian of unfailing truth: the CPSU. We are inclined to call Party interference in such matters presumptuous and authoritarian. Once such a decision has been taken by the Party, it can no longer be criticized, at least not in the communist countries. That situation is incompatible with the tradition of scientific research which adheres to the principle that it should be possible to check any proposition and to discuss and, if necessary, criticize any argumentation.

Criticism of the arguments presented by the neo-Marxists, who accept neither the unfailing authority of the Communist Party nor the infallibility of Marx and Engels, is also gravely hampered. Here it is epistemological rather than political obstacles that prevent an open-minded discussion. However liberal or tolerant they may be, all Marxist and neo-Marxist thinkers—if the epithet is to mean anything at all—accept the dialectical method. It is quite significant that one of the most sophisticated neo-Marxist critics, Theodor W. Adorno, defended the dialectical method against Karl R. Popper's criticism. Their polemic was printed under the title *Der Positivismusstreit in der deutschen Soziologie* (Adorno, 1969).

Although this epistemological discussion has a more general significance and does not apply to literary theory alone, its main themes may be recalled here because of their bearing on Marxist literary theory. Adorno argues as follows:

1. The dialectical method may provide an insight into the totality of society and prevents the artificial isolation of facts and problems. Apart from the matter investigated, it will draw attention to its counterpart. Apart from the scientific problem, it will also study its social context. Besides an investigation of the object it will necessitate an examination of the subject's position in society. In addition to the static moment of observation, it will focus on the historical context of the observed phenomena and their expected future development. *The object of the dialectical method has no limits.* Rather bluntly Adorno declares: "Society is one."[65] Jürgen Habermas explained that Adorno conceives society as a totality in the strictly dialectical sense of the word (Adorno, 1969: 155).

2. The dialectical method is oriented towards the relation between the general and the individual in their historical concretion (Adorno, 1969: 91). This historical concretion is the embedding of any phenomenon in the historical context which has not only a past but also a future. To Adorno, *the future is not open, but determined by a postulated goal (Sinn)* that directs man, society and history. The teleological aspect of his philosophy appears from his view that things have an inherent destination. Science, in his opinion, must uncover the truth or falsity of that which the phenomenon under examination "wants to be".[66] Therefore, according to Adorno, science must be critical *(kritisch)* in the sense of being related or even submitted to a political goal (Adorno, 1969: 97). The same way of thinking transpires when Benjamin warns his readers that a particular scientific observation is progressive (Benjamin, 1936: 11) or not (ibid.: 59), whereas he neglects the question whether these observations are true or false. It is not necessary to show that Adorno's political aims coincide with those of Marxism in order to see the detrimental effect of a political prejudice upon scientific investigations.

3. The teleological aspect relies on the postulated distinction between an apparent *(scheinbar)* and an essential *(wesentlich)* truth. Adorno's dialectics, in fact, attributes a double identity to the subject, who can be split up into one with higher intentions (true consciousness) and one with lower intentions (false consciousness), not unlike the conception of Freud, whom Adorno approvingly cites in a somewhat different context (1969: 96). Only the appearance of phenomena is accessible to empirical investigations;

their outcome may be incompatible with essential truth. In accordance with recent Soviet philosophy, [67] Adorno *postulates a totality which escapes empirical investigation but still yields essential truth* (1969: 93).

4. Rejecting the isolation of problems, Adorno also *rejects the distinction between theory and practice, between object language and metalanguage, and between observed facts and attributed values.* He implies that the subject must become conscious of its own position in society. Habermas saw a role here for hermeneutics (Adorno, (1969: 158). So did Fredric Jameson in his confusing book *Marxism and Form* (1971). Jameson, himself in favour of the dialectical method, brought it to its logical conclusion, namely its self-destruction. He describes dialectical thought as tautological, "tautological in the ontological sense, as part of a dawning realization of the profound tautology of all thought". In the end, "the very act of thinking dissolves away. Here the identity is not that between two words or two concepts, but rather between subject and object itself, between the process of thinking and the very reality on which it is exercised, which it attempts to apprehend" (Jameson, 1971: 341–2).

In fact, the student of Marxist criticism must choose between this high-sounding mystique and the more down-to-earth critical rationalism based on explicit rules that can be checked by anyone, and of which Popper, in answer to Adorno, provided a brief synopsis (Adorno, 1969: 103–25).

Let us recall briefly here that (1) Popper, in his claim that the object of any scientific examination should be clearly delineated, did not deny the complexity of the world as a whole. On the contrary, in his view the world is too complex to be grasped within one single question. (2) In rejecting the teleological aspect of Adorno's epistemology, Popper did not exclude the possibility that we may acquire some knowledge about the future. He only objected to a determinism of which the origin is obscure, if not metaphysical. (3) Of course, Popper's claim that all scientific propositions should be falsifiable prevents him from accepting Adorno's postulate of a totality that escapes empirical investigation. (4) Finally, Popper can not do without the distinction between theory and practice, or between metalanguage and object language. He attempts to eliminate subjectivism and projects the principle of objectivity into the scientific tradition, whereas Adorno includes the subjectivity of the scientist in his epistemology. It is not a simplification to say that the dialectical method as explained by Adorno is incompatible with Popper's critical rationalism.

In conclusion, it must be emphasized that the Marxist attempt to analyse the world in its totality and to relate to each other the various series of experience and knowledge—more or less as Tynjanov and Jakobson (1928) proposed to do within the structuralist framework—, is in itself a legitimate and valuable undertaking. But in the study of the relation between literature and society, between ideology and the economic basis, the postulate that *ultimately* the economic basis determines the developments in the other series, is a severe handicap to open-minded research. Engels' postulate[68] may serve as a criterion to distinguish Marxists and neo-Marxists on the one hand from non-Marxist thinkers on the other hand.

Critical rationalism and all scientific traditions that depart from the Marxist model have been accused of promoting conservatism. There is no basis for the accusation. In fact, as many politicians know, political action should be based on the outcome of neutral research rather than on the biased results of "progressive" analyses, coloured by a particular political view. In order to make revolution with a chance of success, one must first know the facts, as far as one can know them. A scientific tradition that aims at objectivity serves anyone who wants to improve the world. The Marxist tradition, which has abandoned even the intention to heed objectivity in the sense of being open to criticism, is a liability rather than an asset to those who wish to change the world.

This applies also to the dialectical method. In our view there are more direct ways of analysis and knowledge than the dialectical method. Unwittingly Lukács revealed the unfalsifiable nature of dialectical propositions. In his view, "dialectics denies that plainly one-sided causal relations exist anywhere in the world"; even the simplest phenomena are characterized by complex interactions of cause and consequence.[69] So far the dialecticians have failed to show the superiority of their system. Their studies lack the explicitness and precision necessary to continue the debate on literature and society started by highly gifted men who, however, did not succeed in shaking off the burden of dialectics.

5

THE RECEPTION OF LITERATURE: THEORY AND PRACTICE OF "REZEPTIONSÄSTHETIK"

Occasionally reservations have been expressed concerning reception theory. René Wellek, for instance, argued that the survival of literary works, their effect and influence, have always been studied and that the present energetic preoccupation with reception is merely a passing fad (Wellek, 1973: 515–17).

One could counter this criticism with a variety of detailed methodological objections. The following argument, however, might be the decisive one. In the explanation of certain literary facts reception has certainly played a long-standing role, and the knowledge acquired in this way is also thoroughly compatible with contemporary reception theory; what is fundamentally different, however, is the level of abstraction on which reception has been discussed since the 1960s. The recipient has become an integral part of the purpose of literary research, and reception is integrated into the possible definition of literariness. "The object [of literary studies] is created by means of the 'perspective', which is thereby a 'factor' of the structure of the object" (Stempel, 1972: xlv).

A simplified survey of the development of literary research yields the following profile. In positivism the historicity of the object (the texts) was postulated. The historicity of the researcher, on the other hand, was expected to be completely submerged by his "objectivity". In the subsequent reactions of the *geisteswissenschaftliche Methode* and the intrinsic approach, the object was seen primarily as an a-historically constant entity to which an a-historically constant researcher corresponded. From the perspective of reception theory, the facts are reinstated into their historicity, and the historicity of the researcher is acknowledged as well. The researcher/object relationship, coming to expression in the three stages just mentioned, corresponds to a conception of the literary work as *document*, as *monument*, and as *sign* or "*appeal structure*" (*Appellstruktur*).[1] Today we are discovering that the reception-oriented view was already in the offing well before the term *Rezeptionsästhetik* was coined. Russian Formalism played an important role in this respect. However, the orientation towards the reception of literature did not occupy a dominant position in the main publications of the Russian Formalists.

Innumerable attempts to determine "literariness" on the basis of certain characteristics of language have proved inadequate. The results gleaned from linguistics provided no exhaustive definition of the phenomenon of literature, since they offered no possibility of including historicity and value judgement in their theory. A theory of literature cannot, however, lack either of these two aspects.

Theoretical Discussion

Various recent studies on the foundations of literary research include reception in their attempts to determine literariness. Thus Jurij M. Lotman states: "The historical and cultural reality which we call the 'literary work' is not exhausted in the text. The text is only one of the elements of a relation. In fact, the literary work consists of the text (the system of intra-textual relations) in its relation to extra-textual reality: to literary norms, tradition and the imagination" (Lotman, 1972b: 180). And Siegfried J. Schmidt maintains: "Reception [therefore] occurs as a process creating meaning, which realizes the instructions given in the linguistic appearance of the text" (Schmidt, 1973: 28–9).

Accordingly, the object of literary research appears to be not the text but its concretization, not the artefact but the aesthetic object (Mukařovský). Literary research with an orientation toward reception theory will still have to devote itself to textual analysis, and in that respect it will be indebted to linguistics. But, due to its focus on the receiver (who may coincide with the researcher), it will also have to come to terms with methodological problems of modern historiography, of hermeneutics and of structuralism. It cannot avoid discussing problems of historical and cultural relativity, taking a stand on the questions of understanding and the "fusion of horizons", and pondering to what extent the investigation of internal relations, as preferred by structuralism, still offers the possibility of emerging from the limitations of a closed system. Is structuralism to be condemned because, in the words of Paul Ricoeur, it means "working on a corpus already constituted, fixed, closed, and in this sense dead" (Ricoeur, 1967: 801)? Or does the study of the differential relations of the elements of a system enable us to place this system, in turn, in relation to other systems and to open it? The most important opening would be that to diachronic studies. Will the category of the system of relations, the most important organizing principle which structuralism has to offer, suffice to overcome the essentialism inherent in an a-temporal, a-historical way of thinking on the one hand, and on the other to replace the favourite category of historicism, i.e. genetic causality?

Reception theory allows for historical and cultural relativism, since it is fundamentally convinced of the mutability of an object, also of the literary work, within the historical process. Nevertheless it does not for that reason amount to a relapse into the historicism of the nineteenth century. It differs from that historicism in its renunciation of value-free research. The scholar's own epoch is not disqualified in favour of an attitude which prescribes that he creep into the skin of an author of the past. One's own epoch is an essential element in the constitution of the aesthetic object, if only because it decides which works from the past survive as literature. This decision can deviate substantially from one made at the time when the work in question was composed. The differential relation of the past epoch to one's own reveals shifts which give insight into the historical process. On the other hand, the element of historical relativism in reception theory prevents the indiscriminate appropriation of works from the past, an activity which—supported by the postulate of the complete fusion of horizons—in the final analysis leads to the designation of timelessness as the essential characteristic of literature. For Hans Robert Jauss it is the critical withdrawal from two opposite positions which is achieved by the aesthetics of reception: first, the withdrawal from historical objectivism, as it was represented in historical research by Ranke, and secondly, from "classicism", i.e. from a conception of literature which maintains the timeless presence of great literary works, as becomes evident in the publications of Gadamer in spite of his intensive treatment of the historical aspect (Jauss, 1970: 231).

A lack of reflection about one's own historically conditioned perspective characterizes the historical objectivism of the nineteenth century:

The route taken by literary history and art history in the nineteenth century can be characterized by the progressive renunciation of all claims to its own historical knowledge. Under historicism, which accompanied the historical view of ancient and modern art as a new paradigm of historical experience, the historiography of art gradually surrendered its legitimacy as a medium of reflection for aesthetics, philosophy of history, or hermeneutics (Jauss, 1970: 215).

Just how this development finally took another turn Jauss illustrates with the example of Droysen's polemic against Ranke. Droysen's contribution consists in his "reclaiming for the historical fact its event character, which has the openness of the horizon of meaning in common with the event character of the work of art" (Jauss, 1970: 217). A historical objectivism, as rigorous as that of the nineteenth century, today finds its limits and relativization in the openness of the future. In this respect Jauss quotes the analytic philosopher A. C. Danto: "Our knowledge of the past is significantly limited by our ignorance of the future" (Jauss, 1970: 228). The historian Karl-Georg Faber shares Danto's view of the provisional character of scientific knowledge. The study of history is a study of experience which "is retrospective and changes with additional knowledge". For this reason it is incapable of offering definitive statements about the totality of history (Faber, 1971: 22). For Faber "quantitative increase", i.e. the fact that every moment adds new events to the past, means that there is at the same time a "qualitative change in the sum total of the past". He concludes from this that it is necessary for each generation to rewrite history: "The bit of the past which is added each time always includes effects or—if it contains an important caesura—the obliteration of effects from an earlier past. Since the scholarly assessment of a past event must include the effects produced by the event, and since the historian can describe the resultant effects only up to his own time, it is valid to say that every generation must write history anew" (Faber, 1971: 39).

The process of quantitative increase which Faber sketches is also true in all its ramifications for the situation of literary history in which every moment can bring a new work. With the inclusion of the study of effect in scholarly work, a new and distinct rapprochement comes about between general history and literary history. This approach eliminates the commonly assumed difference between, on the one hand, the closed event of history and, on the other, the literary work which is by contrast always accessible for a new actualization. In his essay "Literaturgeschichte als Provokation der Literaturwissenschaft" (1967) Jauss made this difference his point of departure. In "Geschichte der Kunst und Historie" (in Jauss, 1970), however, he claims to see an extensive analogy between the historical event and the work of art of the past, since "every change creates a 'new' and a 'more', which the work of art can also actually accomplish with each new and individual manifestation."[2]

The general concept of the definite character of past events is valid for art as well as for history. That which is written is definite. This one pole in the relation between the literary fact and its effect is also the point of departure for literary research. The possible nuances between the definite entities of history and literature do not suffice to maintain a fundamental difference.

The opposite position, which considers the work of art freed from historicity in its timelessness, is countered by Jauss with a demythologized concept of tradition: "Tradition is incapable of perpetuating itself. It presupposes reception [. . .]. Even the classical models are present only where they are received" (Jauss, 1970: 234). Jauss connects the "timeless question" which a classical text is supposed to ask its reader with the interest of the respective readers. "For whether an old and supposedly timeless question still or again concerns us, while we are indifferent to innumerable other questions, is in the last analysis always determined by an interest which arises from the present situation" (Jauss, 1970: 235).

If the preceding discussion of the questions of hermeneutics is to be relevant for reception theory, it must be noted that we are proceeding from a concept of hermeneutics which has left behind certain premises of traditional hermeneutics. First of all, it is no longer encumbered by the postulate of a hermeneutic method of its own for the humanities, a method which, it must be assumed, had to be irreconcilably at odds with the natural sciences. We are proceeding from a global methodological unity of the empirical sciences, as it is understood by the philosophers of science Popper, Albert, Nagel, Hempel and others. The methodological unity extends to the process of the finding and testing of hypotheses—a process which can be applied just as well in the determination of a context of meaning (which is at stake in the case of written texts), as it can be applied to the phenomena of the natural sciences. It is to Heide Göttner's credit that she has reduced the phenomena which appear peculiar to the humanities to the common denominator of formulating hypotheses.

It is easy to see that the various metaphorical expressions such as *"das Ganze"* of Schleiermacher, *"das Allgemeine"* of Dilthey, *"der Vorentwurf"* of Gadamer and *"das stimmige Gefühl"* of Staiger all intend something very definite and very simple, namely hypothetical statements or complexes of statements which are made by the literary scholar about the text under investigation and which express something about its context of meaning as a whole. Whether they prove correct is subsequently tested against the particulars of the text (Göttner, 1973: 135).

In this quotation Göttner describes the first phase of the scientific process, a process for which she assumes three successive steps: first the psychological one of hypothesis discovery, then the logical-deductive one of systematizing the hypothesis, and finally the inductive step of testing the hypothesis. Göttner shows by illustration that literary research proceeds through all three phases by means of an example of interpretation from the field of medieval German literature. She admits that the way of reasoning peculiar to literary scholarship results in a complicated process of verification, but this need not lead to the conclusion of a fundamental untestability (Göttner, 1973: 60). Göttner criticizes the hermeneutic circle, which seems to separate the humanities from the natural sciences like an unbridgeable gap, and shows that this concept is inaccurate. Only the *logical* circle is meaningful in scientific language. Göttner does not accept the learning process, taking place in the researcher before and during hypothesis formation, as a hermeneutic circle. "This continual to and fro in the practical process of research [. . .] is what the hermeneuticists describe as a circle." To her it appears extremely doubtful whether this is even an instance of a psychological kind of circle, "for the researcher moves forward in the learning process and does not keep turning in circles" (Göttner, 1973: 154).

The concept of objectivity, which earlier hermeneutics to a large extent excluded from the domain of humanities research, finds a new entrée into this field of study as soon as one is prepared to recognize that the process of finding and testing hypotheses can be applied here. The concept of methodological objectivity in the sense of an intersubjective testability has a place here. This methodological objectivism has nothing to do with the historical objectivism that was criticized from the hermeneutic position.

In the same way the process of explanation plays a role in the range of procedures of scientific activity. Explanation and prognosis are not restricted to the natural sciences.[3] The "empathy" evoked by a confrontation with a text, the "imitation of inner mental activity" with the help of the "divinatory method" (Schleiermacher), "empathy with alien states of mind" (Dilthey), and the "intuitive harmony of the double conscious-ness" (Genette) can certainly no longer be considered the goal of research in the humanities. On the contrary, it is a matter of comprehending the "hermeneutic difference between the previous and the present understanding of a work" (Jauss, 1970: 183). The concept of hermeneutic difference is the most important concept which can be transposed from traditional hermeneutics into the new variant. It is indispensable for reception theory, and is in fact one of its fundamental concepts. To obtain the hermeneutic difference— which could perhaps be better designated by the more neutral term of historical distance—it is not necessary to apply a method which is special to the humanities and fundamentally at variance with the natural sciences. The description and explanation of historical distance can be accomplished with the means of the empirical sciences. It is not a matter of "one-dimensional understanding", but of "making that which is understood open to comparison and thus open to criticism" (Hogrebe, 1971: 285). The latter is one of the main tasks of the *history* of reception, which is one of the most important areas of the more comprehensive theory of reception. An identification of the subject and object of knowledge would compromise historical research, just as it compromises all scientific research. To counter that a strict separation of the subject and object of knowledge is unattainable is of no avail, especially since this limitation also holds for the natural sciences. To give up *striving for* such a separation amounts to giving up all scientific exploration.

A hermeneutics understood in the sense indicated above will not prove to be irreconcilable with a structuralist method of thinking. The two were assumed to be incompatible because hermeneutic criticism was ostensibly a creative activity, whereas structuralist criticism achieved only an intelligible reconstruction (Genette, 1965: 369). But, as we have pointed out, the hermeneutic difference cannot be disclosed without an "intelligible reconstruction".

The structuralist tradition offers the concept of "relation" as a central concept for the theory of reception. Structuralism as a method of thinking, as a "noetic standpoint" (Mukařovský), starts from the assumption that a phenomenon cannot be described in isolation but only with the help of relations in which it is embedded.[4]

Also in its historical orientation, reception theory studies relations, not origins; i.e. it first attempts to recognize synchronic systems and subsequently compares them with each other. In this way work can proceed from the synchronic to the diachronic dimension by means of what Jauss calls "synchronic cross-sections"; the history of reception is certainly no history of origins.

The relational system of various elements (of a phonological, lexical, syntactic or thematic kind) of a text is the (synchronic) point of departure for research in reception theory. Ricoeur, who takes a critical stance regarding the structuralist method, speaks in this connection of an "autonomous entity comprising internal dependences", to which he wishes to oppose "the act, the choice, the subject" (Ricoeur, 1967: 807).

For the literary text as it is finalized in writing or in print Jan Mukařovský chose the term "artefact".[5] The complementary concept to "artefact" is for Mukařovský the "aesthetic object":

The artefact is the materially given symbol of meaning, the aesthetic object is the meaning correlate of the artefact in the collective consciousness of the readers. The artefact, unchanging in its structure, is of course the source of the meaning which the reader must constitute, the point of departure for all concretizations of the work by its recipients; and yet the work in its totality cannot be reduced to the artefact. Since it is concretized against the background of fluctuating systems of aesthetic norms, the structure of the aesthetic object is continually shifting as well (Günther, 1971a: 188).[6]

The theory of reception, even though it is interested in the aesthetic object, focusses on the artefact as the point of departure for all concretizations. The aesthetic object, as the point where the artefact and the reader meet, is variable. When the reader's respective systems of norms encounter a text, structuralist methods can describe the varying relations which display something other than "successive immobilities", as Sartre—proceeding from other presuppositions than Ricoeur, but with similar critical intentions—describes it.[7]

Hans Günther proposes the concept "dynamic structuralism' for a structuralism which includes in its investigation not only the closed individual work, but the system of norms of the reader as well. Contrasted with this is the earlier "model structuralism", in which the concept of structure was drawn predominantly from phonology (Günther, 1971a: 189). Dynamic structuralism, as represented by the Czech scholars Mukařovský and Vodička and advocated also outside the study of literature,[8] has succeeded in elaborating some basic postulates for the theory of reception and has thereby bridged the gap between synchronic and diachronic studies. "The work of art manifests itself as sign in its inner structure, in its relation to reality, and also in its relation to society, to its creator and its recipients" (quoted by Günther, 1971b: 226). This statement by Mukařovský could be considered the shortest formulation of the programme of reception theory, from which its basic concepts and its field of research can be derived.

This programme is *structuralist* by virtue of its concept of relation, which is "rather a sign than a causality" (Mukařovský, 1967: 22). It is *semiotic* in its application of the sign concept and in its recognition of a plurality of codes,[9] which allows it to take into account "meanings in varying systems on the basis of varying forms of representation" (Wienold, 1972: 22). Mukařovský's programme is *historical* by virtue of the historical locus of the recipient. This diverges from Roman Ingarden, who grants an important place to the recipient and yet proceeds from an ideal recipient who is as little embedded in history as possible. Mukařovský historicizes Ingarden's approach (Jauss, 1970: 247). Ingarden, who inquires into the adequateness of concretizations, cannot acknowledge a concept as variable as Mukařovský's aesthetic object.

The warning of Sartre—who showed himself to be violently opposed to structuralism in his discussion of Lévi-Strauss—against the idea of successive immobilities is unwarranted as far as Mukařovský's concept of structure is concerned. This becomes evident when Mukařovský, following Tynjanov, places the various structures in relation to each other: "In the history and theory of literature and art, for example, we must view not only the internal artistic form and its development as a structure, but also the relation of this structure to other phenomena, especially of a psychological or social nature" (Mukařovský, 1967: 12). By this route he arrives at a "structural reciprocity", whereby the relations of the individual series unite in a structure of a higher order. The historical dimension then results from the "continual regrouping of reciprocal relations and from the relative importance of the individual elements" (Mukařovský, 1967: 14).

Mukařovský goes one step further and inquires into the motivation for the regroupings and changes, and in so doing he considers an external impetus (social developments and the like) as entirely within the realm of possibility. He does not exclude an interest in causality. Prerequisite for this, however, is the analysis of dominants and transformations within a system.

Jauss cites Mukařovský and Vodička when he sets out to connect structuralist and historical thought. In his view, "structure and process" are not mutually exclusive, but rather complementary concepts: "Consequently, Prague structuralism understands the structure of the work as being a constituent part of the higher structure of literary history, and this in turn as being a process which arises out of the dynamic tension between work and norm, the tension between the historical series of literary works and the series of changing norms or attitudes of the public" (Jauss, 1970: 247).

The structuralist basis helps remove the random character of reception studies, and it can do this for the reason which Günther Schiwy spells out as follows: "Regardless of how the matter stands 'in reality', the structuralist imposes definite limits on his object, even if he has to do that artificially and forcibly (not arbitrarily). It pays off in clear structural rules and describable functions" (Schiwy, 1971: 160). When the theory of reception must rely on cooperative work with other disciplines—and without this cooperation it will hardly be able to master its field—, the structuralist method, with its broad inquiries into the relation and function of parts in the whole, could provide the various disciplines with comparable descriptions. One could speak of a "unification of scientific activities", as Götz Wienold formulates it for semiotics (Wienold, 1972: 14).[10] Without the limits which the structuralist method imposes on those committed to it, reception studies run the risk of infinite expansion. Then it will hardly be able to refute the criticism of Fügen, who maintains that "it is precisely the individualizing procedure which makes studies of this kind seem so random and impressionistic" (Fügen, 1964: 28). Reception studies can be launched on such a broad basis that they cannot be finished unless one limits the goal of one's research. The reply to Fügen's objection we can take from Vodička: "The aim of knowledge cannot consist of all possible concretizations by the individual readers, but of those which display a confrontation between the structure of the work and the structure of the prevailing norms" (quoted by Jauss, 1970: 248).

Theorists of reception exhibit varying degrees of indebtedness to the three fields we have mentioned—history, hermeneutics and structuralism. Although these fields are interrelated in reception theory, the emphases on them vary. If we say that the basis for Mukařovský's theory is to a pronounced extent structuralist and that Jauss appears as the historian, then Wolfgang Iser could be considered the hermeneuticist of reception theory.

Following the lead of Ingarden and Mukařovský, Iser postulates the distinctive features of literature as the absence of an exact correlation between the phenomena described in literary texts and the objects in the world of "real life", and, as a result of this, the impossibility of testing. "At this point", Iser concludes, "there arises a certain amount of indeterminacy which is peculiar to all literary texts, for they permit no referral to any identical real-life situation" (Iser, 1970: 11; cf. also Iser, 1971). It is this quality peculiar to the literary text which the reader encounters with his individual experience. Two possibilities for "normalizing" the indeterminacy are open to him: either he projects his own standards into the text, or he is prepared to revise his own preconceptions (Iser, 1970: 13). The literary text is "open". Or, in Iser's words, "fictional texts are not identical with real situations. They have no exact counterpart in reality. In this respect they could almost be called unsituated, in spite of the historical substratum which accompanies them. And yet it is precisely this openness which makes them capable of shaping the various situations which are completed by the reader in his individual readings. The openness of fictional texts can be eliminated only in the act of reading." Only in the act of reading can indeterminacy be replaced by meaning (Iser, 1970: 34-5).

With regard to Iser's concept of indeterminacy, we shall restrict ourselves to the above-mentioned aspect of the absence of an exact counterpart in reality as a characteristic of literary texts. Iser uses the term indeterminacy in other senses also, e.g. to designate parts of individual texts which are only partly formulated or to describe the thematic indeterminacy of modern literature.

In general, Jauss shares Iser's conception of indeterminacy, of openness and fundamentally inconclusive meaning, as we have already seen. But Jauss handles the concept of indeterminacy in a different way. In his view indeterminacy is the condition for the varying constitutions of meaning in the course of history. This conception comes closest to that suggested by Hannelore Link. She conceives of openness or indeterminacy not as a characteristic of texts, but rather as a characteristic of their history (Link, 1973: 563). Jauss views indeterminacy not so much in individual as in historical-collective terms. The point in Jauss's text which leads us to this conclusion does not, however, refer to Iser but to Roland Barthes and his concept of *critique,* which describes the individual relation between reader and text. On the topic of legitimized subjectivity Iser does not differ from Barthes, whereas Jauss asks whether this subjectivity "or series of interpretations of a work is not itself once again 'institutionalized' by history, and whether, therefore, it cannot form a system in its historical sequence" (Jauss, 1970: 239). He admits that the open structure, characterized by indeterminacy, makes new interpretations continually possible. But on the other hand he maintains that limits are placed on the sheer arbitrariness of interpretations by the historical conditions of question and answer (Jauss, 1970: 241). The historical conditions of interpretations do not enter the picture for Iser, nor does the concretization legitimized by a literary public. In Iser's approach, the reading subject is directly confronted with the text. For this reason Hannelore Link does not consider him representative of the new, historically oriented paradigm in literary scholarship. She would count him rather as one of the older school of intrinsic interpretation (*werkimmanente Interpretation*).

In including the literary public as an object of investigation, Jauss stands in the Czech tradition. For Mukařovský the aesthetic object is defined by that "which the subjective forms of consciousness of the members of a certain collective have in common in their response to the artefact" (quoted by Kačer, 1968: 74). Vodička, too, wants to study "the development of the esthetic consciousness in so far as it has supraindividual qualities and includes within it the attitudes of the times to literary art" (Vodička, 1964: 71). He explicitly excludes from reception studies the subjective elements of evaluation dependent on the momentary attitudes of the reader and his personal preferences. The structuralist point of departure of Mukařovský and Vodička demands a higher degree of historical generalization than the hermeneutic-phenomenological standpoint of Iser. "The object of our cognition are those features which have the character of historic generalities," says Vodička. His concern, ultimately, is to place two structures in relation to each other, one being "the literary norm in its historical development" and the other "the development of the literary structure itself" (ibid.).

The Czechs also regard the specific character of the literary text as the basis of reception. Mukařovský postulates for the literary text a peculiar relation to the referent, which he describes as follows: "The communicative relation between the work of art and the referent has no existential significance, not even in those cases in which this relation maintains or affirms something" (Mukařovský, 1970: 143). Documentary authenticity cannot be demanded for the subject-matter of a work of art. Mukařovský allows for a scale "reality-fiction" on which the relation to the referent, exhibited by the work of art, is located. The particular position on this scale is an important factor in the structure of the work of art (Mukařovský, 1970: 147).

If in the literary work the relation to the referent recedes into the background, then by way of compensation another relation moves to the foreground: the relation of the individual signs to each other. Mukařovský adds to Bühler's three language functions a fourth: the aesthetic function, which focusses attention on the properties of the sign. "The predominance of precisely this function allows the [textual] context to acquire great significance in poetry" (Mukařovský, 1967: 54). In poetry the other three functions are subordinate to the aesthetic function.[11] This is also true of the macrostructural relations of prose.

Implicit in the functional aspect is the dynamic aspect:

As soon as the work is perceived on the basis of the integration into another context (a changed linguistic state of affairs, other literary requirements, a changed social structure, a new set of spiritual and practical values), then precisely those qualities of the work can be perceived as esthetically effective which previously were not perceived as esthetically effective (Vodička, 1964: 79).

In Mukařovský's view as well, art is not a closed domain, and stabilizing the aesthetic function is a matter for the collective (Mukařovský, 1970: 29). Ingarden's standpoint, which does not assign so crucial a role to the historical–cultural situation and which does not take account of the functional aspect, is left farther behind by the Czech representatives of reception theory than by Iser.

Like Jauss (and unlike Iser), Karl Robert Mandelkow opens up the hermeneutic aspect to structuralism, but without using the latter term. The fundamental assumption of reception theory, namely the hermeneutic difference between a previous and a present understanding, he considers more or less common property. But he signals methodological implications "at the point where consideration of the individual phenomenon is converted into historical description of larger contexts and processes which incorporate the individual work into a supra-individual development" (Mandelkow, 1970: 77). Mandelkow then takes up Jauss's concept of the horizon of expectations. He proposes to specify this concept as "expectations regarding the period, expectations regarding the work, and expectations regarding the author". Mandelkow is aware that the differentiation of horizons does not occur in this way in the practical process of reception, but that it rather amounts to a multiplicity of overlapping horizons. Yet he proposes to use this division as a "conceptual construction" in order to disclose certain "dominants of reception". Both Mandelkow's way of conducting his studies and the concepts he employs indicate an indebtedness to the structuralist method.

The concept of the horizon of expectations (*Erwartungshorizont*) plays a central role in Jauss's theory. The reconstruction of this horizon is one of the main concerns of reception history and serves as a frame of reference for the construction of a literary system. Jauss borrows the concept from Karl Popper and Karl Mannheim, and this accounts for the specific significance associated with the term in all of Jauss's work. We are referring to the destruction of the horizon of expectations as a quality of literature. In Soviet semiotics (Lotman) we find instead of "horizon of expectations" the concept of the "cultural code", which is more neutral and not immediately associated with the idea of innovation. Thus Lotman observes two forms of artistic codes, both of equal value; he arrives at a confrontation of an "aesthetics of identity" with an "aesthetics of opposition". Jauss, on the other hand, brings the problem of value into the discussion through his notion that the reconstruction of the horizon of expectations is an aid to understanding precisely the deviating and innovating works of art. Popper makes this same point. In his essay "Natural Laws and Theoretical Systems" he argues that an "expectation" or "hypothesis" (interestingly enough, Popper here uses both concepts as equivalents) lies at the basis of all observation: "In every moment of our pre-scientific or scientific development we possess something which I usually refer to as a 'horizon of expectations' [. . .]. In every case [. . .] the horizon of expectations plays the role of a frame of reference, without which experiences, observations, etc., would have no meaning" (Popper, 1949: 46).

Popper's philosophy of science uses the concept of falsification as a central theoretical postulate. The high value he places on "expectation disappointment" fits in well with this concept: "For we become aware of many expectations only when they are disappointed—for example, when we come upon an unexpected step. (Only the unexpectedness of the step shows us that we expected an even surface.) Expectation disappointments force us to correct our expectations. The process of learning consists largely of such corrections, of the elimination of expectations" (Popper, 1949: 45).

The sociologist Mannheim is, as we mentioned, another source for Jauss's horizon of expectations. In *Man and Society in an Age of Reconstruction* (1940), Mannheim regards disturbing expectation disappointments as characteristic for a society with a highly unstable structure, and therefore as typical of our time.

Besides Popper and Mannheim, the Russian Formalists (especially their concepts of a new perception and differential quality) and the production of modern literature have also been influential for Jauss's thought. Hence his strong emphasis on deviations from the horizon of expectations.

The recognition of a specifically literary text-type is a constant for the theoreticians of reception that we have dealt with, even if they consider the criteria of definition to be variable and culturally conditioned. Therefore they can elaborate the methods which had so far been worked out for describing the structures of a work. The character of texts can "first be described in terms of formal, i.e., immanent-aesthetic categories", as Iser declares in a brief intervention (in Jauss, 1968: 722). This analytical step is usually found in the newer practical studies in reception. But since it is the effect of the structures that counts, there is also a point at which "the aesthetic immanence" must be left behind (ibid.). Reception research must do more than describe the structures of individual works. It must be able to describe which elements of the structure are actualized at a given moment within a prevailing system of literary norms; and it must be able to describe the place which a work, at the time of its appearance, occupies in the frame of reference created by the reader's expectations. This frame of reference reveals itself, according to Jauss, in the "preconception of the genre, in the forms and themes of earlier well-known works, and in the opposition of poetic and practical language" (Jauss, 1970: 173). Reception research must investigate how the position of a work changes with the appearance of new works; it must— and here reception research is to look to other disciplines—be able to explain which extraliterary historical and cultural pre-suppositions pave the way for a certain understanding of a work and for its ranking: "It must describe the effect of structures of the work which lead to a discovery of the presuppositions of understanding. As meta-interpretation it has a diagnostic character for the state of contemporary consciousness" (Iser, in Jauss, 1968: 720).

The relation of the structure of a work and its effect that we have discussed so far can be considered typical of reception theoreticians such as Jauss, Iser, Mandelkow and others, even though there are nuances in their points of view. This relation undergoes a fundamental modification in the work of Götz Wienold, mainly his *Semiotik der Literatur* (1972). He knows of no empirical validity for the text as one of the poles in literary communication. In every case it is a matter of "text use" or "text processing" (*Textverarbeitung*). The initial text as such does not enter the scene; it is always an interpreted text (*Interpretationstext*), i.e. some form of text processing with which the researcher is confronted. By text processing Wienold understands "relatively simple events such as the reception of a text through a reading by one recipient, as well as widely ramified and varying chains of events, from the reception of certain groups of texts in presentation, commentary, translation and revision, to the stimulation of relatively independent new texts by the processed text" (Wienold, 1972: 159). Wienold attempts to formalize the various kinds of text processing and brings them into a clear schematic arrangement. His approach to reception theory is more strongly process-oriented than that of the others. He is concerned not so much with the relation text-reader as with the relation reader-reader as established via a text as mediator. The consequences for literary research are as follows: "The domain of research is now no longer texts, certainly not texts in the form of books. The domain of research is the totality of the processes of text use" (Wienold, 1972: 184). Literary scholarship has to investigate the "classification of literary life into processes of text use" (Wienold, 1972: 171). Its goal is not to draw boundaries around the familiar domain of literature, but to explore the processes which led to codification, evaluation, interpretation, stabilization of meaning, canonization. Wienold sees fewer possibilities for research into the reception processes of the past than for the study of the more tangible processes of the present.

If Jauss saw the possibility of actualizing art from the past as an inherent aspect of the object of research, Wienold considers the various actualizations as forms of text processing which rely on rote learning, inclusion in anthologies, prefaces and programmes, as well as other kinds of sanctioning.

French and Italian semiotic structuralism supplied important stimuli for Wienold's thought. His own conception of sign he calls "strategic". He is interested in "how, via sign media, participants in such sign media together pursue goals and carry out purposeful actions" (Wienold, 1972: 205). But he is not interested in the relation of the sign to the referent, a relation which was traditionally very much a part of semiotic research. Out of this strategic conception of sign there arises a goal, namely "to know the conditions of text-using processes as processes of communicating about literature, to be able to test them and, if the occasion arises, to intervene in them" (Wienold, 1972: 197). Wienold finds that the teaching of literature is unusually suited to this goal, and he therefore understands his theory as a contribution to the didactics of literature.

Wienold's concept of text processing and his classification of various kinds of processing are undoubtedly an interesting contribution to reception research. As mentioned, various passages in his book leave the impression that Wienold considers the initial text (T_0), the formal invariable, the artefact, to be a fiction; and that there is no immediate structure of the work, but only structures which are imparted to the text on the basis of the "structuring capacity" of the various recipients. Although Wienold does not commit himself completely on this question, this interpretation appears to us to be justified. Renouncing the observable and describable starting-point carries with it the danger that the possibility of checking against the text is eliminated, and that the search for processes can go on without end. In our opinion Wienold justifies his renunciation of Text T_0 less as a matter of methodological necessity than as following from his intention to settle accounts once and for all with the tradition of literature as well as with the tradition of literary scholarship. He argues that the "re-evaluation of values in our literary traditions deserves to be repeated with considerable emphasis" (ibid.).

The impetus introduced by the two principal representatives of reception theory in Germany, Jauss and Iser, has found ready acceptance. The theoretical basis was elaborated further, but applied studies (which we shall discuss later) were also undertaken. A critical appraisal of Iser's standpoint was made by Hannelore Link. Her convincing, detached and constructive criticism deserves preference to the critique of Gerhard Kaiser, which is marked by an apologetic bias.

Link first explains the position of Iser within Jauss's scheme of paradigm change in literary scholarship. She concludes that Iser's approach is characterized by an interference of paradigms. On the one hand he belongs to the old paradigm—labelled by us at the outset as the "monument" conception—, and on the other hand to the new paradigm of interest in the reader's response (*Appellstruktur*). Hannelore Link deduces Iser's participation in the old paradigm from his attempt to define literary texts by means of specific characteristics, by a special ontological status, in which his concept of indeterminacy occupies the key position. Methodologically, a critical point is reached when Iser employs the criterion of indeterminacy in terms of reception aesthetics as well: the more places of indeterminacy there are in a text, the greater the participation of the reader in the actualization of meaning (Link, 1973: 539). This viewpoint makes him appear a representative of the new paradigm. But Link finds another reason for regarding Iser as belonging to the older paradigm in his practice of interpretation. As an interpreter,[12] Iser relies primarily on the potential meaning embedded in the text. As a theoretician, he assigns a crucial role to the reader and his imagination (Link, 1973: 548). In this connection it is also important that Iser's reader (the "implicit" reader!), as well as the places of indeterminacy, are in the first place characteristics of the text.

We described Hannelore Link's criticism as constructive, convinced as we are that the semiotic basis which she proposes for the new paradigm is useful for the development of reception aesthetics. In contrast to the over-emphasis on the role of the reader, a semiotic theory of communication offers the possibility of including the sender code in the investigations and of confronting it with the receiver code. The resistance to attrition by the course of time, characteristic of literary works, can be explained on the basis of communication theory. Communication can take place "as long as the two codes are not completely dissociated" (Link, 1973: 558). Once the sender code is reconstructed, Link sees the task of reception history *(Wirkungsgeschichte)* as the study of the various adaptations which a work has undergone in the course of history. This implies the reconstruction of the cultural patterns of thought and reception which govern the respective adaptations. If one wants to proceed beyond description and provide explanations, then one must inquire into the relations which exist between the nature of the work and its reception (Link, 1973: 562).

Link's semiotic approach leaves room for an examination of the nature of the text or sign carrier, and avoids the danger that discrepancies arise between theory and practice, as they do in Iser's approach. Iser's neglect of the historical aspect (on the theoretical level, not in practice) causes, in our opinion, the inconsistency which Link discovers in his work. Jauss and the Czechs, as well as the Russian semioticians, took the historical factor into account right from the beginning. Link historicizes Iser's concept of indeterminacy: "Openness is not a characteristic of texts, but a characteristic of their history" (Link, 1973: 563).

The aspect of indeterminacy is also present in Iser's explanation of the incomprehensibility of certain modern literary texts. Link understands this characteristic of modern texts as the materialization of an attempt to make communication difficult. In terms of the communication model it is a strategy of the sender/author: "Iser, who admits as signifier only that which is explicitly formulated, must consider indeterminacy (that which is not explicitly in a text) as the signified, resulting from the formal nature of the text. In our argumentation, however, indeterminacy is itself, as a conscious strategy of the author, a signifier, of which the signified is to be determined by interpretation" (Link, 1973: 577).

Link chooses the term "apparent indeterminacy" for the indeterminacy which Iser calls a specific characteristic of literary texts. She views this indeterminacy as a "universal of communication theory", which is therefore also true of literary communication (Link, 1973: 580). Behind her suggestion lies the notion that this kind of indeterminacy is in principle capable of being transformed into determinacy by reconstructing the sender code.

The interesting question whether Iser should belong to the older or the newer paradigm might be answered in a more oblique way. The interferences in Iser's work, as signalled by Link, perhaps indicate that paradigm change, in the sense of a revolutionary change of conceptual models, is really an extremely rare phenomenon in literary research—if it occurs at all. Therefore, within an assumed continuity of scholarly tradition a shift in perspective, as we find it in Iser's concept of *Appellstruktur*, is really of great significance.

It is noteworthy that Jauss himself in one of his more recent publications does not in any way call upon the methodology of reception aesthetics to provide a new paradigm, even though this could have been expected on the basis of the intense interest which this method aroused. After Jauss's approach had triggered off criticism regarding not only questions of detail but also his political position (for Marxist literary scholars his theory was disappointingly traditional, for the bourgeois it was suspiciously progressive), Jauss contrasts the all-embracing claims of both idealistic and materialistic theory with the "partiality" of reception aesthetics: "The aesthetics of reception is not an autonomous, axiomatic discipline, sufficient to solve its own problems; rather, it is a partial reflection on method which is open to additions and dependent on cooperation with other disciplines" (Jauss, 1973: 31).

Jauss then goes into some points of his theory which he himself recognized as weaknesses and in need of correction. He considers his concept of tradition, which he simply equated with reception or assimilation of the past, one of these weaknesses. Since it is necessary, however, to distinguish between conscious adaptation and passive assimilation (latent institutionalization), Jauss proposes to introduce selection as a condition of tradition: "Tradition presupposes *selection*, whenever the effect of past art becomes recognizable in contemporary reception" (Jauss, 1973: 37).

Jauss introduces one more supplementary concept, that of actualization, i.e. "the reflected mediation of past and present meaning". Prerequisite for this is the analysis of the process which takes place between the received work and the receiving consciousness (Jauss, 1973: 39). As an example of such a process he cites four historical concretizations of Goethe's *Iphigenie*, of which the harmonizing one is the decisive one, assimilated by modern consciousness; in that way the possible "emancipatory" concretization is removed from consideration.

Further he elaborates on the criticism of his "horizon of expectations". This criticism was mainly directed against the lack of sociological differentiation in the concept, its intraliterary character and its emphasis on the destruction of norms. Jauss admits the possibility of sociological differentiation, but holds firmly to the peculiarity of aesthetic experience which, precisely through this peculiarity, is capable of influencing social life. This idea also places him very close to Mukařovský.

Methodologically speaking, Jauss's concept was less vulnerable than Iser's but due to the aspect of value included in it from the outset (our possible present interest in past art is a question of value), it had to reckon with an ideological discussion.

After these methodological expositions of constants and variables in reception study, we propose to make a short critical survey of "applied" reception theory. In this connection we shall consider only those analytical studies of reception which include reflections on methodology in the sense described above. Of course, there are in addition a number of analyses of reception which contain indispensable material in their investigations of survival and influence, but which make no reference to the problems of reception theory, partly because they antedate the present discussion focussed on reception.

Our selection is made along the following lines. There should be one example of an *historical* study of reception. Further, there should be an *empirical* analysis of the reception of a contemporary text, to be contrasted with a study, also of a contemporary work, which postulates an *implicit reader*. Finally we shall deal with an essay that delves into *political and social* questions.

Historical Study of Reception

In Germany it is in particular scholars in Konstanz *(Konstanzer Schule)* who have concerned themselves with the practical application of Jauss's theory. They have published parts of their results in the series entitled *Poetik und Hermeneutik*. The title of the series indicates their orientation towards both the structures of the literary work and the conditions for understanding it. We shall draw our examples from the 1971 volume entitled *Terror und Spiel: Probleme der Mythenrezeption*. The theme of the conference of which the papers and discussions were compiled in that volume is exemplary for *Rezeptionsgeschichte*. The topic of the conference can best be put in Fuhrmann's words, who asks in his introduction: "What is the function, what is the reality [. . .] of the 'mythical' in no-longer-mythical times?" Thus the focus is on the function of myth rather than on the traditional question about the origin of myths. The opposition myth versus non-mythical times is the common denominator of the volume, and from it several other oppositions are derived. Myth is seen in opposition to dogma (H. Blumenberg), with the freedom of myth appearing as the anti-dogmatic impulse. Myth stands in opposition to allegory (H. R. Jauss); Jauss speaks of the allegorical reduction of the mythical. Another opposition is myth versus aesthetics, in which case we are dealing with the use of traditional myths for purely aesthetic purposes devoid of mythical intention. A possible opposition is that between the creation of new myths and the reactualization of old myths. Furthermore, classical myths enter an oppositional relationship with Christian myth; and, as a general opposition, repetition stands in a reciprocal relation to variation.

The binary oppositions listed here indicate that in various contributions to this volume the structuralist method is linked with the historical problem. No attempt is made to deal exhaustively with individual facts; rather they are described and analysed in terms of their reciprocal relations. Change is seen as a result of changed relations. Striedter illustrates this in his contribution on the 'new myth' of revolution as exemplified in the poetry of Majakovskij. Here he describes the process of reception as follows:

> Such transfers of a mytheme from one system to another are both reductions and generalizations of its traditional potential for meaning. The first reduction occurs already at the moment it is lifted out of the canon of the 'old myth' (Christ no longer as an inseparable part of the triune God, but as a separate figure). Within the many remaining possibilities for meaning, a concentration takes place, focussing on those meanings which are crucial for the transfer into the new system (Striedter, 1971: 415).

Striedter attempts to understand the diachronic change of myth structures by tracing the transposition of Christ "from the religious-metaphysical world of ideas into that of a secular and social-political revolution".

The contributions to the volume on myth would have gained in methodological clarity if use had been made throughout of a structuralist-semiotic terminology, which Striedter indeed uses to a large extent. Because of the lack of such a common terminology, the volume as a whole is less unified than might appear in our short presentation. Our summary, including the emphasis on binary oppositions, will create the impression of a consistency which the reader will hardly be able to find.

Empirical Study of Reception

Text und Rezeption (1972), a study of the reception of lyric poetry—in particular Paul Celan's "Fadensonnen"—by Werner Bauer and others, is a contemporary rather than a historical reception analysis. This difference has an important consequence: the reception analysis can be conducted on an empirical basis (by questionnaires). In this way it can take into account as large and as varied a readership as is desired. Unlike historical reception analysis, it is not primarily locked up within the literary system. Rather, it can make use of the influence of the reader's "life experience". In addition it is at every point scientifically testable (Bauer, 1972: 21). Starting from the communication model, the authors worked with the following basic theoretical concepts: $Text_1$, or the primary text, which corresponds to Mukařovský's artefact; and $Text_2$, or the metatext, which is the equivalent of Mukařovský's aesthetic object. Both the process of reception and $Text_2$, which results from this process, are conditioned by the relation between $Text_1$ and the reader's (or group of readers') syndrome of expectations at the time of reading (Bauer, 1972: 9). The components of this syndrome of expectations are: 1. linguistic experience, 2. experience in dealing with texts, especially literary texts, and 3. individual experiences (emotional, socially determined, and cultural).

The type of reader assumed by this study is not the ideal reader, not the specialist in literature, but an average reader who satisfies a few minimum requirements. "Multivalence" (*Multivalenz*) is postulated as the criterion for literariness, i.e. "a multiplicity of varying, contrasting and, to a certain degree, mutually exclusive strands of meaning in the text, which stand on an equal footing as far as their validity is concerned" (Bauer, 1972: 12). Thus we again encounter the criterion of the fundamental openness of literary texts, which we found in Iser and other critics, and which forms the basis for the concept and the process of reception. In the analysis of the reception of "Fadensonnen", diverse but not unlimited actualizations were assumed: "The real and potential components of meaning contained in Text_1 provide the reader with diverse and yet not unlimited possibilities for response and for the actualization of the text. All activating processes by the reader proceed within the framework of meaning provided by the structure of the text" (ibid.).

From the currently available corpus of reception theory the group selected Riffaterre and Jauss in order to determine their own position. From Riffaterre they chose the essay "Describing Poetic Structures: Two Approaches to Baudelaire's 'Les Chats'" (1966), in which Riffaterre critically assesses the Baudelaire study by Jakobson and Lévi-Strauss (1962). The group considers Riffaterre's essay a reception analysis as opposed to the descriptive structural analysis of the two structuralists. Whereas Jakobson and Lévi-Strauss focussed their attention on the message, Riffaterre concentrates on the response, as he believes that the reader's participation is lacking in structural analysis and that this results in an essential reduction of the text. As was explained in chapter 3, the irony of Baudelaire cannot be determined by careful analysis of the principle of equivalence: it presupposes experience in dealing with literature. Bauer and his associates follow Riffaterre's approach but they do not adopt his concept of the "superreader".[13] They have in mind the average reader from which they demand the fulfilment of "*minimal requirements* as far as *linguistic competence* and *receptive ability* are concerned" (Bauer, 1972: 21).

In contrast to Jauss, the authors intentionally restricted

themselves to a purely synchronic approach, with an eye to the multiple components of expectation which can be accounted for in this way, in particular the personal expectations of the reader (Bauer, 1972: 24). In Jauss's historical reception studies, on the other hand, the expectation determined by previous literature is the primary datum. This historical approach is dependent on an accidental and "possibly incomplete tradition", which constitutes an additional factor of imprecision (Bauer, 1972: 23).

The experiment by Bauer and his associates was conducted as follows. A poem by Paul Celan, chosen for its brevity, was given to various groups of readers who were supposed to carry out a semantic analysis, based on the one hand on free association, and on the other on decisions about semantic differentials (Osgood) given in the questionnaire. In addition, there were questions which were to test the literary experience of the reader. The following results were the most striking. In the so-called microsemantic domain there were associations which as reception constants remained unchanged across socially and educationally diverse groups. Only the subsequent processing of the verbal stimuli, which is steered affectively and subjectively (macrosemantic domain), clearly exhibited the multivalence of word and text: "During this process, in which the reader activates the area of connotations as a focus, the macrosemantic decision of the reader occurs" (Bauer, 1972: 219). It became clear that the various interpretations of the text could not be reduced to a unified scheme with universal validity. Three main clusters of interpretations could be determined: 1. evocation of images, 2. interpretation from the dynamic angle, and 3. an anthropological approach to interpretation with metaphysical components (Bauer, 1972: 217). The reader, when choosing for a certain interpretation, in general knows that there are other interpretations beside his own which are not less "correct". The concept of the horizon of expectations with respect to the literary system, important for historical reception analysis, proved relatively insignificant for contemporary work; also the reader's acquaintance or lack of acquaintance with Celan's poems hardly played a role.

The value of the reception analysis of "Fadensonnen" lies first of all in the exact limitation of its aim and in the consistent pursuit of this aim. It lies furthermore in its attempt to bring interdisciplinary cooperation into the area of literary reception. This study should prove stimulating for the didactics of literature. It is exemplary in the explication of its concepts, even though this does not, of course, exclude errors in the formulation of the questionnaire or in the recording of the semantic potential.[14]

The Implicit Reader

Another kind of reception study is the book by Georg Just (1972) on Günter Grass's *Die Blechtrommel* (Tin Drum). Common to the studies of Celan and Grass is the elimination of historical distance due to the contemporary character of the selected material. In contrast to the experiment by Bauer and associates, Just indicates immediately which element of reception is to be the focal point of his study, namely the question whether *Die Blechtrommel* arouses "critical awareness" in the reader. "Critical" here means going beyond the horizon of expectations of the reader, and refusing to affirm the social and political *status quo*. A further contrast with the analysis of the reception of "Fadensonnen" can be seen in Just's interest in discovering the "intentionality of a literary text" (Just, 1972: 2–4) rather than the factual reception which can be determined empirically.

Just draws his theoretical foundation from the works of Iser, Jauss, Schaff, Mukařovský and Šklovskij. Although he adopts Iser's concept of indeterminacy, he criticizes Iser for localizing the conditions of reception exclusively in the text, whereas "strategies can be understood only in relation to a reader's historically and sociologically determined horizon of expectations" (Just, 1972: 16, 19). The private experiences of individuals are of no consequence for this approach, but "the values which are common and specific to a certain social group permit the necessary construction of the reader's 'horizon of expectations'" (Just, 1972: 19–20).

Just criticizes Iser for neglecting the historical concreteness of the reception process and ignoring the fact that the text does not always evoke the response of the reader in the same way (Just, 1972: 21). Just considers Mukařovský's approach more useful than the phenomenological viewpoint of Iser or the hermeneutic perspective of Gadamer. But this judgement entangles him in contradictions. At the beginning he had focussed his investigation on the "intentionality" of a literary text—not at all far from Iser's position—, but by joining Mukařovský and especially by adopting his concept of the "conflict of value systems" he arrives at a position which transcends the intentionality of the text. He offers what in our opinion is an inadequate compromise: he constructs a reading public, a certain group of contemporaries of the author; this public must have at its disposal attitudes which "*a priori* are contrary to those offered by the narrative perspective" (Just, 1972: 48). Thus Just constructs his group of readers on the basis of an interpretation of *Die Blechtrommel*. He comes to the conclusion that a conflict of value systems is a factor in the structure of the novel, from which a public with "contrary" attitudes then "logically" follows. He assumes the expectational horizon of the petit bourgeois and offers to the reader who is not a petit bourgeois the solution that he feign the attitudes of the petit bourgeois during his reading (Just, 1972: 50).

An empirical basis for reader groups is lacking. In the last analysis characters from novels become readers. Consequently Just's interpretation, which is otherwise excellent, remains just as "formalistic" as that of Iser, whom Just accuses of formalism. Also his criticism of Jauss remains without consequence for his study, since there is no historical distance in the case of *Die Blechtrommel*. By way of contrast, the same criticism of Jauss was meaningful when it was made by Bauer *et al.*, since they in principle gave precedence to the empirical reader over the historical reconstruction.

Of the theoretical studies which form the basis of Just's study, most extensive and fruitful use was made of Viktor Šklovskij and Adam Schaff. As a starting point Just uses Šklovskij's idea that automatized perception means the identification of language sign and referent, or at least "repressing the awareness of the ever-present discrepancy between the two" (Just, 1972: 35). He sees the "stereotype" (Schaff) as the "most complete and thus most dangerous kind of 'automatized' perception", and in his interpretation of *Die Blechtrommel* focusses on the alienating effect of stereotypes. Like Iser's interpretations, Just's study is essentially the reaction of an experienced reader and literary scholar who can utilize his store of knowledge of the literary system and his extensively developed theoretical frame of reference. Such a reader is interesting enough in terms of reception theory. But he has little in common with the "petit bourgeois horizon of expectations" of Just's fictitious reader, and consequently he should not be forced into this scheme.

The Social-Political Approach

Durzak's study of *Örtlich Betäubt* (Local Anaesthetic), another novel by Günter Grass, differs from Just's approach in that it does not deal at all with questions of textual interpretation (Durzak, 1971). The author juxtaposes two different critical attitudes towards the same text and reveals the different presuppositions of the respective critical opinions. These presuppositions are of a social-political kind and reflect different cultural traditions. In his contrasting of the German and American reactions to *Örtlich Betäubt*, Durzak comes to the following conclusions. The attitude of the German critics is to a large extent determined by the "image" of Grass. Having placed the author on a pedestal, they cannot easily arrive at an unbiased evaluation of an individual novel. Their judgement, however, is decisively influenced by their knowledge of the social-political processes. They know that a very serious political problem of our time has been described as a rather comical revolt (Durzak, 1971: 495). The negative evaluation of *Örtlich Betäubt* among the German critics is completely reversed in the American reception which began a year later, prompted by the English translation of the novel. "Whereas the German critics, on the basis of their knowledge of domestic political events, consider Grass's 'Ballad of a Badger-dog' a simplification of the political theme, the American critics interpret the story right from the beginning in a non-literal way; for them it is a veiled portrayal, in parable form, of domestic political events of a specifically American kind" (Durzak, 1971: 498). Durzak points out that in both the German and the American reaction it is not the verdict on form but on content that prevails. His conclusion is that an aesthetics of reception which investigates the conditions of critical judgement must pay all due attention to the realm of political and social awareness (Durzak, 1971: 503).

Concluding Observations

Having presented both the theoretical considerations and some practical examples, we can proceed to sum up. The theoretical starting points of reception studies allow for many different applications. Ideally one can hope for a convergence of systematic and historical research. As far as theory is concerned, it will be necessary to elucidate to what extent one is willing to accept an "objective" structure of the texts. On the one hand the "interest" (of a subjective or collective kind) that is essential to reception studies cannot serve as a theoretical foundation, but on the other hand it cannot be eliminated either. From the point of view of reception theory, the analysis of the structure of the work is no longer acceptable as the final goal of research. This is not to say, however, that the structure, the artefact, has to be treated as a fictitious entity. The various concretizations can be the object of literary research only to the extent that they are justified by properties of the text. If one accepts the artefact as a testable entity, one gains—without wanting to derive normative claims from this—a phenomenon susceptible to analysis which can be placed in more comprehensive correlations. Umberto Eco describes from a semiotic viewpoint the "objective" structure in its relation to the message and the code. The basic structure is "empty", but in its emptiness it represents "the availability of a significant apparatus which has not yet been clarified by the codes, which I select in order to let them converge in the message." "Empty" is here used metaphorically; it does not suggest the renunciation of an objective foundation. The work of the scholar in the humanities who correlates code and message would then consist of the "determination of the *cultural code*, against the background of which he can investigate the [. . .] structuring of every *message*, as well as the variations to which the exchange of messages in time and space subjects the systems of cultural conventions" (Eco, 1972: 418). The special task of the literary scholar becomes visible if we replace in the latter quotation the term "message" with "the literary text". One can study which elements in a literary work appear dominant as a result of a prevailing code and which other elements appear perspectively foreshortened or even completely hidden (Ingarden).

Let us briefly mention an example to make this position a little clearer. At the time when Nietzsche's *Zarathustra* began to make an impact, the following hierarchy resulted from the prevailing aesthetic and ideological system of norms: the concept of *der neue Mensch*/Jugendstil (structural element 1) appeared dominant, the biblical parody (structural element 2) perspectively foreshortened, and the aphorism (structural element 3) hidden. In the meantime the literary system underwent a considerable "quantitative growth". First to follow was Expressionism, later—and this is more relevant to our example—there appeared the works of Thomas Mann. The most important elements of Mann's work can be identified as essayism/aphorism and irony/parody. Whatever can be found of Jugendstil and biblical reminiscences in Thomas Mann is subjected to the parodistic principle. In *Zarathustra*, Jugendstil and the ironic/parodistic principle are often found parallel and without transition (which promoted the concealment of these elements and led later to the label "unbalanced work"). In Thomas Mann's work, on the other hand, Jugendstil is integrated through the predominant and comprehensive ironic/parodistic structural element. Reading experience is stimulated as far as this structural element is concerned, and the reader is trained in the recognition of ironic style. It must be added that Thomas Mann, whom Nietzsche greatly influenced, in turn plays an important role in the interpretation of Nietzsche. With the increased experience resulting from the knowledge of Mann's works (but not only his; Mann stands for a series of modern authors), the same object—*Zarathustra*—appears under a different perspective. Now the ironic/parodistic elements come into view and become dominant. The biblical parody also becomes more apparent; *der neue Mensch*/Jugendstil, on the other hand, is concealed. In this case we are dealing with one of the factors which Ingarden lists when he talks about the modification of the concretizations of a work of art; the factor, that is, of an influential individual who consciously concretizes a literary work and thereby guides the concretizations by others (Ingarden, 1931: 371).

The assumption of the artefact as a testable entity implies, as Jauss has correctly observed, that the individual work of art, even when the plurality of meanings is explicitly given, only permits a choice of certain possibilities of interpretation at the cost of others (Jauss, 1973: 37). But what cannot be excluded is the possibility that future generations will have no more questions to put to *Zarathustra*, and that temporarily, or for a long period of time, the work will recede into obscurity. For the old questions—to use Jauss's phrase—never suggest themselves; rather it is the readers that bring them to the text.

6

PROSPECTS FOR FURTHER RESEARCH

Now there are two things about the history of science. One is that only a man who understands science (that is, scientific problems) can understand its history; and the other is that only a man who has some real understanding of its history (the history of its problem situations) can understand science.

—Popper (1972b)

In the preceding chapters the more vital theories of literature have been expounded, including their developments in recent years. We now go one step further and evaluate the present situation, as well as the opportunities for further research. As we do so, personal convictions claim a somewhat larger role. The reader who has to map out his own road of research may be interested in our judgement of the various possibilities offered in recent publications and their mutual compatibility.

The world of science, including the scientific study of literature, has been expanded enormously over the last decades. We hold that only through cooperation combined with an intelligent division of labour can the study of literature make progress. However, any scientific cooperation should take place within a well-defined framework. As one may have gathered from the preceding chapters, our experience is that important elements for such a framework can be provided by semiotics and the theory of reception. But to what extent are the traditions of semiotics and the aesthetics of reception indeed compatible? Is it just, as Segers (1975) has argued, "a logical step" from *Rezeptionsästhetik* to semiotics? To answer that question we should further investigate the epistemological foundations of both schools, their concepts of sign and of literature, and their capacity to join other disciplines in inter-disciplinary research.

The unqualified acknowledgement of the autonomy of the literary text and its corollary, the claim of the superior truth of the poet and the emphatic assimilation of that truth by the interpreter, will hardly be found in recent publications. The old, indeed traditional conviction that literature has a cognitive and communicative function has come to the fore again and has freed the literary text from its artificial isolation. As a particular form of

165

organizing the semantic universe, literature has been attributed a more relative, but at the same time a more significant place. Literature has been accepted again as part of a more comprehensive cognitive process. As such, it also justifies the attempts to increase our knowledge about literature through scientific investigation. But this position entails an extension of the field of interest of literary studies. The student of literature must have access to all those disciplines that are engaged in the systematic organization of the semantic universe: linguistics, history, sociology, philosophy, and anthropology.

The Challenge of Semiotics

In acquiring and communicating knowledge, language has an important function. As regards the relation between signifier and signified, the idea has been accepted that the signifier represents a schematic simplification of an extremely complex state of affairs. The awareness of the imperfection of language has been reflected in the criticism of poets as well as philosophers such as Bergson and Nietzsche (Kunne–Ibsch, 1972). But the fundamentally schematic character of language has also justified the endeavour to design— with some hope of success—explanatory models which likewise rely on schematic simplifications.[1]

If the intention to preserve the full complexity of the signified were to prevail, the possibilities for communicating knowledge might in certain cases be impaired. On the other hand, if the schematic simplification of language is overemphasized, resulting in an almost exclusive reliance on the construction of abstract scientific models, the possibilities for expressing new experiences are drastically reduced. The latter case may result in an apparent objectification of reality which obstructs the insight in the role of human creativity. Anyway, the comparison and communication of facts are possible only by means of abstractions referring to individual phenomena and based on convention and standardization. There is no natural link between sign and concept. The predominantly *symbolic* relation between signifier and signified appears to be both resistant and flexible.[2] On the one hand, a linguistic community preserves its conventional signs for a very long time; on the other hand, it can adapt these signs to the particular social and cultural situation (cf. the various words for "snow" in Eskimo).

Semiotics has recently shown a keen interest in the production of signs by linguistic and cultural communities. In contradistinction to Saussure's rather static concept of sign and Peirce's taxonomical approach of semiotics, Umberto Eco sets himself to explore the dynamic character of the sign in his *Theory of Semiotics* (1976). He explains his epistemological position by means of a comparison. The object of semiotics may resemble either the surface of the sea where a ship's wake disappears as soon as it has passed, or a forest where cart-trails or footprints have brought about more or less lasting modifications. Eco (1976: 29) considers the task of the semiotician as being rather like exploring a forest, and wants to focus on the modifications of sign systems. This leads him to replace the concept of sign by that of sign function. An "expression item" can be correlated to different "content items". In the case of the English word *plane*, Eco observes three sign functions: "carpentry tool", "level" and "aircraft". He concludes that "a sign is not a fixed semiotic entity but rather the meeting-ground for independent elements (coming from two different systems of two different planes [expression and content] and meeting on the basis of a coding correlation)" (Eco, 1976: 49).

The sign function is the result of the interaction of various codes: "Codes provide the conditions for a complex interplay of sign functions" (ibid.: 56). According to Eco, the system of rules that is a code consists of a complex hierarchy of subcodes, of which some are strong and stable whereas others are weak and transient. Connotative couplings belong to the latter group. The colours red and green of the traffic lights have a meaning established by an international convention and are part of a "strong" code. In addition the red and green lights have weak connotational meanings of "obligation" versus "free choice", "fine" versus "hurry" (127). A similar comment can be made on the name Napoleon. It denotes a cultural unit that is well-defined and has a place in a semantic field of historical data. In addition, different cultures can attribute a great variety of connotations to this particular name (87). Eco believes that "the code is not a natural condition of the Global Semantic Universe, nor a stable structure underlying the complex of links and branches of every semiotic process" (126). Therefore, according to Eco, semiotic research is mainly concerned with signs as "social forces" (65).

In order to explain the expansion and renewal of codes, Eco resorts to Peirce's concept of "abduction". This is a kind of provisional reaction to facts and situations which have not been codified, or the code of which is not accessible to the recipient. (He knows that Peirce joins two rather different cases here; Eco does not elaborate on the case of the inaccessibility of the codes.) Eco observes that "a consistently interpreted ambiguous uncoded context gives rise, if accepted by a society, to a convention, and thus to a coding coupling" (132). It is here that the principle of the flexibility and creativity of language originates. The mutual relationship between code and message, whereby codes control the emission of messages and new messages can restructure the codes, constitutes the basis for the double aspect of language as "rule-governed creativity" and "rule-changing creativity" (161). Made out of arbitrary and conventional linguistic signs, literature (at least in modern Europe and America) in employing specific organizing principles has assumed the role of representing complex, not yet objectifiable phenomena which warrant a flexible response. Literary texts, therefore, are particularly suited to being studied with reference to Eco's concept of code, in particular his notion of "coding coupling".

The applicability of his theory to the field of literature also appears from his concept of "overcoding", i.e. the process by which, as a result of the convergence of various codes in a particular element, additional meanings are produced. The convergence and/or interference of rhetorical-stylistic or iconological codes with the linguistic code are cases in point. As mentioned earlier, Lotman has elaborated on the convergence of various overlapping codes in literary texts.

The methodological restriction which already characterizes the Italian edition (1968) of Eco's *Einführung in die Semiotik* (1972), is repeated with great emphasis in *Theory of Semiotics*: the question of truth is excluded from the field of interest of semiotic theory. Eco rejects Frege's concept of meaning and wants to investigate the *content* of an utterance, not the referent, i.e. the object to which the utterance refers. Truth and falsity are important differentiations, but they belong to the realm of pre- or post-semiotic problems. Eco rejects what he calls the "referential fallacy". Ignoring the extension of meaning, he aims at an "intensional semantics" (Eco, 1976: 58–9). However, he is not primarily in search of the intrinsic order of semantic elements (as, for instance, the New Critics were), but places the message rather in its cultural context. Eco views the semantic content as a *cultural unit*. The expressions "evening star" and "morning star", which may have the same denotatum, imply two different cultural conventions.

Having excluded the referent from semiotic theory, Eco can

include literary texts and ideological discourse (which convey "impossible worlds") into the range of objects to be studied by semiotics. As regards the study of literature, this offers the advantage that the literary text is not isolated from other texts,—on the basis of the non-existent unicorn, or the non-existent Mephistopheles. Literature can be considered as a constituent part of culture, and culture can be defined here as the specific way in which semantic space is divided. The work of Lévi-Strauss provides examples of such divisions by means of semantic oppositions.

As a consequence of the elimination of the referent as a factual correlate, Eco rephrases Peirce's concept of iconic sign.[3] As a motivated non-arbitrary sign, the iconic sign represents the perceptual conditions of an object, but not the object itself; these perceptual conditions are determined by cultural convention. In this respect he refers to E. H. Gombrich's *Art and Illusion* (1960), also a source of inspiration for the German theory of reception.

Eco represents a branch of semiotics which has been influential in the field of literary studies. It appears from our brief review of his recent work that the active role of sender and receiver as members of a cultural community are emphasized more than before. But this does not imply that in the past all research into the nature of linguistic signs focussed on static and logical aspects. That would certainly not be true for Edmund Husserl, whose *Logische Untersuchungen* (1900) has proved to be seminal for much recent work in the humanities. One should recall that Husserl, in his search for the universality of meanings and a universal grammar, had to come to terms with the casual subjective utterance. This is an utterance of which the meaning largely depends on the occasion or situation, as well as the person speaking.[4] Different from the casual utterance, theoretical and mathematical expressions are independent of the situational context and should be called "objective". Husserl raises the question whether the very existence of subjective utterances with multiple meanings interferes with the ideality of meanings. His answer is that in casual utterances the meanings do not change, but the subjective acts which attribute meaning to the utterances do change (Husserl, 1901: II, i, 91). Here one has come very close indeed to Eco's field of interest. Both in his earlier work and in *Theory of Semiotics,* Eco proposes to investigate to what extent the concept of meaning in the phenomenology of perception is compatible with the semiotic notion of cultural unit. "A rereading in this light of Husserl's discussions might induce us to state that semiotic meaning is simply the socialized codification of a perceptual experience [. . .]" (Eco, 1976: 167).

Epistemological Assumptions of the Historical Sciences

The crucial point in Eco's observations is the codified cultural unit, which appears to be an abstraction of perceptual experience. But does the subjective perceptual experience and its role in the constitution of meaning induce us to design a methodology different from that of the deductive and natural sciences? If so, we would again be under the spell of the old separation of the humanities and the sciences, which in effect denies the humanities a "scientific method". Or would it be possible for a subject to formulate testable hypotheses about the perceptual experiences of other subjects? If the latter question can be answered in the affirmative, the humanities may claim to have a scientific method.

The problem has been discussed within the framework of the methodology of the study of history. In the preceding chapters the critical rationalism of Karl Popper has been a recurring point of orientation. Here too we wish to refer to his observations on the study of history. Popper's rejection of "historicism" in *The Poverty of Historicism*, originally published in 1944–5, should not mislead us. His definition of the term departs considerably from the historicism or historical relativism defended by Friedrich Meinecke and other German historians (as defined by us in chapter 1). Popper's criticism of "historicism" (we shall distinguish his concept by means of quotation marks) does not at all imply a rejection of relativism. He explains "historicism" as "an approach to the social sciences which assumes that *historical prediction* is their principal aim, and which assumes that this aim is attainable by discovering the 'rhythms' or the 'patterns', the 'laws' or the 'trends' that underlie the evolution of history" (Popper, 1969a: 3). The idealist and, even more, the materialist version of such historical determinism fall under Popper's verdict. In his view, the so-called universal laws in history have usually remained vague, implicit assumptions and are often of a trivial nature. Anyway they are inadequate for guiding our scientific observations. The opposite extreme of historical determinism, viz. a chronicle or anecdotal account of unrelated facts, would not be a satisfactory alternative. History must be written from a selective, problem-oriented point of view. Popper only objects to a premature identification of the results of historical research on the basis of selective points of view with theories in the theoretical sciences.

Although there may be some functional similarity between the two, a crucial difference is that as a rule selective points of view cannot be tested. One can test the material that a historian at a particular juncture and with a particular interest may have at his disposal. The selective point of view of the historian, which lies at the basis of his "historical interpretation", can only in very rare cases be caught in a falsifiable hypothesis (Popper, 1969a: 147–52).

In *Objective Knowledge* (1972b) Popper sees somewhat more of an analogy between the study of history and—as he calls them— the theoretical sciences. Here he deals with the problem of understanding in the humanities, in particular the subjective re-enactment of past experiences as suggested by Collingwood. The "sympathetic repetition of original experience" is rejected by Popper (1972b: 188) as a task for the historian, because of its psychological and intuitive nature. The psychological process of re-enactment is not essential for scientific purposes, though Popper admits that it may help as a kind of intuitive check: "What I regard as essential is not the re-enactment but the situational analysis" (ibid.). By situational analysis Popper means:

a certain kind of tentative or conjectural explanation of some human action which appeals to the situation in which the agent finds himself. It may be a historical explanation: we may perhaps wish to explain how and why a certain structure of ideas was created. Admittedly, no creative action can ever be fully explained. Nevertheless, we can try, conjecturally, to give an idealized reconstruction of the *problem situation* in which the agent found himself, and to that extent make the action "understandable" (or "rationally understandable"), that is to say, *adequate to his situation as he saw it* (Popper, 1972b: 179).

Here the principle of rationality can be applied as in the natural sciences: "Action, and therefore history, can be explained as problem solving." Popper claims that his "schema of conjectures and refutations" is applicable also in the field of history, and even art. One may "conjecture what the artist's problem was". Popper too refers here to the work of Gombrich (Popper, 1972b: 168, 180).

Two recent publications elaborate on Popper's observations with respect to the methodology of the study of history: Schupp (1975) and Skagestad (1975). More than Popper, Schupp wants to emphasize the epistemological analogy between theory and historical interpretation. He argues that in the field of historical interpretation competing theories based on a similar selective point of view can be compared. But, says Schupp, a critical discussion of these selective points of view is also possible in the case of *different* selective points of view (oriented towards different problems), which lead to divergent and, strictly speaking, non-competing theories (1975: 172). (This, in fact, is what we have attempted in our chapter concerning Marxist theories of literature.) Schupp, however, finds it difficult to reconcile Popper's assumption of a symmetry of explanation and prediction as well as his rejection of the verification of hypotheses with historical research. Both positions seem related to the possibility of experiments in the natural sciences, which is lacking in the historical sciences; nevertheless these points have also been questioned outside the historical sciences. In the study of history probably a lower degree of exactness will be acceptable as against Popper's more severe claims (cf. Helmer and Rescher, 1959).

Another difficulty that may intrigue the historian is the seeming contradiction in Popper's system between his methodological conventionalism (inherent in the situational analysis)—which allows for historical relativism—and his acceptance of Tarski's definition of truth which appears to exclude all relativism (cf. Skagestad, 1975). Although we cannot elaborate on this point here, we presume that the contradiction can be solved, perhaps in accordance with Rescher's argument for a "coherential" perspective on truth and his criticism of Tarski's correspondence theory of truth (Rescher, 1973).

The emphasis of semiotics on the investigation of cultural codifications, the interest of the philosophy of science in the foundations of the study of history, and, last but not least, the acknowledgement of the "steering" or "structuralizing" activity of the observing subject in selecting facts in the natural sciences (as emphasized by Geurts, 1975),—all these efforts to terminate the isolation of the various disciplines prove that scholars from widely different fields of interest are prepared to listen to each other and learn from each other. Certain problems are now common to all disciplines, including the discipline of the scientific study of literature. Literary scholarship cannot isolate itself any longer: wherever in recent years it has reached important results, these were the product of a cooperation or confrontation with other disciplines. Semiotic studies, for instance, recognized the importance of epistemological problems, although not every branch of the semiotic study of literature pays equal attention to epistemology, and Russian semiotics in particular stays somewhat behind Western European studies in this respect.[5]

The aesthetics of reception, with its basis in hermeneutics, has always shown a keen interest in epistemological problems. But hermeneutics itself has changed in the course of time and its epistemological position has changed with it. We may first distinguish early hermeneutics (Schleiermacher), which aimed at a truthful representation of texts from the past. Next, in Dilthey's hermeneutics and also in later developments (Heidegger), the subjective "horizon" of the interpreter came to the fore: texts became a means to self-knowledge. Elmar Holenstein (1975; 1976) has elaborated on the various stages of hermeneutics. While Dilthey argues for an experience in which "act and object coincide", Heidegger proclaims the existentialist credo of the "unsurmountable situation" (Holenstein, 1976: 236). Holenstein expects a new stage in hermeneutics as a result of its confrontation with structuralism, especially that of Roman Jakobson. Holenstein emphasizes the interaction between invariants and variables which is also essential to Jakobson. "The whole in regard to which a part is understood is now a system or a code with a universal basis and a convertible superstructure" (ibid.: 237). The communicative competence of man consists precisely in the "convertibility of his code". This can be considered a criticism of Heidegger's notion of the "unsurmountable situation". The fusion of horizons, as defended by Dilthey, was criticized by other scholars and with other arguments. It is sufficient to mention Norbert Groeben (1972), who within the framework of empirical psychology argued for a separation between recipient and researcher, between understanding and the description of understanding.

A later offspring of hermeneutics, namely the transcendental hermeneutics of Habermas and Apel, was recently criticized by Siegfried J. Schmidt from the position of analytical philosophy and critical rationalism. It is inconceivable that transcendental hermeneutics, which attributes a transcendental character and an unquestionable authority to colloquial language and the community of communication, should provide a theoretical basis for the study of literature.[6]

Schmidt shares the position of analytical philosophy with respect to the historical sciences, as expressed by Helmer and Rescher (1959). Historical laws resemble laws, but are loose at the same time. They are not rigid and admit exceptions. In fact, they can be termed "quasi-laws". Because of their complexity, they often cannot even be made fully explicit in words. Because of this inexhaustive formulation, the criterion of mathematical precision will not be met. What is essential is that the exceptions brought forward by the historical laws demand "an explanation demonstrating the exceptional characteristic of the case in hand by establishing the violation of an appropriate (if hitherto unformulated) condition of the law's applicability" (Helmer and Rescher, 1959: 184).

Jauss and the Sociology of Knowledge

In history, the study of literature, and linguistics, the discussion of method receives a particular sharpness because of the nature of their material, which consists predominantly of texts. In contradistinction to the study of art and music, or the natural sciences, the disciplines that work with linguistic material require the distinction between object language and metalanguage. A change in method immediately affects the status of metalanguage, or, if there was no metalanguage, produces the necessity to construct one. A crucial moment arrives if a science abandons a methodological complex without being forced to do so under the pressure of a new, well-prepared theory. This was the case with literary scholarship, when—merely because of a change of interest, a dissatisfaction with existing conventions, and an awareness of developments in neighbouring disciplines—it gradually gave up the ideal of the intrinsic interpretation in its German version *(werkimmanente Interpretation)*, as well as in its American variety *(New Criticism)*.

This was the situation in which Hans Robert Jauss took issue with traditional literary scholarship in his lecture "Literaturge-schichte als Provokation der Literaturwissenschaft" (1967, in Jauss, 1970). His argument for an aesthetics of reception is a stimulating essayistic challenge. Certainly it does not claim the status of an elaborated theory. But whatever the essayistic approach lacks in consistency, it gains in flexibility. Only gradually do the problems which require theoretical disentangling become apparent. A parallel in the history of literary theory can be found in the *Querelle des Anciens et des Modernes:* the literary polemics of those days only gradually produced the problem of historical consciousness, which subsequently became an object of theoretical speculation. Of course, Jauss's ideas are more than literary polemics; from the very beginning they have been characterized by theoretical reflection. However, the theoretical framework of the aesthetics of reception is still incomplete and awaits further elaboration either by Jauss himself or by others.

Meanwhile this theoretical construct has been applied to literary material. The student of literature is not inclined to wait until a theory has reached a degree of consistency or even elegance that would satisfy the *pur sang* theoretician. As a rule the literary scholar is more interested in the applicability of a theory. But this eagerness for concrete results should not blind us to the danger that the premature application of theoretical propositions may lead to simplifications, eclecticism, and wrong conclusions. The research into the reception of literature, which heavily relied on Jauss's ideas, has not been able to avoid the pitfall of premature application. We shall not give an enumeration of negative examples here; rather we will examine whether in recent years Jauss himself has developed views which contribute to the consolidation of his theoretical conceptions.

His recent publications "La douceur du foyer—Lyrik des Jahres 1857 als Muster der Vermittlung sozialer Normen" (Jauss, 1975a) and "Der Leser als Instanz einer neuen Geschichte der Literatur" (Jauss, 1975b) should be considered here. In the latter, originally a lecture at a German conference of French Studies, Jauss focusses on the necessity of metatheoretical reflection and takes his cue from the Habermas-Gadamer debates, the work of Paul Ricoeur and, in his own words, "the claims of logical empiricism of the so-called unified science". He aims at both a "sociological completion" and a "hermeneutic elaboration in depth" *(hermeneutische Vertiefung)* of his original concept (Jauss, 1975b: 327). Put off by a prejudice against logical empiricism and spellbound by the concept of hermeneutics, Jauss is unable to commit himself to an open-minded examination of the positions of analytical philosophy and critical rationalism, in particular where the latter touches on the possibilities of the historical sciences. It appears as if Jauss would prefer to reserve a separate scientific method for research into "the linguistic nature of human experience of the world, which makes communication a condition of understanding" (ibid.). Elsewhere, however, he intends to dismiss the "false opposition between empiricism and hermeneutics". He considers the understanding of texts in both empirical and hermeneutic terms. The understanding of texts cannot rely solely on a testing of observational data through trial and error, but must also engage in a "question-and-answer play" between reader and text (Jauss, 1975b: 333). The "hermeneutic conditions" of experience should not be excluded from reflection and cannot be replaced by empirical research into readers' response by means of questionnaires. The latter polemic comment is directed against Hillmann (1972).

Jauss's observations should be viewed as motivated by the intention to defend himself against an opposition of widely different provenance. This consideration, however, cannot justify his tendency to allow an interference of the roles of reader and researcher. The proposed question-and-answer play is concerned with "*my* questions about meaning and form" and with answers by other readers, as far as they "confirm or question *my* aesthetic judgement" (Jauss, 1975b: 333, italics added). As long as the reflection on the conditions of *one's own* experience remains the ultimate goal, Jauss will be unable to reach the metatheoretical position that could eliminate the opposition between empiricism and hermeneutics. Meanwhile his epistemological position will be a vulnerable compromise.

This somewhat negative consideration does not apply to Jauss as a historian of literature. What he announces as "horizon analysis" *(Horizontanalyse)* is a reconstruction of the literary system at a particular juncture and can certainly be submitted to inter-subjective checking. This approach goes back to his early book on medieval literature *(Untersuchungen zur mittelalterlichen Tierdichtung,* 1959), and in fact has much in common with Popper's "situational analysis". The "intraliterary" horizon can be reconstructed with due attention to methodological objectivity, and in the process of this reconstruction in principle no appeal is made to the personal experience.

The access to the "extraliterary" or "lifeworldly" *(lebenswelt-liche)* horizon is more difficult, but here, as Jauss suggests, other disciplines may be of assistance. As briefly mentioned in chapter 5, Jauss agreed that his concept of the horizon of expectations was in need of a differentiation between horizons of literary and of social (general) expectations. He distinguishes now between an "implicit" reader and a historically, socially and biographically determined "explicit" reader. He suggests the reconstruction first of the implicit reader because of the accessibility of the basic data of such a reconstruction. Secondly, the preconceptions of the various groups of readers should be clarified. He proposes to speak in this respect of a first and a second code (1975b: 339). If Jauss in the first part of his lecture appears indecisive in epistemological matters, he reaches firm ground in the latter part and formulates a convincing research programme with a solid basis in literary history and sociology.

In "La douceur du foyer" (1975a), Jauss places Baudelaire's "Le crépuscule du soir" within the literary context of poetry about the idle hours of bourgeois family life. Jauss sees a similarity between his own work and that of Michael Riffaterre. He aims to broaden and specify their common methodological position and to solve the problem how "communicative functions can be discovered in the presentational efforts of lyric poetry" (Jauss, 1975a: 401). Of course, he is well aware of the fact that poetry does not refer directly to things; it does however convey notions of things.

In accordance with the reader's expectations, Baudelaire evokes the atmosphere of bourgeois leisure, but already in the first lines contrasts that atmosphere with the world of criminals, prostitutes and sick people. We shall not elaborate here on Jauss's comparison of Baudelaire with the *douceur-du-foyer* poets. However, from a methodological point of view it is of major interest that Jauss does not restrict himself to the literary series but crosses the boundaries of the literary material by using the conceptual framework of the sociology of knowledge, mainly as this has been developed by Peter Berger and Thomas Luckmann (1967). Jauss regards his article as an attempt to bridge the gap between the theory of the reception of literature and the sociological theory of knowledge about the life world *(Lebenswelt)*.

This inclusion of the sociology of knowledge within the field of inquiry of the student of literature is promising indeed; in our view, more promising than research into the domain of the sociology of literature, of which the foundations as well as the delimitations have so far remained unclear. Moreover, the connection between the theory of reception and semiotics can perhaps be provided by the sociology of knowledge. Both semiotics and reception studies are interested in the social distribution of the stock of knowledge by means of language and in the differentiation of experiences of everyday life according to different degrees of relevance. As a result of the particular distribution of knowledge, the world of everyday life strikes the person living in that world now as familiar, then again as remote. Similarly, but from the semiotic point of view, Lotman argues for a description of reality by means of different codes. "A detective of a criminal investigation department and a young admirer of the fair sex who are walking in the same street at the same time each see a completely different reality" (Lotman, 1975: 21).

It is in particular the institutionalization of habitualized actions (Berger and Luckmann, 1967: 70–85) that may interest the student of literature. Habitualized human activity demands only a minimum of decision-making, in contradistinction to new and deliberate actions. In the process of transmission of experience to a new generation, the human responsibility which was originally present is obscured. The man-made social world appears to be objectified: "An institutional world, then, is experienced as an objective reality" (ibid.: 77). Language is one of the primary means of transmitting experiences and adjusting them to the available stock of knowledge. Berger and Luckmann have reserved the term "reification" for the extreme form of objectification. The objective world is now apprehended "as a non-human, non-humanizable, inert facticity" (ibid.: 106). The authors hold that reification is a modality of consciousness and argue that "an apprehension of reification *as* a modality of consciousness is dependent upon an at least relative de-reification of consciousness, which is a comparatively late development in history and in any individual biography" (ibid.: 107).

Although Berger and Luckmann hardly touch on problems of the aesthetic experience, the student of literature may discover common ground in their findings. Šklovskij's concept of "automatization" and "making strange" are analogous to "reification" and "de-reification". Art is a constructive activity, which as a result of its innovative character may, at least temporarily, counter the trend towards objectification.

Art may also question the established "symbolic universes", which "integrate the different provinces of meaning and encompass the institutional order in a symbolic totality" (ibid.: 113). In modern times art has developed the function of transmitting new experiences through new sign relations, which destroys the symbolic (i.e. conventional) sign relation and thereby simultaneously the symbolic universe. Other forms of art (mainly pre-Romantic) served as a legitimation of the symbolic universe. Outside the sphere of European culture, Chinese literature of the Maoist era produced the legitimation of the symbolic universe accepted by the social hierarchy. As we argued in chapter 4, the cultural leaders in China have cherished the ideal that words and concepts be one and that things exist in reality if words only say so often enough. That kind of art, based on the principle of incantation, belongs—in Lotman's terminology—to the aesthetics of identity. The aesthetics of opposition is a rather late development in literary history, which coincides with the observation by Berger and Luckmann that the relative de-reification of consciousness occurs comparatively late in history. It seems very possible to identify the cognitive functions of art belonging to the aesthetics of identity by means of concepts borrowed from the sociology of knowledge. But it will be a greater challenge to attempt the same with respect to the cognitive functions of art belonging to the aesthetics of opposition. The various relevance structures of sender and receiver, author and reader, can become objects of investigation. Obviously linguistics of a semiotic and pragmatic orientation must play a crucial role in this type of research.[7]

A Semiotic Analysis of Structures of Communication
Interesting research into avant-garde art was undertaken by the semioticians O. G. Revzina and I. I. Revzin (1975) in their analysis of Ionesco's plays *La cantatrice chauve* (The Bald Soprano) and *La leçon* (The Lesson). The authors examine the communicative function of these texts, although they do so on the basis of a largely intrinsic analysis. They analyse how in these plays certain expectations essential to conventional communication are destroyed. The communicative function of this semiotic experiment with respect to the audience is, among other things, to make it aware of the conventions underlying normal communication. Within the framework of the aesthetics of opposition, Ionesco's plays reveal the existence of implied social values (in which also the sociology of knowledge would be interested).

The authors base their analysis on Jakobson's communication model and show which components of the model are questioned. With respect to reality (the referential function) they draw attention to the negation of the postulate of determinism in *La leçon*. The authors use the concept of determinism in its "weakest" form. Determinism implies here that "reality is organized in such a way that for some phenomena there are causes; i.e. not all events are equally probable (in the case of 'strong' determinism for any phenomenon a cause may be established)" (Revzina and Revzin, 1975: 256). An example of the negation of "weak" determinism is provided by the pupil who cannot solve an elementary subtraction problem, but who is easily capable of multiplying two large numbers in his head. Organized reality—in this case the hierarchically determined structure of knowledge: first simple subtraction, then complicated multiplication—is called in question by Ionesco. But this is not all. A further postulate closely connected with that of determinism is negated, namely that of a common memory. When sender and receiver share a particular world view, they also have some shared amount of information about the past at their disposal. In the case of a married couple this common memory can certainly be assumed to exist. However, it appears from a conversation between Mr. and Mrs. Martin (in *La cantatrice chauve*) that a shared experience—in this case the departure from Manchester—is not recognized as such, but seen merely as a coincidence: "What a bizarre coincidence!" says Mrs. Martin, "I too, sir, left the city of Manchester about five weeks ago."

A third postulate negated by Ionesco is that of the possibility of foretelling the future in more or less the same way. This postulate is also based on the presence of a shared model of the world: sender and receiver appraise the world in the same categories. Like determinism, the prognosis for the future is based on the assumption of a specific relation between cause and effect. This relation is called in question in *La cantatrice chauve* when the clock strikes irregularly, even in a reverse order, and more than twelve times.

We will not follow the argument of the Revzins in detail and must restrict ourselves to a enumeration of the other postulates which are negated in Ionesco's dialogues and identify the absurd character of his plays:

4. The postulate of informativeness: the sender must relate some new information to the receiver.
5. The postulate of identity: the sender and the receiver have in mind the same reality, i.e. the identity of a subject does not change while we talk about it.
6. The postulate of truthfulness: between the text and reality there must be a correspondence, i.e. the text must contain a truthful statement about reality.
7. The postulate of the incompleteness of description: a text must describe reality with some degree of reduction, being based on the existence of a common memory and the ability to predict the future in a more or less similar fashion.
8. The postulate of the semantic connectedness of the text: the text must be organized so that between two statements which immediately follow each other, and within statements and phrases, one should be able to establish a connection of content (Revzina and Revzin, 1975: 256).

Although they do not refer to the sociology of knowledge, the authors clearly base their analysis on the categories of the distribution of knowledge. Other research, such as that by Bremond (1973) and Doležel (1976), likewise deals with the basic structures of the semantic universe that must serve as a point of reference for any interpretation of literary texts.

Conclusion

The distance between the aesthetics of reception and the semiotic approach is not unbridgeable. On the contrary, the problems that both schools try to solve are comparable or even similar. But in solving these problems they have different equipment at their disposal. On the basis of linguistic assumptions and the theory of signs, semiotics is well equipped to analyse an isolated text as the intersection of different codes. The empirical subject does not interfere with such an analysis, either in the theories of Eco and Lotman or in the application of these theories in Russian or Italian semiotics (Kapp, 1973).

However, the theory of reception—at least, certain branches of it—does not rigorously exclude the empirical subject from the problem situation; and if confronted with an examination of extra-textual relations, reception theory is exposed to the danger of an extreme expansion of its field of inquiry. In our view the sociology of knowledge may provide the theoretical framework for research into the semantic world of the recipient and for organizing the wealth of extra-textual material. Tendencies to fuse the roles of researcher and of reader should be dismissed.

The study of literature has so many aspects that one scholar can no longer encompass the whole field. Only a coordinated division of labour can be an answer to the huge amount of problems confronting us, but it is unlikely that in the humanities such cooperation will quickly materialize, except incidentally and on a small scale. This has various reasons, such as the fact that the principle of the separation of analysis and evaluation—of researcher and recipient—has not yet been widely accepted. If we wish to further scientific cooperation in literary studies, a prime requirement is to establish criteria of testability and to reach agreement on the use of a metalanguage. So far there have been few coordinated efforts in the scientific study of literature; we have dealt with some of them: Russian Formalism, the aesthetics of reception, semiotics. However, without any planned coordination the field of interest of innumerable individual scholars has shifted away from the isolated text to problems of text and context, and of the communication situation. A new metalinguistic terminology has been established parallel to this development, or is in the process of being formulated. This should not blind us to the fact that large areas of potential interest to the study of literature are being neglected, simply because no one—the present authors included—thinks of asking the relevant questions.

Looking at the preceding pages, one will notice that most space is taken up by problems of analysis and interpretation, while very little has been said on the procedure and problems of evaluation. We have dealt with the various functions of language, including the poetic function (Jakobson's terminology). But very little space has been devoted to the aesthetic effect of texts in which the poetic function dominates. Yet that aesthetic effect can be studied as part of the communication situation, in direct relation to certain qualities of the texts and in cooperation with psychologists. This seems the more necessary as the social relevance of literature depends largely on the aesthetic experience that accompanies the assimilation of cognitive elements presented in the text. As Aristotle already knew, much of the cognitive content of literary texts would never be accepted by the recipients if it were not conveyed in an artistic manner. The link between "literature and society" is established primarily through the aesthetic function of the presentation of the semantic material; the latter being related in one way or another (e.g. by hyperbole or by negation) to the social norms or "relevance structures" of society—or, to be more precise, of particular social groups. Various indications have been given above of how this complex of problems can be disentangled. We know, however, that before a firm methodology for solving these problems can be established, further research is necessary, particularly into the conditions of the aesthetic function.

At least one more vital question remained unanswered. Throughout this book we have acquiesced in the semiotic position that the problem of truth belongs to the domain of logic, and not to that of semiotics. The semiotician is not interested in extensional meaning and is not prepared to investigate the truth or falsity of the propositions or texts he subjects to a semiotic analysis; and, if he were to step into the shoes of the logician in order to distinguish true from false, a fellow-semiotician might examine his judgement of the truth value of texts as part of a cultural code, i.e. just another semiotic system. The danger of indecisive subjectivity looms large here. A similar subjectivist tendency can be found in Eco's view, as well as in the view inherent in the aesthetics of reception, that meanings can be assigned to signs which have never been intended by the sender. Convincing as this observation is, it also opens the door to a hypertrophied growth of significations. Where should the participant of a cultural code stop assigning meanings, and where should the scholar stop? Are we in the danger of wilfully expanding the world of the mind, and do we encounter new problems just on that account?

Of course, the proliferation of significations can be restricted by the demand that they are justified by properties of the text. Moreover, the various significations should go through the process of inter-subjective testing. In addition, however, settlement of the truth problem—by means of establishing a theory of truth as well as criteria for distinguishing the various types of truthful relations—is of crucial importance, particularly in view of the traditional claims of literature to a poetic or fictional truth (Špet's "third kind of truth" as described in chapter 2). For the solution of this problem we must, of course, rely on support from the logicians.

Obviously this book was not written in order to answer all questions. However, we hope that some ground has been cleared so that the vital problems of the scientific study of literature can be envisaged in a new light.

NOTES

Chapter 1: *Introduction*

1. We accept Rescher's view that "a definition is an explanation of the meaning of a word" (Rescher, 1964: 30). The word "descriptive" is used in analogy of Ernest Nagel (1961: 83, 349).
2. Cf. Jan Mukařovský's position that "eine Erscheinung, die zu einer bestimmten Zeit oder in einem bestimmten Land eine priviligierte Trägerin einer ästhetischen Funktion war, kann zu einer anderen Zeit oder in einem anderen Land für diese Funktion ungeeignet sein" (Mukařovský, 1970: 13–14).
3. Lu Chi (A.D. 261–303), *Rhymeprose on Literature (Wen-fu)*, trans. Achilles Fang, in Bishop, 1965: 3–43. See p. 8: "He gathers words never used in a hundred generations; he picks rhythms never sung in a thousand years."
4. This definition is based on Friedrich Meinecke's concept of historicism (1936).
5. "Die Interpretation des Werkes [. . .] richtet sich auf das Kunstwerk und braucht eine besondere Einstellung auf das Dichterische, die von der historischen wesensmässig verschieden ist" (Kayser, 1958: 52).
6. "Jede Wertungslehre ruht auf einer Theorie der Dichtkunst, ja auf einer Ästhetik, ob sie nun ausgesprochen wird oder nicht" (Kayser, 1958: 45); "Und doch bedeutet die Anerkennung einer gewissen Bindung des Interpreten an seine Zeit keinen Absturz in völligen Subjektivismus und in Relativität" (ibid.: 54).
7. "Die andere Arbeitsweise, von der nun zu sprechen ist, strebt zunächst gar nicht nach Wertung. Sie sieht das Werk als Ganzheit— das ist ein Teil ihrer Auffassung von der Dichtung—und will das Gefüge dieser Ganzheit begreifen und durchsichtig machen. Sie heisst dieses ihr Verfahren Interpretation schlechthin (Kayser, 1958: 45).
8. "Die Wertung liegt in der Interpretation beschlossen" (Kayser, 1958: 51).
9. Cf. T. A. van Dijk's conclusion: "For the moment we only want to stress that the requirement of generality is not satisfied in poetics. We do not have laws or rules formulating properties of a general, let alone universal character, and even if we have some of them, e.g. in the theory of narrative, they are hardly explicit enough to be tested" (Van Dijk, 1972: 177-8).
10. Except for rather trivial generalities such as "the number of genres is limited".
11. "Man müsste die *allgemeinen* Faktoren finden, die das *Individuelle* erklären" (Seiffert, 1972: 210).

Chapter 2: *Russian Formalism, Czech Structuralism and Soviet Semiotics*

1. *Opojaz* is the abbreviation of *Obščestvo izučenija poetičeskogo jazyka* (Society for the Study of Poetic Language).
2. Compare Šklovskij's view that "artistry [...] results from what kind of perception we have" (1916a: 7) with Jakobson's position that "a scientific poetics becomes possible only when it forgoes all valuation" (1921: 23).
3. Although not mentioned by Šklovskij, Belinskij (1811-48), as well as Potebnja (1835-91), expressed the view that "art is thinking in images" ("iskusstvo est' myšlenie v obrazach") (Belinskij, 1954: IV, 585), a definition firmly rejected by Šklovskij.
4. Probably the same as G. von Spett, mentioned by Husserl in a letter of August 6, 1921, to Roman Ingarden (Husserl, 1968: 21).
5. "Setzen wir zwei, bereits kategoriale Objecte, z. B. zwei Sachverhalte, in eine Beziehung, so sind diese Sachverhalte der Stoff, relativ zu der sie beide in Eins setzenden Beziehungsform. Dieser Bestimmung der Begriffe Stoff und Form entspricht genau die traditionelle Unterscheidung zwischen Materie und Form bei den Aussagen" (Husserl, 1901: II, ii, 182).
6. The question whether science really explains, i.e. supplies reasons for regarding the explicandum as intrinsically necessary, is not a trivial one (cf. Nagel, 1961: 26-8).
7. "In einem wahren Kunstwerk gibt es keine einzelne Schönheit, nur das Ganze ist schön," quoted Mukařovský (1935: 73) from F. W. J. von Schelling's *Schriften zur Philosophie der Kunst* (Leipzig, 1911).
8. In the tradition of Husserl and Saussure, Mukařovský would immediately be prepared to admit that, strictly speaking, the *signifiant* is not a purely physical entity, but the psychic impression of a physical entity. The impression of the physical entity is correlated to psychic concepts as a result of which it has the capacity to operate as a carrier of meaning or signifier (Saussure, 1915: 98).
9. Ingarden (1968: 280n) provides one of the very few references to Russian Formalism.
10. We have already referred above to the first German edition (Lotman, 1972a) and shall continue to do so; however, all quotations have been checked with the Russian original (Lotman, 1970).
11. "Eine Struktur ist ein Modell, das nach Vereinfachungsoperationen konstruiert ist, die es ermöglichen verschiedene Phänomene von einem einzigen Gesichtspunkt aus zu vereinheitlichen" (Eco, 1972:63).

Chapter 3: *Structuralism in France: Criticism, Narratology and Text Analysis*

1. This programme has been outlined in "Thèses", *Mélanges linguistiques dédiés au Premier Congrès des Philologues Slaves*, Travaux du Cercle linguistique de Prague, 1(Prague, 1929): 7-29.

2. This essay later became part of the volume entitled *Anthropologie structurale* (1958).
3. *Die Zeit,* October 13, 1967.
4. The year 1965 can be said to mark a caesura as far as Germany too is concerned in view of the publication of works dealing with the problem of literary evaluation, and in view of Bierwisch's "Poetik und Linguistik"; as for Switzerland, the so-called Zurich Literary Debate (*Zürcher Literaturstreit*) marks the caesura. In this debate Emil Staiger's speech entitled "Literatur und Öffentlichkeit", which he delivered on December 17, 1966, has a central position. This speech was published in *Neue Zürcher Zeitung* of December 21, 1966.
5. See above pp. 30–8 and below pp. 136–64.
6. Peter Demetz writes of a "rediscovery" of their ideas by Barthes (*Die Zeit,* October 13, 1967).
7. For criticism of the postulate of the fixed order of the functions see above p. 28.
8. Our opinion that French structuralism (and not only Julia Kristeva) has dealt with the problem of diachrony is confirmed by Karlheinz Stierle (1972).
9. "As R. O. Jakobson has convincingly shown, the search for the artistic function of grammatical structures in some respects resembles the play of geometrical structures in the spatial arts" (Lotman, 1972a: 233).
10. We will not discuss the concept of "superreader" at this place. Riffaterre gives a clear explanation (1966: 204).
11. The proliferation of equivalence relations was also criticized by Jonathan Culler (1975: 62) and Roger Fowler (1975a).
12. See above, pp. 31–5.

Chapter 4: *Marxist Theories of Literature*

1. "Es handelte sich bei dieser meiner Rekapitulation der Mathematik und der Naturwissenschaften selbstredend darum, mich auch im einzelnen zu überzeugen—woran im allgemeinen kein Zweifel für mich war—, dass in der Natur dieselben dialektischen Bewegungsgesetze im Gewirr der zahllosen Veränderungen sich durchsetzen, die auch in der Geschichte die scheinbare Zufälligkeit der Ereignisse beherrschen" (Friedrich Engels, *Herrn Eugen Dührings Umwälzung der .Wissenschaft: Dialektik der Natur, 1873–1882* [1935; rpt. Glashütten im Taunus: Auvermann, 1970]; Karl Marx und Friedrich Engels, Historisch-kritische Gesamtausgabe, [XIII], Sonderausgabe, p. 11).
2. "Die Produktionsweise des materiellen Lebens bedingt den sozialen, politischen und geistigen Lebensprozess überhaupt. Es ist nicht das Bewusstsein der Menschen, das ihr Sein, sondern umgekehrt ihr gesellschaftliches Sein, das ihr Bewusstsein bestimmt. Auf einer gewissen Stufe ihrer Entwicklung geraten die materiellen Produktivkräfte der Gesellschaft in Widerspruch mit den vorhandenen Produktionsverhältnissen, oder, was nur ein

juristischer Ausdruck dafür ist, mit den Eigentumsverhältnissen, innerhalb deren sie sich bisher bewegt hatten. Aus Entwicklungsformen der Produktivkräfte schlagen diese Verhältnisse in Fesseln derselben um. Es tritt dann eine Epoche sozialer Revolution ein. Mit der Veränderung der ökonomischen Grundlage wälzt sich der ganze ungeheure Überbau langsamer oder rascher um" (Marx and Engels, 1967: I, 74, 75).

3. "Du hättest dann von selbst mehr *shakespearisieren* müssen, während ich Dir das *Schillern*, das Verwandeln von Individuen in blosse Sprachröhren des Zeitgeistes, als bedeutendsten Fehler anrechne" (Marx and Engels, 1967: I, 181).

4. "Aber diese kritisch-philosophische Geschichtsanschauung, in der sich eherne Notwendigkeit an Notwendigkeit knüpft und die eben deshalb auslöschend über die Wirksamkeit *individueller* Entschlüsse und Handlungen hinwegfährt, ist eben darum kein Boden, weder für das *praktische revolutionäre Handeln* noch für die *vorgestellte dramatische Aktion*" (Marx and Engels, 1967: I, 191).

5. Marx phrased this phenomenon literally as "the unequal relation between the development of material production and, for instance, artistic production" ("das unegale Verhältnis der Entwicklung der materiellen Produktion, z.B. zur künstlerischen") (Marx and Engels, 1967: I, 123).

6. In Marx's own words: "Bei der Kunst bekannt, dass bestimmte Blütezeiten derselben keineswegs im Verhältnis zur allgemeinen Entwicklung der Gesellschaft, also auch der materiellen Grundlage, gleichsam des Knochenbaus ihrer Organisation, stehn" (Marx and Engels, 1967: I, 123-4).

7. "Warum sollte die geschichtliche Kindheit der Menschheit, wo sie am schönsten entfaltet, als eine nie wiederkehrende Stufe nicht ewigen Reiz ausüben?" (Marx and Engels, 1967: I, 125).

8. In Engels' own words: "Aber ich meine, die Tendenz muss aus der Situation und Handlung selbst hervorspringen, ohne dass ausdrücklich darauf hingewiesen wird, und der Dichter ist nicht genötigt, die geschichtliche zukünftige Lösung der gesellschaftlichen Konflikte, die er schildert, dem Leser an die Hand zu geben" (Marx and Engels, 1967: I, 156).

9. In Engels' words: [. . .] "jeder ist ein Typus, aber auch zugleich ein bestimmter Einzelmensch, ein 'Dieser', wie der alte Hegel sich ausdrückt, und so muss es sein" (Marx and Engels, 1967: I, 155).

10. Cf. the following observation by Mao Tse-tung: "Some works which politically are downright reactionary may have a certain artistic quality. The more reactionary their content and the higher their artistic quality, the more poisonous they are to the people, and the more necessary it is to reject them" (Mao Tse-tung, 1942: 89). From this passage it appears that a particular literary work, which cannot be judged positively even on historicist grounds, may still possess a very high artistic quality.

11. Cf. Erlich, 1969: 42. German translation of the poem "My" (We) by V. T. Kirillov in Lorenz (1969: 78-9).

12. This was one of the differences between Stalinist orthodoxy and

Russian Formalism. The idea that scientific analysis may "separate" form and content was still being defended recently by Moissej Kagan (1971: 279). Cf. Engels' separation of form and content in his letter to Lassalle (Marx and Engels, 1967: I, 185).

13. "O žurnalach 'Zvezda' i 'Leningrad'; iz postanovlenija CK VKP(b) ot 14 Avgusta 1946g" (On the journals 'Zvezda' [Star] and 'Leningrad'; from the resolution of the Central Committee of the Communist Party of the Soviet Union [Bolsheviki] of August 14, 1946), Bol'ševik, No. 15 (1946): 11-14. A. Ždanov, "Doklad o žurnalach 'Zvezda' i 'Leningrad' " (Report on the journals 'Zvezda' and 'Leningrad'), Bol'ševik, No. 17-18 (1946): 4-20.

14. Cf. L. Timofeev and N. Vengrov (1955: 148): "The writer's opinion on what constitutes the typical in life, the features described by him as typical, that which he typifies in his work,—all this reflects first and foremost the writer's political views." Also quoted by Friedberg (1959: 21).

15. From quite another angle H. R. Jauss (1975c) reached similar conclusions.

16. Hegel described the creative act as "geistige Thätigkeit [. . .], welche jedoch zugleich das Moment der Sinnlichkeit und Unmittelbarkeit in sich hat" (Hegel, 1956-65: XII, 68-9). René Wellek has observed that the second part of Belinskij's formula is reminiscent of A. W. Schlegel's definition of poetry as "bildlich anschauender Gedankenausdruck" (Wellek, 1955-65: III, 363).

17. The quotations are translated from the German: "Der Nutzen wird mit dem Verstand erkannt, das Schöne mit dem Kontemplationsvermögen. Das Gebiet des ersteren ist die Berechnung; das Gebiet des zweiten ist der Instinkt . [. . .] Das wichtigste Kennzeichen des ästhetischen Genusses ist seine Unmittelbarkeit" (Plechanov, 1955: 196-7).

18. "Vom Character des Themas dagegen ist der Wert des Werkes unmittelbar abhängig. Es ist unbestreitbar, dass das Interesse der Menschen für das Kunstwerk bestimmt wird durch die Tiefe des Themas, seine soziale Bedeutung, durch das Mass, in dem es den wichtigsten Bedürfnissen der Gesellschaft, der Klasse, der Nation, der Menschheit entspricht" (Kagan, 1971: 285). In this respect Rita Schober, an East German scholar, agrees with Kagan: "Das höchste Prädikat ästhetischer Wertung käme dann einem Werk zu, in dem der Künstler das für seine Zeit [. . .] wesentlichste Thema aufgreift, die für seine Entfaltung optimale künstlerische Idee findet [. . .] und es ihm zugleich gelingt, diese in der künstlerischen Ausführung voll zu realisieren." A similar priority of ideological content appears from the concept of the image of (socialist) Man as a criterion in literary judgement (Schober, 1973: 241-4).

19. See Cheng Chi-ch'iao, "Wen-i ling-yü li pi-hsü chieh-ch'ih ma-k'o-szu-chu-i ti jen-shih-lun; tui hsing-hsiang szu-wei lun ti p'i-p'an" (It is necessary to persist in Marxist epistemology in the realm of literature and art; a critique of the theory of thinking in images), Hung ch'i (Red Flag), No. 5(1966): 34-52; translated in Survey of China Mainland Magazines, No. 523(1966): 23-47. Also: T'an P'ei-

sheng, "Chou Yang ho O-kuo ti san-ko 'szu-chi' " (Chou Yang and Russia's three '-skys'), *Chieh-fang-chün wen-i* (Literature and Art of the Liberation Army), No. 18(1967): 15-18; translated in *Survey of China Mainland Magazines,* No. 608(1968): 14-20.

20. This has been elaborated by Karel van het Reve in his book *Het geloof der kameraden* (Amsterdam: Van Oorschot, 1969).

21. Quoted from the essay "Literature and Revolution" ("Wen-i yü ko-ming," 1928), *Selected Works,* III (Peking: Foreign Language Press, 1959): 22. Original text in Lu Hsün, *Ch'üan chi* (Complete works), IV (Peking: Jen-min wen-hsüeh ch'u-pan-she, 1973): 95.

22. An editorial in *Kuang-ming jih-pao* (Kuang-ming Daily) of June 6, 1966, criticized the view that "before the truth all men are equal" *(tsai chen-li mien-ch'ien jen-jen p'ing-teng).* It explained that not all people can be equal before the truth, since there are different kinds of truth defended by different classes, instead of one "abstract" truth. This view makes it impossible to check whether an assertion is in accordance with that which it purports to say, and therefore it ends all scientific discussion.

   Accordingly, any objective, truthful representation of facts is considered suspect, unless it is indicated that the represented "truth" coincides with the truth of the Party. If the "truth" is a "bourgeois truth", the orthodox Maoist reaction runs as follows: "How can they talk of being 'objective', 'truthful' and 'impartial'! Beguiling words like 'objective', 'truthful' and 'impartial' are but so many soiled fig-leaves to hide the fact that they are serving the bourgeoisie and safeguarding its interests!" ("Carry the Great Revolution on the Journalistic Front Through to the End", *Peking Review,* No. 37(1968): 20).

23. In an address to the Second Chinese Writers' Congress (1953) Chou Yang emphasized that the writers "should master the creative method of Socialist Realism" *(Wen-i pao* (Literary Gazette), No. 19 (1953): 7-17). In the same year Mao Tse-tung's "Yenan Talks" of 1942 were reprinted as part of the Chinese edition of his selected works. Although Mao Tse-Tung in 1942 had not mentioned "Socialist Realism" (as reflected in the 1950 American translation of the "Yenan Talks" [Mao Tse-tung, 1950]), the 1953 Chinese edition of the "Yenan Talks" made it appear as if already in 1942 Mao Tse-tung had been in favour of "Socialist Realism" (cf. Mao Tse-tung, 1942: 87).

24. Wang Jo-wang, "P'ing 'she-hui-chu-i shih-tai ti hsien-shih-chu-i'" (Critique of 'realism of the socialist epoch'), *Wen-i pao* No. 6 (1957): 6-7.

25. Chou Yang, "Hsin min-ko k'ai-t'o-le shih-ko ti hsin tao-lu" (The new folk songs cleared a new road for poetry), *Hung ch'i,* No. 1 (1958): 33-9.

26. *Wen-hsüeh p'ing-lun* (Literary Criticism), No. 2(1959): 124.

27. "Chien-li Chung-kuo tzu-chi ti ma-k'o-szu-chu-i-ti wen-i li-lun ho p'i-p'ing", *Wen-i pao,* No. 17 (1958): 7-12. Italics added.

28. "Ma k'o-szu i-shu sheng-ch'an yü wu-chih sheng-ch'an fa-chan ti pu p'ing-heng kuei-lü shih fou shih-yung yü she-hui-chu-i wen-hsüeh"

(Is Marx's law of unbalanced development of artistic and material production applicable to socialist literature?), *Wen-i pao,* No. 2 (1959): 20-4.

29. See above, note 19.
30. *Hung ch'i,* No. 9 (1967): 2–10. English translation in Ch'en (1970: 77–82, 86, 97).
31. *Hung ch'i,* No. 6 (1967): 25–8. English translation in *Chinese Literature,* No. 8 (1967): 118–25.
32. *Hung ch'i,* No. 9 (1967): 11–21. English translation in *Important Documents on the Great Proletarian Cultural Revolution in China* (Peking: Foreign Languages Press, 1970): 201-38.
33. See, for instance, the criticism of Chou Yang by Wen Kung in *Jen-min jih-pao* (People's Daily), February 2, 1972. Wen Kung's article criticizes Lu Ting-i and Chou Yang for rejecting the view that "subject–matter decides" *(t'i-ts'ai chüeh-ting).*
34. Chinese: *tang-hsing* (Mao Tse-tung, 1942: 70).
35. D. W. Fokkema, "Chinese Literature under the Cultural Revolution", *Literature East and West,* 13 (1969): 335-59.
36. Yün Lan discussed the problem of the typical and (without much basis) accused the "frauds of the Liu Shao-ch'i type" of having propagated the mistaken view that "literature is identical with politics" (Yün Lan, "I-shu-shang yao ching i ch'iu ching" (In artistic work one must always seek refinement), *Jen-min jih-pao* (People's Daily), April 28, 1973).
37. "ein in jeder Hinsicht reaktionäres Werk voll von idealistischer Mystik, falsch in allen seinen Einschätzungen der historischen Entwicklung" (Lukács, 1963-75: IV, 334).
38. See above, p. 100.
39. For a different opinion see H.-J. Schmitt (1973).
40. "[. . .] das Unwesentliche, Scheinbare, an der Oberfläche Befindliche verschwindet öfter, hält nicht so 'dicht', 'sitzt' nicht so 'fest' wie das 'Wesen'" (Lukács, 1963-75: IV, 109).
41. "Vielleicht ist die echte Wirklichkeit auch Unterbrechung" (ibid.: IV, 316). Cf. Bloch, 1962: 270.
42. "Surrealismus ist erst recht—Montage. [. . .] Sie ist die Beschreibung des Durcheinanders der Erlebniswirklichkeit mit eingestürzten Sphären und Zäsuren" (Lukács, 1963-75: IV, 320). Cf. Bloch, 1962: 224.
43. "Jeder Marxist weiss, dass die grundlegenden ökonomischen Kategorien des Kapitalismus sich in den Köpfen der Menschen unmittelbar stets verkehrt spiegeln" (Lukács, 1963–75: IV, 317).
44. "dauernden Züge [. . .], die als objektive Entwicklungstendenzen der Gesellschaft, ja der ganzen Menschheitsentwicklung, durch lange Perioden hindurch wirksam sind" (ibid.: IV, 332).
45. "Kein Realist begnügt sich damit, immerfort zu wiederholen, was man schon weiss; das zeigt keine lebendige Beziehung zur Wirklichkeit" (Brecht, 1968: XIX, 295).
46. "Verkündet nicht mit der Miene der Unfehlbarkeit die allein seligmachende Art, ein Zimmer zu beschreiben, exkommuniziert nicht die Montage, setzt nicht den *inneren Monolog* auf den Index!

Erschlagt die jungen Leute nicht mit den alten Namen! Lasst nicht bis 1900 eine Entwicklung der Technik in der Kunst zu und ab da nicht mehr!" (ibid.: XIX, 294).

47. Brecht, 1968: XIX, 298. Cf. Klaus Völker (1969: 138): "Lukács dagegen geht es nicht um Einflussnahme auf die Wirklichkeit, er sucht das 'Kunsterlebnis'."

48. "Erpresste Versöhnung; Zu Georg Lukács: 'Wider den missverstandenen Realismus'," reprinted in Adorno, 1958–74: II, 152–188.

49. Lukács, 1963-75: X, 539-787. Cf. Lukács' revealing self-criticism on pp. 788-9.

50. "sinnfällige, sinnbildliche Gestalten eines Besonderen, das sowohl seine Allgemeinheit wie seine Einzelheit organisch in sich fasst, in sich aufhebt [. . .], (und) auf eine universelle Nacherlebbarkeit gerichtet ist" (Lukács, 1963–75: X, 712). It is extremely difficult to do justice to the original formula in a translation. Parkinson, who has also struggled with this text, suggests that *"das Besondere"* should be translated as "the special", a suggestion which we have not followed (Parkinson, 1970: 115).

51. "Kunst erkennt nicht dadurch die Wirklichkeit, dass sie sie, photographisch oder 'perspektivisch', abbildet, sondern dadurch, dass sie vermöge ihrer autonomen Konstitution ausspricht, was von der empirischen Gestalt der Wirklichkeit verschleiert wird" (Adorno, 1958–74: II, 168).

52. "Das Wesentliche jedoch, wodurch das Kunstwerk als Erkenntnis sui generis von der wissenschaftlichen sich unterscheidet, ist eben, dass nichts Empirisches unverwandelt bleibt, dass die Sachgehalte objektiv sinnvoll werden erst als mit der subjektiven Intention verschmolzene" (ibid.).

53. "So schliesst die von der Kunst widerspiegelte und gestaltete Wirklichkeit von vornherein als Ganzes bereits eine Parteinahme zu den historischen Kämpfen der Gegenwart des Künstlers ein" (Lukács, 1963–75: X, 713-14).

54. "inhaltlich–richtige Stellungnahmen zu den grossen Problemen der Zeit" (ibid.: X, 716).

55. "Der Akzent auf dem autonomen Werk jedoch ist selber gesellschaftlich–politischen Wesens" (Adorno, 1958–74: III, 134).

56. "Das Asoziale der Kunst ist bestimmte Negation der bestimmten Gesellschaft" (Adorno, 1970: 335).

57. "Andererseits wird der Typus stets so erfasst, dass die Einheit mit dem Individuum, in der es im Leben erscheint, nicht aufgehoben, sondern im Gegenteil vertieft wird" (Lukács, 1963–75: XII, 241).

58. "Was ist eigentlich Aura? Ein sonderbares Gespinst von Raum und Zeit: einmalige Erscheinung einer Ferne, so nah sie sein mag" (Benjamin, 1970: 83).

59. "In dem Augenblick aber, da der Massstab der Echtheit an der Kunstproduktion versagt, hat sich auch die gesamte Funktion der Kunst umgewälzt. An die Stelle ihrer Fundierung aufs Ritual tritt ihre Fundierung auf eine andere Praxis: nämlich ihre Fundierung auf Politik" (Benjamin, 1936: 21).

60. "In der Sowjetunion kommt die Arbeit selber zu Wort" (Benjamin, 1936: 34).

61. In "Über einige Motive bei Baudelaire", published in 1939-40, Benjamin devoted many pages to the motif of the urban masses in the work of Baudelaire, although he had to admit at the same time that "the masses are so much internalized by Baudelaire that their representation does not occur in his work" ("Die Masse ist Baudelaire derart innerlich, dass man ihre Schilderung bei ihm vergebens sucht") (Benjamin, 1969: 128).

62. "Er drückt in keiner Weise seine Epoche aus, nicht einmal zehn Jahre" (Brecht, 1968: XIX, 408).

63. "La conscience collective perd progressivement toute réalité active et tend à devenir un simple reflet de la vie économique et, à la limite, à disparaître" (Goldmann, 1964: 30).

64. "L'homologie entre la structure romanesque classique et la structure de l'échange dans l'économie libérale" (Goldmann, 1964: 16).

65. "Die Gesellschaft ist eine" (Adorno, 1969: 90).

66. "Wissenschaft hiesse: der Wahrheit und Unwahrheit dessen innewerden, was das betrachtete Phänomen von sich aus sein will" (Adorno, 1969: 97).

67. In his criticism of Karl Popper, I. S. Kon (1966: I, 287) postulates "a system of social relations which exists independent from the human consciousness" ("ein System gesellschaftlicher Verhältnisse, das unabhängig vom menschlichen Bewusstsein existiert").

68. In a letter of January 25, 1894, to W. Borgius, Engels explained the primacy of the economic basis as follows: "We consider the economic conditions as determining the historical development in the last instance. [. . .]. The political, legal, philosophical, religious, literary, artistic etc. development is based on the economic development. But they all also react to each other and to the economic basis. It is not so, that the economic condition is a *cause*, *active alone*, whereas the rest has a passive role. But there is interaction on the basis of the *in the last instance* determining economic necessity." ("Wir sehen die ökonomischen Bedingungen als das in letzter Instanz die geschichtliche Entwicklung Bedingende an. [. . .]. Die politische, rechtliche, philosophische, religiöse, literarische, künstlerische etc. Entwicklung beruht auf der ökonomischen. Aber sie alle reagieren auch aufeinander und auf die ökonomische Basis. Es ist nicht, dass die ökonomische Lage *Ursache*, *allein aktiv* ist und alles andere nur passive Wirkung. Sondern es ist Wechselwirkung auf Grundlage der *in letzter Instanz* stets sich durchsetzenden ökonomischen Notwendigkeit.") (Karl Marx und Friedrich Engels, *Werke*, XXXIX (Berlin: Dietz Verlag, 1968): 206). Cf. also Engels' letter of September 21-22, 1890, to Joseph Bloch (ibid., XXXVII (1967): 462-6).

69. "Die Dialektik bestreitet, dass irgendwo auf der Welt rein einseitige Ursache-Folge-Beziehungen existieren; sie erkennt in den einfachsten Tatsachen komplizierte Wechselwirkungen von Ursachen und Folgen" (Lukács, 1963-75: X, 207-8).

Chapter 5: *The Reception of Literature: Theory and Practice of "Rezeptionsästhetik"*

1. "Sign" in this context refers to the term as used in the Russian and Czech tradition, as well as in Italian semiotics. *Appellstruktur* is a concept more specific to German reception theory (Iser); it would also fit into Roland Barthes' conception of literature.
2. Here Jauss quotes Droysen (Jauss, 1970: 231). Both essays in Jauss (1970).
3. On the problem of explanation in the various disciplines see the chapter "Problems in the Logic of Historical Inquiry" in Nagel (1961).
4. Thus structuralism, at its beginnings in phonology, worked from the conception that a phoneme was in itself meaningless and that its significance was derived only from its relation with other phonemes and in opposition to them.
5. Other theorists use the term "text" or "Text$_1$".
6. As a complementary concept to "text" or "Text$_1$" there appear variously "metatext" (Roland Barthes and others), "work" (Jurij Lotman), "text processing" (Götz Wienold), and "Text$_2$" (Werner Bauer).
7. "Jean-Paul Sartre antwortet", interview by Bernard Pingaud in *Alternative* 54 (1967): 129.
8. Jean Piaget views structure as "a system of 'transformations' rather than of static 'forms' " (Piaget, 1968: 10).
9. Further developed in Lotman (1972a).
10. A survey of structuralist thought in various disciplines is available in Ducrot (1968), Lane (1970), and Naumann (1973). For structuralist semiotics and comparative literature see Fokkema (1974).
11. Already in 1921 Roman Jakobson characterized poetry as an "utterance with a set towards the expression" (Jakobson, 1921: 31). Bühler's three functions of language are the expressive, conative and referential functions (*Ausdruck, Appell* and *Darstellung*) (Bühler, 1934:28).
12. Cf. Iser's collection of essays *Der implizite Leser* (1972).
13. On Riffaterre's concept of the "superreader" see Roland Posner (1972). Posner weighs the advantages and disadvantages of the two possibilities: "description of the sign carrier" (structuralist interpretation) and reception analysis as Riffaterre conceives of it. If the former can avoid the sources of error of the latter ("multivalence, vagueness, minimal testability and theoretical imprecision"), then reception analysis, by way of contrast, offers the possibility of determining literary value and conditions for the writing of literary history.
14. From quite another angle comparable research has been undertaken in the field of the reception of art by the psychologist D. E. Berlyne (1971; 1974).

Chapter 6: *Prospects for Further Research*

1. Cf. Eimermacher (1973) and Klaus (1969); the latter in particular s.v. *Modell*.
2. The word symbolic is understood here as referring to an "imputed, learned contiguity between signans and signatum". This connection "does not depend on the presence or absence of any similarity or physical contiguity" (Jakobson, 1965: 24).
3. Jakobson explains Peirce's concept of icon as follows: "*Icon* acts chiefly by factual similarity between its signans and signatum, e.g. between the picture of an animal and the animal pictured; the former stands for the latter 'merely because it resembles it' " (Jakobson, 1965: 23).
4. Or, in Husserl's words, an utterance which "eine begrifflich einheitliche Gruppe von Bedeutungen so zugehört, dass es ihm [dem Ausdruck] wesentlich ist, seine jeweils aktuelle Bedeutung nach der Gelegenheit, nach der redenden Person und ihrer Lage zu orientieren" (Husserl, 1901: II, i, 81).
5. As posited by Boris Ogibenin in a lecture to the Dutch Association of Comparative and General Literature (1976).
6. A brief comment on Habermas' concepts of inter-subjectivity and objectivity may be inserted here. In his view inter-subjectivity consists in a communicative consensus in colloquial language of at least two subjects. The relation between the two subjects is that of participating subject and counterpart. Habermas sees "understanding" primarily as a communicative experience, which may usher in objectivity; and in doing so he expresses reservations *vis-à-vis* the, in his view, "positivistic" position of Dilthey, who in "empathy" (*Einfühlung*) and "re-enactment" (*Nacherleben*) had found a kind of equivalent to "observation" amounting to a non-committed attitude (Habermas 1969: 226-33). We shall not elaborate here on Habermas' criticism of Dilthey. Suffice it to note that when Habermas demands from the interpreter that he "reflect at the same time both the object and himself" as potentialities of an objective totality (ibid.: 228), he comes dangerously close to the fusion of researcher and recipient.
7. Karlheinz Stierle (1975b) has combined semiotic categories with those of the sociology of knowledge.

BIBLIOGRAPHY

This bibliography lists only works that have been mentioned in the text. In general the various titles by the same author are listed in chronological order, in accordance with the date of first publication. If in fact a later edition has been used, the year of that edition is mentioned after the name of the publisher or, in the case of reprinted articles, after the name of the editor.

ABRAMS, M. H.
1972 "What's the Use of Theorizing about the Arts?" in Bloomfield, 1972b: 3–54.

ADORNO, Theodor W.
1958–74 Noten zur Literatur, 4 vols. (Frankfurt: Suhrkamp).
1970 Ästhetische Theorie, Gesammelte Schriften VII (Frankfurt: Suhrkamp).

ADORNO, Theodor W., et al.
1969 Der Positivismusstreit in der deutschen Soziologie, 3rd ed. (Darmstadt and Neuwied: Luchterhand, 1974).

ALBERT, Hans, ed.
1972 Theorie und Realität: Ausgewählte Aufsätze zur Wissenschaftslehre der Sozialwissenschaften, 2nd ed. (Tübingen: Mohr).

BAKKER, R.
1973 Het anonieme denken: Michel Foucault en het structuralisme (Baarn: Wereldvenster).

BARTHES, Roland
1953 Le degré zéro de l'écriture, suivi de Éléments de sémiologie, Bibliothèque médiations (Paris: Gonthier, 1970).
1963 Sur Racine (Paris: Seuil). This volume includes "Histoire ou littérature", pp. 145–68.
1964a Essais critiques (Paris: Seuil). This volume includes "L'Activité structuraliste" (1963), pp. 213–21.
1964b On Racine, trans. Richard Howard (New York: Hill and Wang).
1966 Critique et vérité (Paris: Seuil).

BAUER, Werner, et al.
1972 Text und Rezeption: Wirkungsanalyse zeitgenössischer Lyrik am Beispiel des Gedichtes "Fadensonnen" von Paul Celan (Frankfurt: Athenäum).

BAUMANN, Hans Heinrich
1969 "Über französischen Strukturalismus: Zur Rezeption moderner Linguistik in Frankreich und Deutschland", Sprache im technischen Zeitalter 30: 157–83.

BEARDSLEY, Monroe
1970 The Possibility of Criticism (Detroit: Wayne State University Press).

196   Bibliography

BELINSKIJ, V. G.
1953–9   Polnoe sobranie sočinenij, 13 vols. (Moskva: Izd. Ak. Naŭk
          SSSR).
BENJAMIN, Walter
1936   "Das Kunstwerk im Zeitalter seiner technischen Repro-
          duzierbarkeit", in Benjamin, 1970: 7–65.
1969   Charles Baudelaire: Ein Lyriker im Zeitalter des Hochkapitalismus
          (Frankfurt: Suhrkamp).
1970   Das Kunstwerk im Zeitalter seiner technischen Reproduzierbarkeit:
          Drei Studien zur Kunstsoziologie, 4th ed. (Frankfurt:
          Suhrkamp).
BERGER, Peter L., and Thomas Luckmann
1967   The Social Construction of Reality (London: Allen Lane The
          Penguin Press).
BERGSON, Henri
1889   Essai sur les données immédiates de la conscience (Paris: Felix
          Alcan). English translation: Time and Free Will: An Essay on the
          Immediate Data of Consciousness, trans. F. L. Pogson (New
          York: Harper and Row, 1960).
BERLYNE, D. E.
1971   Aesthetics and Psychobiology (New York: Appleton–Century–
          Crofts).
BERLYNE, D. E., ed.
1974   Studies in the New Experimental Aesthetics: Steps Toward an
          Objective Psychology of Aesthetic Appreciation (Washington
          D.C.: Hemisphere Publishing Corporation, and New York:·
          John Wiley).
BERNŠTEJN, Sergej
1927   "Ästhetische Voraussetzungen einer Theorie der De-
          klamation", in Stempel, 1972: 339–86. Translation of
          "Esteticeskie predposylki teorii deklamacii".
BIERWISCH, Manfred
1965   "Poetik und Linguistik", Sprache im technischen Zeitalter 15:
          1258–73.
BISHOP, John L., ed.
1965   Studies in Chinese Literature (Cambridge, Mass.: Harvard
          University Press).
BLOCH, Ernst
1962   Erbschaft dieser Zeit, Erweiterte Ausgabe (Frankfurt:
          Suhrkamp).
BLOOMFIELD, Morton W.
1972a   "The Two Cognitive Dimensions of the Humanities", in
          Bloomfield, 1972b: 73–90.
BLOOMFIELD, Morton W., ed.
1972b   In Search of Literary Theory (Ithaca and London: Cornell
          University Press).
BLUMENSATH, Heinz, ed.
1972   Strukturalismus in der Literaturwissenschaft (Köln: Kiepenheuer
          and Witsch).

BRECHT, Bertolt
1968   *Gesammelte Werke,* 20 vols. (Frankfurt: Suhrkamp).
BREMOND, Claude
1964   "Le message narratif", *Communications* 4: 4–32.
1966   "La logique des possibles narratifs", *Communications* 8: 60–77.
1973   *Logique du récit* (Paris: Seuil).
1974   "L'Étude structurale du récit depuis V. Propp", paper read at
        the First Congress of the International Association for
        Semiotic Studies (Milano, June 2–6).
BRIK, Osip
1927   "Rythmus und Syntax", in Striedter, 1969: 163–222.
        Translation of "Ritm i sintaksis".
BRONZWAER, W. J. M., D. W. Fokkema and Elrud Kunne-Ibsch
1977   *Tekstboek Algemene Literatuurwetenschap* (Baarn: Ambo).
BROOKS, Cleanth
1947   *The Well-Wrought Urn: Studies in the Structure of Poetry* (New
        York: Harcourt, Brace and Co).
BROOKS, Cleanth, and Robert Penn Warren
1938   *Understanding Poetry,* 3rd ed. (New York: Holt, Rinehart and
        Winston, 1961).
BROWN, Lee B.
1968–9 "Definition and Art Theory", *The Journal of Aesthetics and Art
        Criticism* 27: 409–17.
BRÜTTING, Richard, and Bernhard Zimmermann, eds.
1975   *Theorie—Literatur—Praxis: Arbeitsbuch zur Literaturtheorie seit
        1970* (Frankfurt: Athenaion).
BUBNER, Rüdiger, *et al.,* eds.
1973   *Theorie literarischer Texte,* Neue Hefte für Philosophie 4
        (Göttingen: Vandenhoeck).
BÜHLER, Karl
1934   *Sprachtheorie: Die Darstellungsfunction der Sprache* (Jena: Gustav
        Fischer).
CASSIRER, Ernst A.
1945   "Structuralism in Modern Linguistics", *Word* 1: 99–121.
ČERNYŠEVSKIJ, N. G.
1950   *Ob iskusstve: stat'i, recenzii, vyskazyvanija* (Moskva: Izd. Ak.
        Chudožestv SSSR).
CHATMAN, Seymour
1967   "The Semantics of Style", *Social Science Information* 6, No. 4:
        77–100. Reprinted in Koch, 1972: 343–66.
CH'EN, Jerome
1970   *Mao Papers: Anthology and Bibliography* (London: Oxford
        University Press).
CHRISTIANSEN, Broder
1909   *Philosophie der Kunst* (Hanau: Clauss und Feddersen).
CULLER, Jonathan
1975   *Structuralist Poetics: Structuralism, Linguistics, and the Study of
        Literature* (London: Routledge and Kegan Paul, 1975).

CURTIS, James M.
1976   "Bergson and Russian Formalism", *Comparative Literature* 28: 109–22.

DEMETZ, Peter
1967   *Marx, Engels, and the Poets*, trans. Jeffrey L. Sammons (Chicago and London: University of Chicago Press). Translation of *Marx, Engels und die Dichter* (1959).
1970   "Wandlungen der marxistischen Literaturkritik: Hans Mayer, Ernst Fischer, Lucien Goldmann", in Paulsen, 1969: 13–33.

DIEMER, A., ed.
1971   *Der Methoden- und Theorienpluralismus in den Wissenschaften* (Meisenheim am Glan: Anton Hain).

DOBROLJUBOV, N. A.
1961   *Literaturnaja kritika* (Moskva: Gos. izd. chudožestvennoj literatury).

DOLEŽEL, Lubomír
1972   "From Motifemes to Motifs", *Poetics* 4: 55–91.
1973   *Narrative Modes in Czech Literature* (Toronto: University of Toronto Press).
1976   "Narrative Semantics", *PTL* 1: 129–51.

DORSCH, T. S., ed.
1970   *Classical Literary Criticism* (Harmondsworth: Penguin).

DOUBROVSKY, Serge
1966   *Pourquoi la Nouvelle Critique? Critique et objectivité* (Paris: Mercure de France).

DUCROT, Oswald, *et al.*
1968   *Qu'est-ce que le structuralisme?* (Paris: Seuil).

DUNDES, Alan
1962   "From Etic to Emic Units in the Structural Study of Folktales", *Journal of American Folklore* 75: 95–105. Reprinted in Koch, 1972: 104–15.

DURZAK, Manfred
1971   "Plädoyer für eine Rezeptionsästhetik: Anmerkungen zur deutschen und amerikanischen Literaturkritik am Beispiel von Günter Grass Örtlich Betäubt", *Akzente* 6: 487–504.

ECO, Umberto
1968   *La struttura assente: Introduzione alla ricerca semiologica* (Milano: Bompiani).
1972   *Einführung in die Semiotik*, ed. Jürgen Trabant (München: Fink). Translation of Eco, 1968.
1976   *A Theory of Semiotics*, Advances in Semiotics (Bloomington, Ind. and London: Indiana University Press).

EHRMANN, Jacques, ed.
1970   *Structuralism* (Garden City, N.Y.: Doubleday).

EIMERMACHER, Karl
1971   "Entwicklung, Charakter und Probleme des sowjetischen Strukturalismus in der Literaturwissenschaft", in Karl Eimermacher, ed., *Teksty sovetskogo literaturovedčeskogo strukturalizma*, Centrifuga, Russian Reprintings and Printings, 5 (München: Fink): 9–40.

1973 "Zum Problem einer literaturwissenschaftlichen Metasprache", *Sprache im technischen Zeitalter* 48: 255–77. Revised Dutch version in Bronzwaer, 1977.

EIMERMACHER, Karl, ed.
1972 *Dokumente zur sowjetischen Literaturpolitik 1917–1932*, mit einer Analyse (Stuttgart: Kohlhammer).

EJCHENBAUM, Boris
1918a "Wie Gogol's 'Mantel' gemacht ist", in Striedter, 1969: 123–60. Translation of "Kak sdelana 'Šinel'"·Gogolja".
1918b "Die Illusion des Skaz", in Striedter, 1969: 161–8. Translation of "Illjuzija skaza".
1926 "The Theory of the Formal Method", in Matejka and Pomorska, 1971: 3–38. Translation of "Teorija 'formal'nogo metoda' ".
1929 "Literary Environment", in Matejka and Pomorska, 1971: 56–66. Translation of "Literaturnyj byt".

EMPSON, William
1930 *Seven Types of Ambiguity* (Harmondsworth: Penguin, 1973).

ERLICH, Victor
1955 "Social and Aesthetic Criteria in Soviet Russian Criticism", in Simmons, 1955: 398–417.
1969 *Russian Formalism: History, Doctrine*, with a preface by René Wellek, 3rd ed., Slavistic Printings and Reprintings, 4 (The Hague: Mouton). First edition 1955.

ESCARPIT, Robert, *et al.*
1970 *Le littéraire et le social: Éléments pour une sociologie de la littérature* (Paris: Flammarion).

FABER, Karl-Georg
1971 *Theorie der Geschichtswissenschaft* (München: Beck).

FISCHER, Ernst
1971 *Überlegungen zur Situation der Kunst und zwei andere Essays* (Zürich: Diogenes).

FIZER, John
1963 "Art and the Unconscious", *Survey* 46: 125–134.

FOKKEMA, D. W.
1965 *Literary Doctrine in China and Soviet Influence 1956–1960*, with a foreword by S. H. Chen (The Hague: Mouton).
1971 *Cultureel relativisme en vergelijkende literatuurwetenschap* (Amsterdam: Arbeiderspers).
1972 "Cultural Relativism and Comparative Literature", *Tamkang Review* 3, No. 2: 59–72. Translation of Fokkema, 1971.
1974 "Method and Programme of Comparative Literature", *Synthesis, Bulletin du Comité National de Littérature Comparée de la République Socialiste de Roumanie* 1: 51–63.

FOWLER, Roger
1975a "Language and the Reader: Shakespeare's Sonnet 73", in Fowler, 1975b: 79–123.

FOWLER, Roger, ed.
1975b *Style and Structure in Literature: Essays in the New Stylistics* (Oxford: Blackwell).

FRIEDBERG, Maurice
1959   "Recipe for Writers: Tipichnost and Narodnost", *Soviet Survey* 27: 20–4.
FÜGEN, Hans Norbert
1964   *Die Hauptrichtungen der Literatursoziologie und ihre Methoden* (Bonn: Bouvier).
FUHRMANN, Manfred, ed.
1971   *Terror und Spiel: Probleme der Mythenrezeption* (München: Fink).
GALLAS, Helga
1969   "Ausarbeitung einer marxistischen Literaturtheorie im BPRS und die Rolle von Georg Lukács", *Alternative* 67/68: 148–74.
GARVIN, Paul L., ed.
1964   *A Prague School Reader on Esthetics, Literary Structure, and Style*, translated from the Czech (Washington: Georgetown University Press).
GENETTE, Gérard
1965   "Strukturalismus und Literaturkritik", in Naumann, 1973: 354–77. German translation of "Structuralisme et critique littéraire".
GEURTS, J. P. M.
1975   *Feit en theorie: Inleiding tot de wetenschapsleer* (Assen and Amsterdam: Van Gorcum).
GÖTTNER, Heide
1973   *Logik der Interpretation: Analyse einer literaturwissenschaftlichen Methode unter kritischer Betrachtung der Hermeneutik* (München: Fink).
GOLDMANN, Lucien
1955   *Le dieu caché: Étude sur la vision tragique dans les pensées de Pascal et dans le théâtre de Racine* (Paris: Gallimard).
1964   *Pour une sociologie du roman* (Paris: Gallimard).
GOMBRICH, E. H.
1960   *Art and Illusion: A Study in the Psychology of Pictorial Representation* (London: Phaidon).
GREENLEE, Douglas
1973   *Peirce's Concept of Sign*, Approaches to Semiotics, 5 (The Hague and Paris: Mouton).
GREIMAS, A.-J.
1963   "La description de la signification et la mythologie comparée", *L'Homme: Revue française d'anthropologie* 3, No. 3: 51–66.
1966a   *Sémantique structurale: Recherche de méthode* (Paris: Larousse).
1966b   "Éléments pour une théorie de l'interprétation du récit mythique", *Communications* 8: 28–59.
GROEBEN, Norbert
1972   *Literaturpsychologie: Literaturwissenschaft zwischen Hermeneutik und Empirie* (Stuttgart: Kohlhammer).
GRYGAR, Mojmír
1969   "Bedeutungsgehalt und Sujetaufbau im *Pekař Jan Marhoul* von Vladislav Vančura: zur Poetik der lyrischen Prosa", *Zeitschrift für Slawistik* 14: 199–224.

1972   "Remarques sur la dénomination poétique chez Khlebnikov",
        Poetics 4: 109–19.
GÜNTHER, Hans
1969   "Zur Strukturalismus-Diskussion in der sowjetischen
        Literaturwissenschaft", *Die Welt der Slaven* 14: 1–21.
1971a   "Die Konzeption der literarischen Evolution im tschechischen
        Strukturalismus", *Alternative* 80 (1971): 183–201.
1971b   "Grundbegriffe der Rezeptions- und Wirkungsanalyse im
        tschechischen Strukturalismus", *Poetica* 4: 224–43.
GUÉPIN, J. P.
1972–73 "Propp kan niet en waarom", *Forum der letteren* 13: 129–48; 14:
        30–52.
GUILLÉN, Claudio
1971   *Literature as System: Essays toward the Theory of Literary History*
        (Princeton, N. J.: Princeton University Press).
GULJAEV, N. A., A. N. Bogdanov and L. G. Judkevič
1970   *Teorija literatury v svjazi s problemami estetiki* (Moskva: Izd.
        "Vysšaja škola").
HABERMAS, Jürgen
1969   *Erkenntnis und Interesse* (Frankfurt: Suhrkamp).
HASSAN, Ihab
1975   *Paracriticisms: Seven Speculations of the Times* (Urbana etc.:
        University of Illinois Press).
HEGEL, G. W. F.
1956–65 *Sämtliche Werke,* ed. Hermann Glockner, 4th ed., 22 vols.
        (Stuttgart-Bad Camstatt: Friedrich Frommann).
HELMER, Olaf, and Nicholas Rescher
1959   "Exact vs. Inexact Sciences: A More Instructive Dichotomy?"
        in Krimerman, 1969: 181–203.
HEMPEL, Carl G.
1966   *Philosophy of Natural Science* (Englewood Cliffs, N. J.: Prentice
        Hall).
HILLMANN, Heinz
1972   "Rezeption—empirisch", in Müller-Seidel, 1975: 433–49.
HIRSCH, Jr., E. D.
1972   "Value and Knowledge in the Humanities", in Bloomfield,
        1972b: 55–73.
1976   *The Aims of Interpretation* (Chicago and London: The
        University of Chicago Press).
HOGREBE, Wolfram
1971   "Theorienpluralismus in der Literaturwissenschaft", in
        Diemer, 1971: 265–86.
HOLENSTEIN, Elmar
1975   *Roman Jakobsons phänomenologischer Strukturalismus* (Frankfurt:
        Suhrkamp).
1976   "The Structure of Understanding: Structuralism versus
        Hermeneutics", *PTL* 1: 223–38.
HUSSERL, Edmund
1900–1 *Logische Untersuchungen,* 5th ed., 2 vols., 3 bindings (Tübingen:
        Niemeyer, 1968).

202   *Bibliography*

1968   *Briefe an Roman Ingarden,* mit Erläuterungen und Erin-
            nerungen an Husserl, ed. Roman Ingarden (Den Haag:
            Nijhoff).
INGARDEN, Roman
1931   *Das literarische Kunstwerk,* 3rd ed. (Tübingen: Niemeyer,
            1965).
1968   *Vom Erkennen des literarischen Kunstwerks* (Darmstadt:
            Wissenschaftliche Buchgesellschaft). Adapted translation of *O
            poznawaniu dziela literackiego* (1937).
1969   *Erlebnis, Kunstwerk und Wert: Vorträge zur Ästhetik 1937–1967*
            (Darmstadt: Wissenschaftliche Buchgesellschaft).
ISER, Wolfgang
1970   *Die Appellstruktur der Texte: Unbestimmtheit als Wirkungsbedin-
            gung literarischer Prosa* (Konstanz: Universitätsverlag).
1971   "Indeterminacy and the Reader's Response in Prose Fiction",
            in Miller, 1971: 1–45.
1972   *Der implizite Leser* (München: Fink).
IVANOV, Vjačeslav Vs.
1973a   "The Category of Time in Twentieth-Century Art and
            Culture", *Semiotica* 8: 1–46.
1973b   "On Binary Relations in Linguistic and Other Semiotic and
            Social Systems", in Radu J. Bogdan and Ilkka Niiniluoto, ed.,
            Logic, Language, and Probability (Dordrecht: D. Reidel):
            196–201.
1973c   "Značenie idej M. M. Bachtina o znake, vyskazyvanii i dialoge
            dlja sovremennoj semiotiki", *Trudy,* 1973: VI, 5–44.
IVANOV, V. V., and V. N. Toporov
1962   "Ketskaja model' mira", in *Simpozium,* 1962: 99–103.
JAKOBSON, Roman
1921   "Die neueste russische Poesie", in Stempel, 1972: 19–136.
            Translation of "Novejšaja russkaja poezija".
1934   "Was ist Poesie", in Stempel, 1972: 393–418. Translation of
            "Co je poesie".
1939   "Signe zéro", in *Mélanges de linguistique offerts à Charles Bally*
            (Genève: Georg). Reprinted in Jakobson, 1971: II, 211–20.
1960   "Linguistics and Poetics", in Sebeok, 1960: 350–78.
1965   "Quest for the Essence of Language", *Diogenes* 51: 21–38.
1971   *Selected Writings, II, Word and Language* (The Hague and Paris:
            Mouton).
JAKOBSON, Roman, and Claude Lévi-Strauss
1962   "'Les chats' de Charles Baudelaire", *L'Homme: Revue française
            d'anthropologie* 2: 5–21. English translation in Lane, 1970:
            202–21.
JAMESON, Fredric
1971   *Marxism and Form: Twentieth-Century Dialectical Theories of
            Literature* (Princeton, N. J.: Princeton University Press).
JARRY, André
1974   "Aujourd'hui, Lotman et le 'texte' artistique", *Le monde,*
            March 8, 1974.

JAUSS, Hans Robert
1970 *Literaturgeschichte als Provokation* (Frankfurt: Suhrkamp).
1973 "Racines und Goethes Iphigenie: mit einem Nachwort über die Partialität der rezeptionsästhetischen Methode", in Bubner, 1973: 1–47.
1975a "La douceur du foyer—Lyrik des Jahres 1857 als Muster der Vermittlung sozialer Normen", in Warning, 1975: 401–34.
1975b "Der Leser als Instanz einer neuen Geschichte der Literatur", *Poetica* 7: 325–44.
1975c "The Idealist Embarrassment: Observations on Marxist Aesthetics", *New Literary History* 7: 191–209.

JAUSS, Hans Robert, ed.
1968 *Die Nicht Mehr Schönen Künste: Grenzphänomene des Ästhetischen* (München: Fink).

JUST, Georg
1972 *Darstellung und Appell in der 'Blechtrommel' von Günter Grass: Darstellungsästhetik versus Wirkungsästhetik* (Frankfurt: Athenäum).

KAČER, M.
1968 "Der Prager Strukturalismus in der Ästhetik und Literaturwissenschaft", *Die Welt der Slaven* 13: 64–87.

KAGAN, Moissej
1971 *Vorlesungen zur marxistisch-leninistischen Ästhetik* (Berlin: Dietz). Translation of *Lekcii po marksistsko–leninskoj estetike*.

KAPP, Volker, ed.
1973 *Aspekte objektiver Literaturwissenschaft: Die italienische Literaturwissenschaft zwischen Formalismus, Strukturalismus und Semiotik* (Heidelberg: Quelle und Meyer).

KATZ, Jerrold J.
1972 *Semantic Theory* (New York: Harper and Row).

KAYSER, Wolfgang
1958 *Die Vortragsreise: Studien zur Literatur* (Bern: Francke).

KLAUS, Georg, ed.
1969 *Wörterbuch der Kybernetik*, 2 vols. (Frankfurt: Fischer).

KOCH, Walter A., ed.
1972 *Strukturelle Textanalyse, Analyse du récit, Discourse Analysis* (Hildesheim and New York: Georg Olms).

KOESTLER, Arthur
1970 "Literature and the Law of Diminishing Returns", *Encounter* 34, No. 5: 38–46.

KON, I. S.
1966 *Die Geschichtsphilosophie des 20. Jahrhunderts: Kritischer Abriss*, 2 vols. (Berlin: Akademie-Verlag).

KONSTANTINOVIĆ, Zoran
1973 *Phänomenologie und Literaturwissenschaft: Skizzen zu einer wissenschaftstheoretischen Begründung* (München: List).

KOSELLECK, R., and W.-D. Stempel, eds.
1973 *Geschichte: Ereignis und Erzählung* (München: Fink).

204   Bibliography

KRIMERMAN, Leonard, ed.
1969   The Nature and Scope of Social Science: A Critical Anthology
        (New York: Meredith).
KUNNE-IBSCH, Elrud
1972   Die Stellung Nietzsches in der Entwicklung der modernen
        Literaturwissenschaft (Assen: Van Gorcum, and Tübingen:
        Niemeyer).
1974   "Form und Bedeutung: Eine Kritik der 'Form-Inhalt'
        Dichotomie", Degrés 2, No. 5: i 1–12.
KUO Mo-jo
1971   Li Po yü Tu Fu (Li Po and Tu Fu) (Peking: Jen-min wen-hsüeh
        ch'u-pan-she).
LANE, Michael, ed.
1970   Structuralism: A Reader (London: Cape).
LANSON, Gustave
1910   Essais de méthode de critique et d'histoire littéraire, ed. Henri Peyre
        (Paris: Hachette, 1965).
LEENHARDT, Jacques
1973   Lecture politique du roman: La Jalousie d'Alain Robbe-Grillet
        (Paris: Éditions de Minuit).
LENIN, V. I.
1967   On Literature and Art (Moscow: Progress Publishers).
LÉVI-STRAUSS, Claude
1945   "L'Analyse structurale en linguistique et en anthropologie",
        Word 1:33–54. Reprinted in Lévi-Strauss, 1958: 37–63, and
        1972: 31–55.
1955   Tristes tropiques (Paris: Plon).
1958   Anthropologie structurale (Paris: Plon).
1960   "La structure et la forme: Réflexions sur un ouvrage de
        Vladimir Propp", Cahiers de l'Institut de Science Économique
        Appliquée, 99: 3–37.
1962   Pensée sauvage (Paris: Plon).
1972   Structural Anthropology, trans. Claire Jakobson and Brooke
        Grundfest Schoepf (Harmondsworth: Penguin). Translation
        of Lévi-Strauss, 1958
LEVIN, Harry
1966   Refractions: Essays in Comparative Literature (New York:
        Oxford University Press).
LEVIN, Samuel R.
1962   Linguistic Structures in Poetry (The Hague and Paris: Mouton).
LINK, Hannelore
1973   " 'Die Appellstruktur der Texte' und ein 'Paradigmawechsel
        in der Literaturwissenschaft'?" Jahrbuch der deutschen
        Schillergesellschaft 17: 532–83.
LORENZ, Richard, ed.
1969   Proletarische Kulturrevolution in Sowjetrussland 1917–1921:
        Dokumente des 'Proletkult' (München: DTV).

LOTMAN, Jurij M.
1964   *Lektsii po struktural'noi poetike: Vvedenie, Teoriia stikha,*
        Introduction by Thomas G. Winner, Brown University Slavic
        Reprint, 5 (Providence, R. I.: Brown University Press, 1968).
1970   *Struktura chudožestvennogo teksta* (Moskva: Izd. "Iskusstvo").
1972a   *Die Struktur literarischer Texte,* trans. Rolf-Dietrich Keil
        (München: Fink). Translation of Lotman, 1970.
1972b   *Vorlesungen zu einer strukturalen Poetik: Einführung, Theorie des
        Verses,* ed. Karl Eimermacher und Waltraud Jachnow,
        Theorie und Geschichte der Literatur und der schönen Künste,
        14 (München: Fink). Translation of Lotman, 1964.
1972c   *Analiz poetičeskogo teksta: Struktura sticha* (Leningrad:
        Prosveščenie).
1975   *Die Analyse des poetischen Textes,* trans. Rainer Grübel
        (Kronberg, Ts.: Scriptor). Translation of Lotman, 1972c.

LOWENTHAL, Leo
1957   *Literature and the Image of Man: Sociological Studies of the
        European Drama and Novel, 1600–1900* (Boston: Beacon Press).

LUKÁCS, Georg
1958   *Wider den missverstandenen Realismus* (Hamburg: Claassen).
1962   *Die Theorie des Romans: Ein geschichtsphilosophischer Versuch
        über die Formen der grossen Epik* (Neuwied: Luchterhand). First
        published in 1916.
1963–75 *Werke,* 17 vols. (incomplete) (Neuwied: Luchterhand).

MAGUIRE, Robert A.
1968   *Red Virgin Soil: Soviet Literature in the 1920s* (Princeton, N. J.:
        Princeton University Press).

MANDELKOW, Karl Robert
1970   "Probleme der Wirkungsgeschichte", *Jahrbuch für inter-
        nationale Germanistik* 2: 71–85.

MAO Tse-tung
1942   "Talks at the Yenan Forum on Literature and Art", *Selected
        Works,* III (Peking: Foreign Languages Press, 1967): 69–99.
        Translation of "Tsai Yen-an wen-i tso-t'an-hui shang ti
        chiang-hua" (edition of 1953).
1950   *Problems of Art and Literature* (New York: International
        Publishers). Translation of "Tsai Yen-an wen-i tso-t'an-hui
        shang ti chiang-hua" (pre-1950 edition).

MARGOLIS, Joseph
1965   *The Language of Art and Art Criticism* (Detroit: Wayne State
        University Press).

MARKOV, Vladimir
1968   *Russian Futurism: A History* (Berkeley and Los Angeles:
        University of California Press).

MARX, Karl, and Friedrich Engels
1953   *Über Kunst und Literatur: Eine Sammlung aus ihren Schriften,* ed.
        Michail Lifschitz, mit einem Vorwort von Fritz Erpenbeck
        (Berlin: Henschelverlag).
1967–8 *Über Kunst und Literatur,* 2 vols. (Berlin: Dietz).

206   Bibliography

MATEJKA, Ladislav, and Krystyna Pomorska
1971   Readings in Russian Poetics: Formalist and Structuralist Views
        (Cambridge, Mass. and London: M.I.T. Press).
MEINECKE, Friedrich
1936   Die Entstehung des Historismus, 2 vols. (München and Berlin:
        R. Oldenburg).
MELETINSKIJ, E. M.
1969   "Zur strukturell-typologischen Erforschung des Volks-
        märchens", in Propp, 1972: 179–215. Translation of
        "Strukturno-tipologičeskoe izučenie skazki".
MELETINSKIJ, Elizar, and Dmitri Segal
1971   "Structuralisme et sémiotique en URSS", Diogène 73: 94–118.
MERLEAU-PONTY, Maurice
1945   Phénoménologie de la perception (Paris: Gallimard).
MILLER, J. Hillis, ed.
1971   Aspects of Narrative (New York and London: Columbia
        University Press).
MORRIS, Charles
1964   Signification and Significance: A Study of the Relations of Signs and
        Values, Studies in Communication (Cambridge, Mass.: M.I.T.
        Press).
MORRIS, Wesley
1972   Toward a New Historicism (Princeton, N. J.: Princeton
        University Press).
MÜLLER-SEIDEL, Walter, ed.
1975   Historizität in Sprach- und Literaturwissenschaft: Vorträge und
        Berichte der Stuttgarter Germanistentagung 1972 (München:
        Fink).
MUKAŘOVSKÝ, Jan
1929   "Über die gegenwärtige Poetik", in Mukařovský, 1974:
        84–100.
1934   "Die Kunst als semiologisches Faktum", in Mukařovský,
        1970: 138–46. Translation of "L'art comme fait sémi-
        ologique".
1935   Aesthetic Function, Norm and Value as Social Facts, trans. by
        Mark E. Suino, Michigan Slavic Contributions (Ann Arbor:
        Department of Slavic Languages and Literature, University of
        Michigan, 1970). Translation of "Estetická funkce, norma a
        hodnota jako sociální fakty".
1938   "Die poetische Benennung und die ästhetische Funktion der
        Sprache", in Mukařovský, 1967: 44–55. Translation of
        "Dénomination poétique et la fonction esthétique de la
        langue".
1940   "Der Strukturalismus in der Ästhetik und in der
        Literaturwissenschaft", in Mukařovský, 1967: 7–55. Trans-
        lation of "Strukturalismus v estetice a ve vědě o literatuře".
1947   "Zum Begriffssystem der tschechoslovakischen Kunst-
        theorie", in Mukařovský, 1974: 7–20.
1967   Kapitel aus der Poetik, trans. Walter Schamschula (Frankfurt:
        Suhrkamp).

1970   *Kapitel aus der Ästhetik,* trans. Walter Schamschula (Frankfurt: Suhrkamp).
1974   *Studien zur strukturalistischen Ästhetik und Poetik,* trans. Herbert Grönebaum und Gisela Riff, mit einem Nachwort: "Die strukturalistische Ästhetik und Poetik Jan Mukařovskýs" (München: Carl Hanser).

NAGEL, Ernest
1961   *The Structure of Science: Problems in the Logic of Scientific Explanation* (London: Routledge and Kegan Paul).

NAUMANN, Hans, ed.
1973   *Der moderne Strukturbegriff: Materialien zu seiner Entwicklung* (Darmstadt: Wissenschaftliche Buchgesellschaft).

"ON THE PROBLEM of the Typical in Literature and Art" (in Russian)
1955   "K voprosu o tipičeskom v literature i iskusstve", *Kommunist* 18: 12–24.

OOMEN, Ursula
1973   *Linguistische Grundlagen poetischer Texte* (Tübingen: Niemeyer).

OVSJANNIKOV, M. F., ed.
1973   *Marksistsko-leninskaja estetika* (Moskva: Izd. Moskovskogo Universiteta).

PARKINSON, G. H. R., ed.
1970   *Georg Lukács: The Man, His Work and His Ideas* (London: Weidenfeld and Nicolson).

PAULSEN, Wolfgang, ed.
1969   *Der Dichter und seine Zeit: Politik im Spiegel der Literatur,* Drittes Amherster Kolloquium zur modernen deutschen Literatur (Heidelberg: Lothar Stiehm).

PEARCE, Roy Harvey
1969   *Historicism Once More: Problems and Occasions for the American Scholar* (Princeton, N. J.: Princeton University Press).

PEIRCE, Charles Sanders
1958–60 *Collected Papers,* 8 vols., 2nd printing (Cambridge, Mass.: Harvard University Press). Vol. 1–6 edited by Charles Hartshorne and Paul Weis, vol. 7–8 by Arthur W. Burks.

PIAGET, Jean
1968   *Le structuralisme* (Paris: Presses universitaires de France).

PICARD, Raymond
1965   *Nouvelle Critique ou nouvelle imposture* (Paris: Jean-Jacques Pauvert).

PLECHANOW, G. W.
1955   *Kunst und Literatur,* Vorwort M. Rosental, Redaktion und Kommentar N. F. Beltschikow, trans. Joseph Harhammer (Berlin: Dietz). Translation of *Iskusstvo i literatura* (1948).

POMORSKA, Krystyna
1968   *Russian Formalist Theory and Its Poetic Ambiance* (The Hague: Mouton).

POPPER, Karl R.
1949 "Naturgesetze und theoretische Systeme", in Albert, 1972: 43–59.
1969a *The Poverty of Historicism* (London: Routledge and Kegan Paul). First edition 1944–45.
1969b "Die Logik der Sozialwissenschaften," in Adorno *et al.*, 1969: 103–25.
1972a *The Logic of Scientific Discovery,* revised ed. (London: Hutchinson). Revised translation of *Logik der Forschung* (Wien, 1934).
1972b *Objective Knowledge: An Evolutionary Approach* (Oxford: Clarendon Press).

POSNER, Roland
1972 "Strukturalismus in der Gedichtinterpretation: Textdeskription und Rezeptionsanalyse am Beispiel von Baudelaire's 'Les chats' ", in Blumensath, 1972: 202–42. The first version of this article appeared in 1969.

Problems of Soviet Literature
1935 Reports and Speeches at the First Soviet Writers' Congress, ed. H. G. Scott (Moscow and Leningrad: Co-operative Publishing Society of Foreign Workers in the USSR). Speeches by A. Ždanov, M. Gorkij, N. Bucharin, K. Radek and A. Steckij.

PROPP, Vladimir Ja.
1928 *Morfologija skazki,* 2nd ed., Issledovanija po fol'kloru i mifologii vostoka (Moskva: "Nauka", 1969).
1958 *Morphology of the Folktale,* ed. by Svatava Pirkova-Jakobson, trans. by Laurence Scott, *International Journal of American Linguistics,* vol. 24, No. 4, Part III. Publication 10 of the Indiana University Research Center in Anthropology, Folklore, and Linguistics. Translation of Propp, 1928.
1968 *Morphology of the Folktale,* Second edition ed. by Louis A. Wagner and Alan Dundes, Publication of the American Folklore Society, Bibliographical and Special Series, 9; Indiana University Research Center in Anthropology, Folklore, and Linguistics, 10 (Austin and London: University of Texas Press). Translation of Propp, 1928.
1970a *Morphologie du conte,* trans. Claude Ligny (Paris: Gallimard). Translation of Propp, 1928.
1970b *Morphologie du conte, suivi de "Les transformations des contes merveilleux" et de E. Mélétinski: "L'Étude structurale et typologique du conte",* trans. Marguérite Derrida, Tzvetan Todorov et Claude Kahn, Collection poétique, Sciences humaines, 12 (Paris: Seuil). Translation of Propp, 1928.
1972 *Morphologie des Märchens,* ed. Karl Eimermacher (München: Carl Hanser). Translation of Propp, 1928.

RESCHER, Nicholas
1964 *Introduction to Logic* (New York: St. Martin's Press).
1969 *Introduction to Value Theory* (Englewood Cliffs, N. J.: Prentice-Hall).

1973   *The Coherence Theory of Truth* (London: Oxford University Press).

REVZIN, I. I.
1974   "On the Continuous Nature of the Poetic Semantics", *Poetics* 10: 21–7.

REVZINA, O. G.
1972   "The Fourth Summer School on Secondary Modeling Systems (Tartu, 17–24 August 1970)", *Semiotica* 6: 222–44.

REVZINA, O. G., and I. I. Revzin
1975   "A Semiotic Experiment of Stage: The Violation of the Postulate of Normal Communication as a Dramatic Device", *Semiotica* 14: 245–68.

RICOEUR, Paul
1967   "La structure, le mot, l'événement", *Esprit* 35: 801–22.
1969   *Le conflit des interprétations: Essais d'herméneutique* (Paris: Seuil).

RIESER, Max
1968–9   "Problems of Artistic Forms: The Concept of Art", *The Journal of Aesthetics and Art Criticism* 27: 261–70.

RIFFATERRE, Michael
1966   "Describing Poetic Structures: Two Approaches to Baudelaire's 'Les chats'", *Yale French Studies*, Nos. 36–37: 200–42. Quoted from the reprinted version in Ehrmann, 1970: 188–230.

ROZENTAL', M. M., and P. F. Judin, eds.
1963   *Filosofskij slovar'* (Moskva: Izd. političeskoj literatury).

RÜHLE, Jürgen
1960a   *Literatur und Revolution* (Köln: Kiepenheuer and Witsch).
1960b   "The Soviet Theater: Part II", *Problems of Communism* 9, No. 1: 40–50.

RUWET, Nicolas
1968   "Limites de l'analyse linguistique en poétique", *Langages* 12: 56–70.
1971   "Je te donne ces vers . . .", *Poétique* 7: 355–401. Reprinted in Ruwet, 1972: 228–48.
1972   *Langage, musique, poésie* (Paris: Seuil).

SAPIR, Edward
1949   *Selected Writings in Language, Culture, and Personality*, ed. David G. Mandelbaum (Berkeley and Los Angeles: University of California Press).

SARTRE, Jean-Paul
1948   *Situations*, II (Paris: Gallimard).

SAUSSURE, Ferdinand de
1915   *Cours de linguistique générale*, publié par Charles Bally, Albert Sechehaye et Albert Riedlinger, ed. Tullio de Mauro (Paris: Payot, 1972).
1959   *Course in General Linguistics*, trans. Wade Baskin (New York: McGraw-Hill). Translation of Saussure, 1915.

SCHIWY, Günther
1971   *Neue Aspekte des Strukturalismus* (München: Kösel).

SCHMID, Herta
1970   "Zum Begriff der Konkretisation im tschechischen Struktural-
        ismus", *Sprache im technischen Zeitalter* 36: 290–319.
SCHMID, Wolf
1973   "Poetische Sprache in Formalistischer Sicht: Zu einer neuen
        Anthologie russischer Formalisten", *Zeitschrift für französische
        Sprache und Literatur* 83: 260–71. Review of Stempel, 1972.
SCHMIDT, Siegfried J.
1969   *Bedeutung und Begriff: Zur Fundierung einer sprachphilosophischen
        Semantik* (Braunschweig: Vieweg).
1973   "On the Foundation and the Research Strategies of a Science
        of Literary Communication", *Poetics* 7: 7–36.
1976   "On a Theoretical Basis for a Rational Science of Literature",
        PTL 1: 239–64.
SCHMITT, Hans-Jürgen, ed.
1973   *Die Expressionismusdebatte: Materialien zu einer marxistischen
        Realismuskonzeption* (Frankfurt: Suhrkamp).
SCHOBER, Rita
1973   "Zum Problem der Wertung literarischer Kunstwerke", in
        Brütting and Zimmermann, 1975: 197–251.
SCHOLES, Robert
1974   *Structuralism in Literature: An Introduction* (New Haven and
        London: Yale University Press).
SCHÜCKING, Levin L.
1923   *The Sociology of Literary Taste*, trans. E. W. Dickes (London:
        Kegan Paul etc., 1944). Translation of *Soziologie der
        literarischen Geschmacksbildung.*
SCHUPP, Franz
1975   *Poppers Methodologie der Geschichtswissenschaft: Historische
        Erklärung und Interpretation* (Bonn: Bouvier).
SEBEOK, Thomas A.
1972   "Problems in the Classification of Signs", in Evelyn Scherabon
        Firchow *et al.*, eds., *Studies for Einar Haugen* (The Hague and
        Paris: Mouton): 511–22.
SEBEOK, Thomas A., ed.
1960   *Style· in Language* (New York: Technology Press of the
        M.I.T.).
SEGAL, D. M.
1962   "O nekotorych problemach semiotičeskogo izučenija
        mifologii", in *Simpozium,* 1962: 92–9.
1968   "Nabljudenija nad semantičeskoj structuroj poetičeskogo
        proizvedenija", *International Journal of Slavic Linguistics and
        Poetics* 11: 159–72.
1974   *Aspects of Structuralism in Soviet Philology,* Papers on Poetics
        and Semiotics, 2 (Tel-Aviv University, Department of Poetics
        and Comparative Literature).
SEGERS, Rien T.
1975   "Readers, Text and Author: Some Implications of
        Rezeptionsästhetik", *Yearbook of Comparative and General
        Literature* 24: 15–24.

Bibliography 211

SEIFFERT, Helmut
1972   Einführung in die Wissenschaftstheorie, I (München: C. H. Beck).
SIMMONS, Ernest J.
1961   "The Origin of Literary Control", Survey: A Journal of Soviet and East-European Studies 36: 78–85, and 37: 60–7.
SIMMONS, Ernest J., ed.
1955   Continuity and Change in Russian and Soviet Thought (Cambridge, Mass.: Harvard University Press).
Simpozium
1962   Simpozium po strukturnomu izučeniju znakovych sistem: tezisy dokladov (Moskva: Izd. Ak. Nauk SSSR).
SKAGESTAD, Peter
1975   Making Sense of History: The Philosophy of Popper and Collingwood (Oslo: Universitetsforlaget).
ŠKLOVSKIJ, Viktor
1914   "Die Auferweckung des Wortes", in Stempel, 1972: 3–18. Translation of "Voskrešenie slova".
1916a   "Die Kunst als Verfahren", in Striedter, 1969: 3–36. Translation of "Iskusstvo, kak priëm".
1916b   "Der Zusammenhang zwischen den Verfahren der Sujetfügung und den allgemeinen Stilverfahren", in Striedter, 1969: 37–122. Translation of "Svjaz' priëmov sjužetosloženija s obščimi priëmami stilja".
1921   "Der parodistische Roman: Sternes 'Tristram Shandy'", in Striedter, 1969: 245–300. Translation of "Parodijnij roman: 'Tristram Šendi' Sterna".
1925   Theorie der Prosa, ed. Gisela Drohla (Frankfurt: Fischer, 1966). Translation of O teorii prozy.
ŠPET, Gustav
1922–3 Estetičeskie fragmenty, 3 vols. (Peterburg: Knigoizdatel'stvo "Kolos").
STAIGER, Emil
1971   Die Kunst der Interpretation: Studien zur deutschen Literaturgeschichte (München: DTV).
STEMPEL, W.-D., ed.
1972   Texte der Russischen Formalisten, II: Texte zur Theorie des Verses und der poetischen Sprache (München: Fink).
STIERLE, Karlheinz
1972   "Semiotik als Kulturwissenschaft: A. -J. Greimas' Du sens, Essais sémiotiques", in Stierle, 1975a: 186–219.
1975a   Text als Handlung: Perspektiven einer systematischen Literaturwissenschaft (München: Fink).
1975b   "Was heisst Rezeption bei fiktionalen Texten?" Poetica 7: 345–387.
STRIEDTER, Jurij
1971   "Poesie als 'neuer Mythos' der Revolution am Beispiel Majakovskijs", in Fuhrmann, 1971: 409–35.
STRIEDTER, Jurij, ed.
1969   Texte der Russischen Formalisten, I: Texte zur allgemeinen Literaturtheorie und zur Theorie der Prosa (München: Fink).

212   *Bibliography*

SUS, Oleg
1972   "On the Genetic Preconditions of Czech Structuralist
        Semiology and Semantics: An Essay on Czech and German
        Thought", *Poetics* 4: 28–55.
SWAYZE, Harold
1962   *Political Control of Literature in the USSR, 1946-1959*
        (Cambridge, Mass.: Harvard University Press).
TEESING, H. P. H.
1964   "Der Standort des Interpreten", *Orbis litterarum* 19: 31–47.
TERC, Abram (pseudonym of A. D. Sinjavskij)
1957   "On Socialist Realism", in Abram Tertz, *The Trial Begins, and
        On Socialist Realism* (New York: Vintage Books, 1965): 147–
        220.
TIMOFEEV, L., and N. Vengrov
1955   *Kratkij slovar' literaturovedčeskich terminov*, 2nd ed. (Moskva:
        Gos. učebno-pedagogičeskoe izd. Min. Prosveščenija RSFSR).
TODOROV, Tzvetan
1965a   "L'Héritage méthodologique du formalisme", *L'Homme:
        Revue française d'anthropologie* 5: 64–84.
1966   "Les catégories du récit littéraire", *Communications* 8: 125-151.
1969   *Grammaire du Décaméron*, Approaches to Semiotics, 3 (The
        Hague: Mouton).
1971   *Poétique de la prose* (Paris: Seuil).
TODOROV, Tzvetan, ed.
1965b   *Théorie de la littérature: Textes des Formalistes russes;* préface de
        Roman Jakobson (Paris: Seuil).
TOMAŠEVSKIJ, Boris
1925   *Teorija literatury*, reprinted with introduction by A. Kirilloff
        (Letchworth: Bradda Books, 1971). The original edition was
        published by Gos. izdatel'stvo in Leningrad.
TROTSKY, Leon
1924   *Literature and Revolution* (Ann Arbor: University of Michigan
        Press, 2nd printing, 1966). Translation of *Literatura i revoljucija.*
TRUBETZKOY, Nikolai
1933   "Die gegenwärtige Phonologie", in Naumann, 1973: 57–81.
        Translation of "La phonologie actuelle".
Trudy
1964–73 *Trudy po znakovym sistemam*, 6 vols. (Tartu: Gos. Universitet).
TYNJANOV, Jurij
1924a   "Das literarische Faktum", in Striedter, 1969: 393–432.
        Translation of "Literaturnyj fakt".
1924b   *Problema stichotvornogo jazyka; stat'i* (Moskva: Sovetskij
        pisatel', 1965). Partly translated in Matejka and Pomorska,
        1971: 126–145.
1927   "Über die literarische Evolution", in Striedter, 1969: 433–62.
        Translation of "O literaturnoj evoljucii".
1929   *Archaisty i novatory, Archaisten und Neuerer*, Nachdruck der
        Leningrader Ausgabe von 1929, mit einer Vorbemerkung von

Dmitrij Tschižewskij, Slavische Propyläen, 31 (München: Fink, 1967).

TYNJANOV, Jurij, and Roman Jakobson
1928 "Problems in the Study of Literature and Language", in Matejka and Pomorska, 1971: 79-82. Translation of "Problemy izučenija literatury i jazyka".

USPENSKIJ, B. A.
1962 "O semiotike iskusstva", in Simpozium, 1962: 125-129.
1970 *Poetika kompozicii: Struktura chudožestvennogo teksta i tipologija kompozicionnoj formy* (Moskva: Izd. "Iskusstvo").
1973 *A Poetics of Composition*, trans. Valentina Zavarin and Susan Wittig (Berkeley and Los Angeles: University of California Press). Translation of Uspenskij, 1970.

VAN DIJK, Teun A.
1972 *Some Aspects of Text Grammars: A Study in Theoretical Linguistics and Poetics* (The Hague and Paris: Mouton).

VINOGRADOV, Viktor
1925 "Das Problem des *Skaz* in der Stilistik", in Striedter, 1969: 169-208. Translation of "Skaz v stilistike".

VODIČKA, Felix
1964 "The History of the Echo of Literary Works", in Garvin, 1964: 71-82.
1972 "The Integrity of the Literary Process: Notes on the Development of Theoretical Thought in J. Mukařovský's Work", *Poetics* 4: 5-16.

VÖLKER, Klaus
1969 "Brecht und Lukács: Analyse einer Meinungsverschiedenheit", *Alternative* 67/68: 134-48.

VOLKELT, Johannes
1905-14 *System der Aesthetik*, 3 vols. (München: C. H. Beck).

WARNING, Rainer, ed.
1975 *Rezeptionsästhetik: Theorie und Praxis* (München: Fink).

WATSON, George
1969 *The Study of Literature* (London: Allen Lane The Penguin Press).

WEITZ, Morris
1956 "The Role of Theory in Aesthetics", *The Journal of Aesthetics and Art Criticism* 15(1956): 27-35.
1972 *Hamlet and the Philosophy of Literary Criticism* (London: Faber and Faber).

WELLEK, René
1955-65 *A History of Modern Criticism: 1750-1950*, 4 vols. (New Haven and London: Yale University Press).
1963 *Concepts of Criticism*, ed. Stephen G. Nichols, Jr. (New Haven and London: Yale University Press).
1970 *Discriminations: Further Concepts of Criticism* (New Haven and London: Yale University Press).

1973   "Zur methodischen Aporie einer Rezeptionsgeschichte", in Koselleck and Stempel, 1973: 515-17.

WELLEK, René, and Austin Warren
1956   *Theory of Literature* (New York: Harcourt, Brace and World). First edition 1949.

WETTER, Gustav A.
1966   *Soviet Ideology Today: Dialectical and Historical Materialism*, trans. Peter Heath (London: Heinemann).

WHORF, Benjamin Lee
1950   "An American Indian Model of the Universe", *International Journal of American Linguistics* 16: 67-73.
1956   *Language, Thought, and Reality: Selected Writings*, ed. John B. Carroll, foreword by Stuart Chase (Cambridge, Mass.: M.I.T. Press, 1971).

WIENOLD, Götz
1972   *Semiotik der Literatur* (Frankfurt: Athenäum).

INDEX

ABRAMS, M. H., 3
Achmatova, Anna, 99
Adorno, Theodor W., 82, 115,
123–30, 132–5, 191
Aeschylus, 83, 87
Albert, Hans, 140
Apel, Karl-Otto, 173
Aristophanes, 87
Aristotle, 86, 128, 182

BACHTIN, M. M., 40
Bakker, R., 52
Balzac, Honoré de, 88–9, 95, 98,
100, 117, 120
Barth, John, 132
Barthes, Roland, 45, 55–60, 71, 73,
80, 131, 146, 193
Baudelaire, Charles, 56, 71, 73–5,
77, 130, 158, 176–7, 192
Baudouin de Courtenay, Jan, 52
Bauer, Bruno, 86
Bauer, Edgar, 86
Bauer, Egbert, 86
Bauer, Werner, 157–61, 193
Baumann, Hans Heinrich, 54
Beardsley, Monroe C., 7
Beckett, Samuel, 125
Beethoven, Ludwig van, 92
Belinskij, V. G., 15, 38, 98–9,
101–3, 107, 119, 128, 185, 188
Benjamin, Walter, 115, 128–30,
133, 191–2
Berger, Peter, 177–8
Bergson, Henri, 16, 50–1, 57, 166
Berlyne, D. E., 193
Bernštejn, Sergej, 11, 18, 21, 30, 40
Bierwisch, Manfred, 186
Bishop, John L., 184
Bloch, Ernst, 117–8, 125, 132, 190
Bloch, Joseph, 192
Bloomfield, Morton, 104

Blumenberg, Hans, 156
Boccaccio, Giovanni, 70
Bogatyrëv, Pëtr, 11
Borgius, W., 192
Brecht, Bertolt, 119–21, 128–30,
190–2
Bremond, Claude, 28–9, 61,
64–71, 180
Brik, Osip, 19–20, 40, 43–4
Brooks, Cleanth, 5, 44
Brown, Lee B., 3
Bucharin, Nikolaj, 97–8
Bühler, Karl, 31, 148, 193
Bulgakov, Michail, 95
Bunin, I. A., 98

ČAPEK, Karel, 35
Cassirer, Ernst A., 30
Celan, Paul, 157, 159–60
Céline, L. F., 98
Černyševskij, N. G., 101, 103
Cervantes, Miguel de Saavedra, 87
Chatman, Seymour, 47
Chekhov, A. P., 95, 98
Ch'en, Jerome, 190
Ch'en Yung, 107
Cheng Chi-ch'iao, 107, 188
Chiang Ch'ing, 108–9
Chin Ching-mai, 113
Chlebnikov, Viktor, 10
Chou Lai-hsiang, 106
Chou Yang, 103, 105–6, 114,
189–90
Christiansen, Broder, 14, 17, 21,
24, 30–1
Ch'ü Ch'iu-pai, 105, 114
Collingwood, R. G., 171
Conrad, Joseph, 122
Conrad, W., 33
Cortázar, Julio, 132
Culler, Jonathan, 186

Curtis, James M., 16
Čužak, N., 97

DANTE, 29, 87
Danto, A. C., 139
Delille, Jacques, 77
Demetz, Peter, 55, 84, 86, 89, 131, 186
Dickens, Charles, 117
Dilthey, Wilhelm, 140–1, 173, 194
Dobroljubov, N. A., 89, 101, 103, 106
Döblin, Alfred, 116
Doležel, Lubomir, 29–30, 36, 180
Dorsch, T. S., 4
Dos Passos, John, 116, 118, 120–1
Dostoevsky, F. M., 98, 117
Doubrovsky, Serge, 55
Droysen, Johann Gustav, 139, 193
Ducrot, Oswald, 193
Dundes, Alan, 29, 62
Durzak, Manfred, 161–2

ECO, Umberto, 42, 47, 163, 167–70, 181–2, 185
Eimermacher, Karl, 39, 41, 93–4, 102, 194
Ejchenbaum, Boris, 11–3, 17–9, 22, 25–6, 29, 36, 38
Eliot, T. S., 5–6
Empson, William, 34
Engels, Friedrich, 81–90, 93, 106–7, 111, 115–6, 120, 122–4, 127, 130, 132, 135, 186–8, 192
Erenburg, Il'ja, 95–6
Erlich, Victor, 11, 13, 17, 26, 100, 187
Escarpit, Robert, 131

FABER, Karl-Georg, 139
Fadeev, A. A., 94, 109
Fang, Achilles, 184
Fischer, Ernst, 130
Fizer, John, 104
Fokkema, D. W., 7, 88, 190, 193
Fowler, Roger, 186
Frege, Gottlob, 168
Freud, Sigmund, 54, 133
Friedberg, Maurice, 188
Fügen, Hans Norbert, 145

Führmann, Manfred, 156

GADAMER, Hans-Georg, 138, 140, 160, 175
Gallas, Helga, 129
Garvin, Paul L., 36
Genette, Gérard, 141–2
Geurts, J. P. M., 172
Gladkov, F. V., 94
Goethe, Johann Wolfgang, 83, 117, 155
Göttner, Heide, 140–1
Gogol, N. V., 18, 95, 98, 101–2, 117
Goldmann, Lucien, 115, 128, 130–1, 192
Gombrich, E. H., 169, 171
Gorky, Maksim, 92, 94, 97–8, 106, 119
Grass, Günter, 160–2
Greenlee, Douglas, 44
Greimas, Algirdas Julien, 61, 64–7, 71
Griboedov, A., 98
Groeben, Norbert, 173
Grygar, Mojmír, 36
Günther, Hans, 30, 34, 39, 42, 143
Guépin, J. P., 28
Guillén, Claudio, 118
Guljaev, N. A., 104

HABERMAS, Jürgen, 133–4, 173, 175, 194
Harkness, Margaret, 88
Hassan, Ihab, 132
Havránek, Bohuslav, 36
Hegel, G. W. F., 82, 86, 88, 102, 124, 128, 187–8
Heidegger, Martin, 173
Helmer, Olaf, 172–4
Hemingway, Ernest, 122
Hempel, Carl G., 8, 140
Hillman, Heinz, 175
Hirsch, Jr., E. D., 1, 7
Hogrebe, Wolfram, 142
Holenstein, Elmar, 173
Homer, 6, 85, 95
Horace, 4
Hsiao Chün, 110
Hu Shih, 108

Husserl, Edmund, 14, 16, 21, 31, 36, 57, 169, 185, 194

INGARDEN, Roman, 32–4, 36–7, 57, 144, 148, 163–4, 185
Ionesco, Eugène, 179–80
Iser, Wolfgang, 145–8, 150, 152–5, 160–1, 193
Ivanov, Vjačeslav Vs., 39–40

JAKOBSON, Roman, 10–5, 17, 19–23, 25–6, 29–30, 33, 35, 37, 41, 44–6, 52–3, 56, 71–80, 131, 135, 158, 173, 179, 182, 185–6, 193–4
Jakubinskij, Lev, 11, 15
Jameson, Fredric, 115, 134
Jarry, André, 40
Jauss, Hans Robert, 45, 138–42, 144–56, 158–60, 164, 174–7, 188, 193
Joyce, James, 98, 116, 118–9
Judin, P. F., 83
Just, Georg, 160–1

KAČER, M., 147
Kafka, Franz, 29, 116, 122
Kagan, Moissej, 103, 188
Kaiser, Gerhard, 152
Kant, Immanuel, 102, 124
Kapp, Volker, 181
Katz, Jerrold J., 41
Kautsky, Karl, 87
Kautsky, Minna, 87–8
Kayser, Wolfgang, 4–5, 184
Kirillov, V. T., 95, 187
Koestler, Arthur, 8
Kon, I. S., 192
Konstantinović, Zoran, 34
Kristeva, Julia, 186
Kručënych, Aleksej, 10, 13
Krupskaja, N. K., 93, 102
Kunne-Ibsch, Elrud, 17, 166
Kuo Mo-jo, 113

LANE, Michael, 76–7, 193
Lanson, Gustav, 50, 54
Lao She, 109
Lassalle, Ferdinand, 84–6, 188
Leenhardt, Jacques, 115, 131

Lenin, V. I., 82, 89–95, 99, 111, 115–9
Levin, Harry, 121
Levin, Ju. I., 39
Levin, Samuel R., 75–6
Lévi-Strauss, Claude, 27, 30, 48, 50, 52–4, 56, 58, 60–6, 68–9, 71–9, 144, 158, 169
Li T'ai-po, 113
Lifshitz, M. A., 116
Lin Piao, 108, 113
Link, Hannelore, 146–7, 152–4
Liu Shao-ch'i, 113
Lorenz, Richard, 187
Lotman, Jurij M., 20, 22, 24, 29, 32–3, 38–49, 74–5, 79–80, 119, 125, 137, 149, 168, 177–8, 181, 185–6, 193
Lowenthal, Leo, 131
Lu Chi, 184
Lu Hsün, 105, 111, 115, 189
Lu Ting-i, 190
Luckmann, Thomas, 177–8
Lukács, Georg, 115–129, 131–2, 135, 190–2
Lunačarskij, A. V., 94–5, 101–2, 107

MÁCHA, K. H., 35
Maguire, Robert A., 94
Majakovskij, V. V., 94, 157
Malenkov, G. M., 100
Mandelkow, Karl Robert, 148, 150
Mann, Heinrich, 119
Mann, Klaus, 117
Mann, Thomas, 116, 119, 121–2, 163–4
Mannheim, Karl, 149–50
Mao Tse-tung, 91, 105–112, 114–5, 127, 187, 189–90
Mao Tun, 109
Margolis, Joseph, 3
Markov, Vladimir, 10
Marx, Karl, 54, 81–90, 92–3, 106, 111, 115–6, 118–20, 123–5, 127–8, 130, 132, 186–8, 190, 192
Mathesius, Vilém, 30
Mauron, Charles, 55, 58
Mehring, Franz, 94

Meinecke, Friedrich, 90, 170, 184
Mejlach, M. B., 39
Meletinskij, E. M., 27, 39. 65–6
Merleau-Ponty, Maurice, 56–7
Molière (Jean-Baptiste Poquelin), 95
Morris, Charles, 42
Morris, Wesley, 5
Mukařovský, Jan, 21–2, 31–7, 43–4, 47–8, 57–8, 80, 137, 142–5, 147–8, 155, 157, 160, 184–5

NAGEL, Ernest, 140, 184–5, 193
Naumann, Hans, 193
Nietzsche, Friedrich, 17, 54, 163–4, 166

OGIBENIN, Boris, 194
Oomen, Ursula, 74
Osgood, Charles E., 159
Ovsjannikov, M. F., 99, 104

PA CHIN, 109
Parkinson, G. H. R., 128, 191
Pascal, Blaise, 130
Pearce, Roy Harvey, 5
Peirce, Charles Sanders, 41, 44, 167, 169, 194
Peyre, Henri, 50
Piaget, Jean, 193
Picard, Raymond, 54–5, 58, 60
Pil'njak, Boris, 95–7
Pingaud, Bernard, 193
Pjatigorskij, A. M., 39
Plechanov, G. V., 102, 107, 188
Pomorska, Krystyna, 1
Popper, Karl R., 9, 12, 82, 132, 134–5, 140, 149–50, 165, 170–2, 176, 192
Posner, Roland, 75–6, 79–80, 193
Potebnja, A. A., 15, 185
Propp, Vladimir, 27–30, 61–6, 68–71
Proust, Marcel, 98
Pushkin, A. S., 13, 19

RACINE, Jean, 55, 58–60, 77, 130
Radek, Karl, 98
Ranke, Leopold von, 138–9

Raphael, 95, 103
Rescher, Nicholas, 49, 172–4, 184
Reve, Karel van het, 189
Revzin, I. I., 39, 41, 179–80
Revzina, O. G., 42, 179–80
Ricardou, Jean, 131
Richard, Jean-Pierre, 55
Ricoeur, Paul, 54, 137, 142–3, 175
Rieser, Max, 8
Riffaterre, Michael, 77–80, 158, 177, 186, 193
Robbe-Grillet, Alain, 131
Rolland, Romain, 119, 121
Rozanov, V. V., 19
Rozental', M. M., 83
Rühle, Jürgen, 120–1
Ruwet, Nicolas, 75–6, 79

SALTYKOV-ŠČEDRIN, M. E., 95
Sapir, Edward, 42
Saussure, Ferdinand de, 14, 16, 31, 50–2, 61, 167, 185
Sartre, J.-P., 51, 126, 143–4, 193
Ščeglov, Ju. K., 39
Schaff, Adam, 160–1
Schelling, F. W. J. von, 31, 185
Schiller, Friedrich, 85, 87
Schiwy, Günther, 145
Schlegel, August Wilhelm, 102, 188
Schleiermacher, F. E. D., 140–1, 173
Schmid, Herta, 36
Schmid, Wolf, 16
Schmidt, Siegfried J., 73, 137, 173
Schmitt, Hans-Jürgen, 190
Schober, Rita, 188
Scholes, Robert, 69
Schücking, Levin L., 131
Schupp, Franz, 171–2
Sebeok, Thomas A., 39
Segal, D. M., 20, 39, 42, 65–6
Segers, Rien T., 165
Seghers, Anna, 121, 128
Seiffert, Helmut, 184
Serafimovič, A. S., 94
Shakespeare, William, 83, 85, 88, 95
Shannon, Claude, 40

Simmons, Ernest J., 92
Sinjavskij, A. D., 98
Skagestad, Peter, 171–2
Šklovskij, Viktor, 10–3, 15–21, 23–7, 29–30, 32, 37–8, 40, 45–8, 95, 160–1, 178, 185
Solzhenitsyn, Aleksandr, 117, 123
Špet, Gustav, 21–2, 29, 32, 40–1, 183, 185
Staiger, Emil, 5, 140, 186
Stalin, I. V., 10, 97–9, 123
Steinbeck, John, 122
Stempel, Wolf-Dieter, 11, 136
Stierle, Karlheinz, 186, 194
Striedter, Jurij, 11, 156–7
Sue, Eugène, 86
Surkov, A. A., 92–3
Sus, Oleg, 36
Swayze, Harold, 88, 97, 99–100
Szeliga, see Zychlin

T'AN P'EI-SHENG, 107, 188
Tarski, Alfred, 172
Teesing, H. P. H., 5
Terc, Abram, 98
Timofeev, L., 188
Ting Ling, 110
Todorov, Tzvetan, 27, 29, 38, 61, 69–71
Tolstoy, L. N., 13, 16–7, 89–91, 98, 117
Tomaševskij, Boris, 11, 13, 18, 38
Toporov, V. N., 39
Trotsky, Leon, 24–5, 94, 96, 98
Trubetzkoy, Nikolai, 30, 50, 52–3
Tschižewskij, Dmitrij, 38
Tu Fu, 113
Turgenev, I. S., 17
Tynjanov, Jurij, 1, 3, 10–2, 14, 17–20, 22–6, 29, 31–2, 35, 37–8, 40, 43–4, 46, 57, 135, 144

USPENSKIJ, B. A., 39–41, 43

VAN DIJK, T. A., 184
Vardin, I., 102
Vengrov, N., 188
Veselovskij, A. N., 18, 27, 29
Viëtor, Karl, 4
Vinogradov, Viktor, 11, 19
Vinokur, G. O., 11
Vodička, Felix, 33, 36, 58, 143–5, 147–8
Völker, Klaus, 128, 191
Volkelt, Johannes, 37
Voronskij, A. K., 94–5, 101–2

WALDEN, Herwarth, 117
Wang Jo-wang, 189
Warren, Austin, 5–6
Warren, Robert Penn, 5
Watson, George, 2–3
Weber, Jean-Paul, 55, 58
Weitz, Morris, 2–3, 24
Wellek, René, 2, 5–7, 24, 30, 34–6, 89, 136, 188
Wen Kung, 190
Wetter, Gustav A., 90
Whorf, Benjamin Lee, 42, 47
Wienold, Götz, 144–5, 150–2, 193
Wittgenstein, Ludwig, 3

YÜN LAN, 190

ZAMJATIN, Evgenij, 95, 97, 111
Ždanov, A. A., 97–9, 106, 109, 188
Žirmunskij, Viktor, 11
Zola, Émile, 89
Žolkovskij, A. K., 39
Zoščenko, Michail, 99, 111
Zychlin von Zychlinski, Franz, 86